P9-CQV-586

By VALERIU MARCU

ACCENT ON POWER:

The Life and Times of Machiavelli

Translated By
Richard Winston

Illustrated

FARRAR & RINEHART, INC.
New York *Toronto*

All illustrations in this book used by the courtesy of The Bettmann Archive.

COPYRIGHT, 1939, BY FARRAR & RINEHART, INC.
PRINTED IN THE UNITED STATES OF AMERICA
BY THE FERRIS PRINTING COMPANY, NEW YORK
ALL RIGHTS RESERVED

Printing Statement:

Due to the very old age and scarcity of this book, many of the pages may be hard to read due to the blurring of the original text, possible missing pages, missing text and other issues beyond our control.

Because this is such an important and rare work, we believe it is best to reproduce this book regardless of its original condition.

Thank you for your understanding.

The translator wishes to thank Miss Miriam Sholna for her indispensable assistance in the translation of this book.

CONTENTS

LIST OF ILLUSTRATIONS

TRANSLATOR'S PREFACE

Valeriu Marcu selected Machiavelli as a subject for a new biography because Machiavelli expressed the spirit of an age that in many respects resembles our own. The Florence of the Medici was a microcosm in which operated those forces that were calling into existence a new world. The nationalism, secularism, and individualism which were so evident in the Florentine Republic, characterized the life of Europe at the end of the fifteenth century. In the confusion of the transition from the old to the new, the policies of princes and popes assumed a determining role.

Machiavelli, for most of his official life a subordinate clerk in the Florentine Signory, lived in the anteroom of power. Not in a position to wield power himself, and apparently having little inclination to do so, he studied those who were its executors, appraised their tactics, their intrigues, their objectives. It might almost be said that he spent his life in the School of Power (the title of this book in the original German is *Die Schule der Macht*) and became its most distinguished graduate.

In the current recession of democracy and the concomitant decline of internationalism, the teachings of the School of Power are once more of preeminent importance. In the totalitarian states today the accent is on power just as truly as in the Florence of Lorenzo or Cesare. The life and times of the Medici were in parvo the life and times of the dictators of Europe today. The observations of Machiavelli help us understand what at first glance appear to be the capricious acts of the power politicians who seem to have the destiny of the world in their hands.

ACCENT ON POWER

The American edition of Mr. Marcu's book comes at a time when Americans are realizing that they cannot consider themselves in an isolated world apart. *Accent on Power* reveals the strange continuity of the happenings of yesterday and today. Authoritative in its historical treatment, it helps us understand without recourse to wishful and romantic thinking the progress of events in a world where power once more rules. If the teachings of the little clerk of the sixteenth century Florence have become the guide book for modern dictators, it is important that those of us whose faith is still in democracy should be acquainted with the text.

Richard Winston

I

THE HERITAGE OF THE PAST

CHAPTER I

Florence Penetrates the World

COSIMO DI MEDICI was the most powerful merchant in the bourgeois society of his time and the richest banker in the world. He possessed more than two and a half tons of fine gold; he ended the wars of Venice, Milan, and Naples by withdrawing his credit; his agency in Paris determined the moods of the King of France. He held the miter of the Pope in pawn. . . . Cosimo di Medici was in his 50th year when, in 1439, after a long and eventful political career, he became the ruler of the Florentine Republic.

The Medici had always been opposed to the scattered relics of feudalism and the urban oligarchic families. It appalled them that the old families should squander their fortunes at foreign courts in drunkenness and gluttony, bankrupt themselves through pledges for friends or through the rebellions of their subjects, yet nevertheless pretend to govern the Republic while actually plunging it into senseless adventures. The Medici voiced the sentiments of the *populani,* the rich men who had risen from the common people and who kept the account books of their commercial, domestic, and agricultural affairs with unflagging diligence. But they did not identify themselves with these industrious, hardheaded Florentine business men. The Medici were not afraid to face radical uprisings. Florence saw members of the family become confederates of the fourteen Lesser Guilds. They were capable of calling upon dyers, tailors, woodcutters, lapidaries, carpenters, and cobblers to rise up and fight for

Freedom, Vengeance, and Justice. They permitted barefoot and tattered wool carders, bearing the captured flag of the chief magistrate of the city, the *gonfaloniere,* to penetrate into the Palace of Power. Then they would appear as deliverers from a threatening equalization of poverty.

But the Medici never broke entirely with any of the struggling groups. They lent money at usurious rates to the nobility whom they fought; they gave advice to the Greater Guilds; they helped the parvenus explode traditions; they united themselves with the guild of notaries and magistrates by common intellectual bonds. More material interests linked them with the linen, wool, silk, and fur guilds and with the money-changers. They even maintained secret connections with the administration that banished them from the city.

A singular political tenacity inspired this family. The founders labored for power with the patience of those architects of Tuscan cathedrals who could not hope to live to dedicate their works. One Medici had painted in his palace, as a symbol of his family, a tortoise! From father to son they strove patiently, unswervingly for supremacy.

During a century of opposition the fathers gathered ever-increasing influence for their sons until the strength of their position made them ready for monarchy. Not because the firm "Cosimo di Medici, Figli e Nepoti" was one of the richest in Europe were they able to force their coat-of-arms upon the Republic. Other financial and commercial dynasties of Tuscany were also rich. But none of them had the Medicean faculty for brilliantly utilizing the two popular fears—fear of the storms of civil war and fear of the peacefulness of tyranny. They gave due regard to the longing of the burghers for law and order. They capitalized on the power of money and exploited the glamor of culture.

When Cosimo became ruler of the city the people of Florence said: the new *stato* has arrived. The stato that came to power with him was the old Medicean party. For half a century there had assembled around the Medici, families who grew great together, who had common interests, and who did not abandon each other in moments of financial disaster. The children and grandchildren of these families were destined for definite official positions while they were still in swaddling clothes. This organization of rich populani consisted of no more than fifty or a hundred men; it was a corporation of friends whose laws were never written down. After Cosimo, however, the lion's share of power lay in the camp of the Medici. It was not necessary for these allied leading families to govern directly in order to rule. Through their influence they determined the activities of the men in office. Independence of office was an abstract phrase from the Constitution of 1343, without any real existence.

Even after his accession to power Cosimo did not enlarge the boundaries of this "state" of fifty men. But he extended its benefits far beyond his circle of friends. In the vestibule of power were nearly two thousand adherents, who formed the broadened stato, the extension of the party. For them Cosimo became *pater patriae*.

Under his rule the Republic itself enjoyed a lavish prosperity. The soil of the city, fertilized with tribute from all parts of the world, became fruitful in gardens, villas, and palaces. Monumental works intoxicated the Florentines. Only the poor complained that the congestion of new stone buildings left them no room to stretch their limbs and literally drove them out of the rich Republic. The *miserabili* were forced to live ever closer together because rents and the price of land had tripled within twenty years. More momentous than the new poverty, however, was the novelty of wealth. A proud generation of masters appeared, lovers of color and form, who, under Cosimo, made Florence a city of splendor.

In the Piazza of the Mercato Novo nearly seventy bankers' booths had tables out in the open. Many of these banks owned great buildings in the city. But it was a part of tradition to be represented in the Mercato Novo. For two hundred years money-changing had been carried on here. Here, too, stood the public scales on which all golden florins were weighed and sealed in bags. None doubted the weight of a money-bag which bore the Florentine seal. Most of these banking firms had branches in Venice, Paris, Genoa, London, or Bruges.

To the gentlemen of this market, no mortal debtor's soul weighed more than another's. Florentine peasants who needed money for their retail trade; native grain dealers seeking to dispose of their stock-in-trade; Scottish and Norman barons mortgaging their castles and estates; the crown of Castile pledging its jewels, and the kings of France guaranteeing their loans with the incomes of whole provinces—all were the same.

In the account books of the Mercato Novo the sorrows of all the world could be read: the debts of nobles and prelates from Naples, England, France, Tyrol, Bohemia, and Dalmatia. The feudal lords and their associates, unsettled and uprooted by changed economic conditions, frequently sought their salvation in the Florentine bankers. Men with armor, retainers, and attendants, had no ready cash; to get it they had to convert their castles, woods, and streams into money. Money became in ever-increasing measure the sole standard of all things. Honor and office, salvation and indulgences, fame and soldiers, love and women, solitude and independence, could be had only by purchase. But many of the nobility were ruined by the dangerous assistance of the bankers of Florence.

This assistance, however, was well suited to the growing centralized Powers. These had a broader basis than the smaller states. By means of their widespread connections, the bankers provided the expanding monarchies with the financial prerequisites to power. Public credit and pending debts, such as the Florentines contrived for the kings of England and

France, were a part of the economic structure which the young nations needed for the achievement of political unity.

The Florentine money-aristocracy continued to hold this position as midwife to a new world order even after the springs of wealth of the Mediterranean had begun to dry up. Their affiliates displaced Italian competitors in foreign lands. Before the Signory purchased Siena, Lucca, Pisa, and Arezzo, the banks of these cities had already passed into their control. The Florentine money market could not have shown this tenacity if it had been the meeting place of short-sighted usurers made totally blind by their profits. On the contrary, it was the rallying point for coolheaded adventurers, men of courage with feet firmly on the ground. The wealth in ready money was never the result of a transitory crisis, nor, as a rule, the product of lucky speculation. The Mercato Novo could survive heavy and unexpected financial reverses because it was wisely fed from the life stream of the whole economy.

This lasting wealth was the result of linking the purchase of raw materials with manufacturing. It was a result of frequently daring grants of credit for trade in commodities and money. Other cities, also, had at that time great credit agencies handling large fortunes. But none was so skillful as Florence in combining credit with importation from and exportation to southern and northern Italy, France, England, and the Orient. None had so many ears and eyes to watch for those fluctuations in demand out of which riches arose. None understood so well how to further business interests by anticipating the outbreak of disputes among ambitious potentates. And none could predict to such a nicety the tightness or liquidity of money, the scarcity or surplus of commodities, in the various cities.

Florence itself never encountered a shortage of goods. For its national industry, the making of textiles, Florence imported wool for spinning from Champagne, Cyprus, Flanders, Greece, Sardinia, and Lombardy. It brought materials for dyeing and refining from England and the Provence; silk for the finest embroidery from Syria and China, and ermine and fox fur from Asia Minor.

Countless shops were squeezed into a narrow alley between the Old Market and the Arno. Retailers offered everything at bargain prices. A perpetual fair, reminiscent of the oriental bazaars, was in progress here, but only the smallest part of the goods was visible to the eye. In the tall, square buildings whose shadows darkened the streets and the counters of the shops, labyrinthine corridors were packed with enough goods to supply the needs of whole regions. And all countries had faith in these commodities.

Here the domestic and sartorial fashions of the Occident were fixed. Florence produced not only money but also ever newer demands. A French tapestry with the family coat-of-arms must be woven on the Arno in order to be valuable. A brass or bronze chalice was considered perfect only when it took its mark of origin in the Via di Callimala. Women thought to assist nature most efficiently by having the trimmings for their hats, the combs for their hair, and the buttons for their blouses bought in Florence, while even priests felt that they were administering their office with the maximum of dignity only if their dalmatics had been woven on a Florentine loom. In the organization of the crafts, the rulers of the economy strove to guard the quality of their products. Florence was praised far and wide by lords, barons, and common people for the excellence of its products.

The personality of the worker was not submerged in the shops of the artisans on the Arno. The manual laborer looked upon himself as an artist. The guilds were called *arti.* The character of neither employer nor employee was eclipsed by the mass of their commodities. In domestic industry, where poverty threatened to cripple both producer and product, the urban oligarchy sought, through the Church, to give aid.

The clergy in their sermons had to inform the spinners how they were to reel the yarn in accordance with the regulations of the guilds, and in confession the poor were questioned searchingly as to whether they had committed any sins against the sacred commandment of quality. But this wealth and these methods were still not enough for the Medici. If a well-known populano had suffered unexpected losses, had forfeited his possessions in gambling, was unable to supply his daughter with a dowry, or if usurious rates of interest were threatening to ruin him—then a friendly letter from the generous Cosimo rescued him.

He would have liked best, said Cosimo, to have God also among his debtors. He helped all those who were financially shipwrecked and who in desperation were inclined to throw in their lot with the banished chiefs of the Albizzi or Strozzi parties. For Cosimo fought his enemies by entering their names in the great family ledger of the Medici where the accounts of gifts of money were kept. In struggle, too, "this great sage and equally great merchant"—as his son, Piero, called him—clung to statistics. From his father, Cosimo had inherited the book of defunct loans, which bore only indirect political interest; and in time the names of many opponents were included among those of his very close friends. Instead of persecuting his enemies or throttling them in prison, he stifled their rebellious instincts. He did not buy, he helped. He demanded no return, but the conscience of the recipient was touched. Above all, he did not cloud his days with useless struggles. His bank took over the larger part of the work of the police: the establishment of absolute order and a moderate degree of contentment.

The new ruler of Florence was not to be seen at the place where the city discussed its affairs. Cosimo avoided the palace of the Signory. He did not like to appear in public; he hated everything official; and applause disturbed him like a sudden intimacy from a stranger. Ambition directed him to conceal his power. He did not consider himself infallible, but he once declared, as if in apology, that the city could not be governed by the Lord's Prayer. Another time, he said that honor was part of one's dress—and cloth was purchasable in any quantity. Cosimo never considered himself a success. No one ever heard him talking about himself; he never quoted himself; never dramatized his past for his friends. He worked as it were necessary to reconquer his position every day.

From early morning Cosimo sat regularly in the counting room of his bank. From here the city was governed. From here he kept track of funds invested throughout Europe. Here all news reports arrived and here he received the citizenry. Here Florence and his private enterprises became a unity; in every man he saw only his creature and in every organ of the city he looked upon his creation. Cosimo had discovered that appearance was a convenient device by which to rule. He permitted the Florentines the appearance of liberty, the appearance of participation in government, the appearance of equality. Toward the end of his reign he left them only the appearance of wealth itself. He respected vanities, traditions, and habits but nevertheless molded everything to his will. In political life it is astonishing how successful the Medici were at being more than they seemed. An ordinary citizen like Cosimo, with neither crown nor scepter, with no attested and recorded legitimation—an equal among equals—nevertheless controlled a community divided against itself. Without violence he gained supremacy over the souls of the simple and the subtle. By opportunism, Cosimo added wheel after wheel to a complex, indirect administrative machinery such as the Middle Ages had never known. He bred in the Florentines a gift for pliancy, for opportunism; he made skillful bargaining, *combinazione,* a matter of course in all questions. Thus he was able to satisfy a people which, in the past, had settled its quarrels by weapons, not words, and which had solved the problems of the Republic not by laws but by exile and the death penalty.

Cosimo often retired to the well-guarded tranquility of the monastery of San Marco, not far from the Medicean bank. He had had this ancient, decaying home of the Dominicans rebuilt. Here he established for his own and future generations the richest library of the West. At no time before or after him were drafts and credits for the purchase of manuscripts and codices so gladly honored by a bank as they were by his firm.

Wherever a trace of a Greek or Roman manuscript was suspected, he opened up a promised land to the Florentines. The eyes of the Republic, the ninety trade and banking agencies throughout the world, spied out remote monasteries where Plutarchs and Aristotles, without commentaries and unfalsified by secondhand translations from the Arabic, lay packed in chests, thwarting time by the power of the word. After the patient industry of a half century the Florentines were able to restore the past to the western world. In the houses of the *nobili* the library came more and more to occupy the most important place. Frequent jealousies over books flared up among the aristocrats. Strozzi, an enemy of Cosimo Medici, avenged himself by outfitting a ship for Constantinople and so bringing the first copy of Aristotle's *Politics* to the West. For the Medicean bibliophile this was the last straw and led him to banish his fortunate rival from the Republic!

In San Marco, in the center of Florence, Cosimo provided the humanists with a congenial environment in which their impulse toward a revival of the Greek and Roman civilizations might take root and blossom. San Marco was removed from the world, but was nevertheless stirred by the intellectual forces of the time. Cosimo was no scholar. His mind sought humbly, however, for the content and the forms of Hellenic clarity. In the culture of the ancient world he saw how man had conquered his own instability, the fear of his own aimlessness and ephemerality. Consequently, in him, as in his learned protegés, Christianity was compounded with Platonism. San Marco became the best school for the mind of a benevolent autocrat. It taught discretion through knowledge, individual morality born of independent thought. All day Cosimo conversed in his cell with half-Platonic, half-Christian disciples. A pious man from the monastery of San Marco who knew how ruinous sovereignty was to men, how the fullness of power poisoned the individual with spitefulness, vanity, and superficiality, declared that only the monastery had saved Cosimo from becoming "a common despot."

Cosimo's originality, however, did not lie in his love of culture; he paid tribute here to necessity. By becoming enthusiastic about a desire of the many he made his rule first possible and then increasingly easy.

For this impulse toward culture was as much a part of this republic as the geographical position, the antifeudal, commercial temper and the institution of the city. It harmonized with the distaste for antique monuments which would have burdened creative initiative, with the love of the republican form of government, with the century-old independence from Pope and Emperor, and with the industrious, forward-looking instincts of the citizens and their inclination to political experiment. Desire for culture was as native to Florence as the melodic dialect out of which modern Italian had arisen, and as the light which from the heights overlooking Florence revealed the city in silver clarity, promising all the allurements of the earth.

A feverish excitability had been growing since the early Middle Ages in Europe. It was born of suffering and the yearning for a purified, rejuvenated piety. The cry of Francis of Assisi for the rebirth in Christ and the plea of Dante for the empire of peace had expressed this yearning. In the

Medicean Republic it became the humanistic reverence for the classical world.

This world of culture was maintained by the Florentine commercial nobility. The advantages of power and wealth were supplemented by the advantages of culture. Education, and all that accompanied it, bore the stamp of the patrician and the noble. To walk with a book in one's hands afforded the same security in the streets of Florence as the wearing of a sword in another city. In the eyes of all, the more educated a man became, the more man and therefore the more human he seemed.

Any education and taste that prevailed outside of noble circles owed its existence to the moral and esthetic influence of the aristocracy. To be like the oligarchs, the Medici, Caponi, Albizzi, Strozzi, Pazzi, Salvati, Frescobaldi, Gualteroti, Bartolini, Antonori, and Soderini—this was the dream of the saddlers, dyers, bell casters, beltmakers, and moneychangers. In the workshops of these men, the authority of the nobili in matters of taste was less challenged than in political matters. As there is always a center of rule—a stato—so also is there a center of culture. And culture, like government, can never be a really popular concern. In Florence, sovereignty and learning became identified—a phenomenon which history finds elsewhere only in Greece in the fourth century before the birth of Christ. And both epochs are but short moments, mere sixty-year minutes in the life of mankind.

Education and culture are most frequently an affair of the palace when sovereignty does not freeze hard in the muteness of a dictatorship. Wealth buys education. It can afford culture. In Florence, however, culture and learning corresponded not only to the power and wealth, but also to the spirit and ideals of the nobility. Those who lent the money and those who supplied the impulse could no longer be distinguished from each other. Culture was part of

Power's ideals and illusions about itself. Wealth found its justification in culture. An uncultivated noble was considered by his peers a degenerate. He was merely part of the mob.

For a Florentine noble, culture was a social distinction in the same way that the possession of a large militia was a distinction for a German knight and the decapitation of many Moors was a mark of honor for a Castilian. The muse of sovereignty did not carry a golden scales or a sword in her hand; she carried a book.

In this striving for learning and culture, the Florentines manifested their infinite joy in life. It was the peaceful culture of the freeman whose society had no caste of the learned, no mandarins. To be sure, humanistic science did not serve the acquisition of wealth and gave no "right to office". Its mission was the extension of the boundaries of pleasure and the possibilities of sensation. It attempted to teach the appreciation of the beautiful; scholars were the cavaliers of a magnificent society. They possessed a sense of individual forcefulness, not the impotence of poverty which usually binds men of science to their rooms. The scholars were doers, optimists. It was absolutely necessary to own Greek and Roman books, absolutely necessary to spend many wakeful nights reading them; but it was no less necessary to experience things of the flesh, to go hunting and riding, to love, to fish, and to travel.

"We love," wrote Marsilio Ficino, "unmixed colors, lights, voices, the gleam of gold, the whiteness of silver, learning, and the soul."

The standard-bearers of this new movement, the patricians of the Medicean decades, were for all of that no daydreamers. They nowhere sought the absolute in order to crown it with glory. They did not desire, for the sake of the ancient world, to fall into the arms of a vain and barren phantasy. Latinism and Hellenism were for them no revivals of a lost world, but the practical forms for their own individual existences. The enthusiasm for patriarchal, republican Rome simplified even the domestic, private severity of the patricians. Hypocrisy, the normal, faithful follower of every civilization, won in Florence a new unclouded conscience. From an art it turned into a virtue. The nobili lived in equal measure for learning and for power.

The features of the Florentine oligarchy, with their variety and individuality, had one common, stern line. The frigidity began with the red, regular tilestones of the façades of the palaces. These lords loved a regulated life, days run by the clock. Morning and afternoon were taken up with official matters. In the early morning the Florentine heard mass first. "Then he went," as a chronicler recounts, "through the streets to the market or to the palace of the Signory in pursuit of his business, in summer in a black *lucco,* folded at the throat, and a black silk beret with a long tassel, and in winter in a black cloak and severe cape." He rarely failed to be at home for the midday meal and always spent fully an hour afterwards with his children and his wife. In the family he was a stern master. Severity towards his wife came easy to him. He ordinarily had no greater inclination toward her than toward the scribe who immortalized the names of the newly wed in the church register—as if it were a burial urn. His spouse was the inevitable, the price he must pay for ruling the city. For every noble family formed a cornerstone in the building of the stato and the extended party. If a man were so tortured or so insolent as to divorce his wife, he might be forced out of the party, driven into the opposition, and economically ruined.

All the love and care which the nobleman had left over for his home belonged to his children. Among manuscripts and statues he preached the cult of study and humanism. He taught his children not to desire a change of political conditions, to avoid conflict both with the men in the street and with the ruling family, and to endeavor to find liberty in

Power. This education rose simultaneously out of love for his children and loyalty to Florence.

His real life began within the circle of his friends. Here he lost the gravity of duty, the dignity of responsibility; here he expected from women other virtues and from humanism lighter forms.

The aristocrat had spent his youth with literati. He had learned grammar and rhetoric with them from the same teacher. He believed in the same ideals and he had been inspired by the same manuscripts. Now the noble received in his salon, whose friezes, ceiling, tables, and chairs manifested the monumental temper of the Republic, the horde of the inconstant and swiftly productive.

The throng of talented persons, for whom Florence was the center of secular culture, exchanged the solid heritage of their ancestors for the glittering ideas of the day. They hatched aristocratic opinions more ruthlessly than the nobili. They coined the pregnant phrases that expressed the new consciousness of their age; they said: we and Cicero, we and Plato. They divided mankind into two parts, separated by a bottomless abyss: those who understood the antique world, and the ignoramuses. With the former, the men of learning throughout the world, the humanists felt themselves to be fraternally united, although they reviled one another unsparingly in Florence. In all cities they saw centers of learning being built, far from the mob. This intellectual archipelago was consolidated and inspired by a similar striving for the aristocratic ideal.

The humanism which had its capital on the Arno could not be other than cosmopolitan. The literati were not Florentines, not Italians, but Latins. Until shortly before the end of Lorenzo's reign, Italian was considered the language of animals. Dante was doomed to wither in his own inferno because he had written the *Divine Comedy* in Italian. Latin was for them the reconquered homeland of their thoughts and emotions.

The present, with its cities, fortresses, and boundaries, its popular assemblies and tyrants, appeared far too limited to these men to permit of their binding themselves in space and time. They could afford the wonderful and rare luxury of not acknowledging things in existence or in the making. They opposed their talents and often their genius to the course of events and to history.

Their longings were directed toward the new, colorful, and immediate, to all things between heaven and earth that were bathed in light. Their inquiring minds wanted to see and to feel; general concepts were dimmed in their eyes. The common abstractions of the Middle Ages, the moral pillars which had supported the beliefs of ordinary men, were blasted. In the papacy they saw only the pope, in empire only the emperor, in love only a Solomon's Song of the senses, and in war only murder. The villas, the palaces, the homes of the republic on the Arno were the unfortified citadels of anti-war sentiments. Here the peaceful men of letters met with the lords of the banks and politics.

The motives of the merchants did not have a purely humanistic basis as did those of the literati. They rarely forgot that peace was the most healthful atmosphere for wealth, and this knowledge of the cosmopolitan requirements of business made them even more receptive to the vehement Greco-Roman enthusiasms of their guests. The abstract ideals and the animal impulses of personal, daily life became one. The merchants and their literati did not want to live as heroes, warriors, or ascetics, but as epicureans, as wise men, and, if they could do no better, as dilettanti.

They celebrated man as the miracle that strove to decipher all the other miracles of nature. And here, in the mild air of Florentine nights, they derided as barbarian the warlike Europe of the Spaniards, the Germans, the Mohammedans, and the French—peoples driven by their own whims, misled by ideas and prejudices. They saw no trace of poetry in war and spoke only with pity of the line of Spanish poets and painters who found their highest inspiration in the battlefield.

"I do not hold it my duty," the historian, Valla, declared, "to die for a citizen of my city, not even for two or for three. Least of all do I consider it my duty to suffer death for the sum of all the citizens whom I do not know and who mean nothing to me."

"He who serves the community," Alberti stated, "serves no one; the more a thing is a common good, the less it is divine."

"When the citizens of a city come together in the piazza to decide upon a war," says Simonetta, "a herald ought to cry out, 'All rational men and all who know how to read and write shall immediately leave our assemblage. We, animals and ignoramuses, desire to be by ourselves.' "

All the collective virtues which made of battle the eternal abode of power, the sole possible, the sole incorruptible scale of justice, the tester of all phrases, ambitions, and endeavors, seemed to the humanists the very negation of dignity and nobility. The honorable man, the strong-willed man, the man who had but a spark of spirit, the man who deserved the rewards of fate, and any man who had ever felt the might of ideas, despised battle. There was no cowardice or dissimulation which would not be counted the highest virtue if it made possible a man's withdrawal from the struggles of the armed mob. Battle belonged to the lowest order of all activities. A brow crowned with the laurel became an ass's head. As long as he lived the individual had infinite potentialities, and every potentiality, every form, every beauty, was destroyed by battle. For the humanist, a man was great only because he lived, not because he died.

And when man's abundance of days is nevertheless interrupted by battle, when the condottiere gathers his men, when the streamers of flags are fluttering and the warriors, awaiting the battle morning with turbulent souls, kiss the soil in the face of the enemy, cross themselves thrice and then cut, plunder, or die—in such times the humanist seeks a friendly refuge, far from the tumult of the battle. The humanist never fought against anything, not even against war. His disposition did not allow him the joy of the reformer. He merely withdrew the more; he tended the garden of his learning and conceded to the world its consuming, incalculable impulses. From the time of the victory of the Medici, Florence was no longer animated by a warlike spirit. The traffic of the bankers and the ideals of the humanists caused the city on the Arno to follow in its foreign policy, the dictum of Leonardo da Vinci, "Avoíd the tempest!"

Wars for a neighboring piece of territory, or against an enemy city or threatening prince, seemed to the Florentines causes unworthy of thought or desire. An entirely different ambition burned in them: to invade the furthest corners of the world and everywhere in the East and West, wherever profits lured, to set up an enterprise of the city in order to share in those profits.

And if nevertheless it was an immediate necessity to conquer in order to assure the safety of the commerce routes that radiated from Florence into Liguria, Siena, and Umbria, or to control the Arno from source to mouth, the Signory sent battle-wagons filled, not with soldiers but with gold to combat the obstacle. They brought about the victory of one party in an enemy city and their gold then bought the victor. Thus towns which had once been prosperous and active throughout the Mediterranean—Siena, Pisa, Lucca, and Arezzo—were chained by Florence.

The driving force of these peaceful conquerors—their commercial élan—was effectively more warlike, revolutionary, and unified than the strongest army. It was a process which in Florentine daily life had nothing solemn about it; they were not even consciously aware of it. The invasion of the world's markets was completed both materially by the coinage the Republic minted—the "florin"—and spiritually by the new attitude towards life, by the power of the individual.

It was the great breach in the consciousness of man which had been preparing for three hundred years. Like everything of significance in the West, the process began with the Catholics. "He who loves God with an ardent soul," one of the mystic doctrines of St. Bernard had declared, "transforms himself into Him." And now man also proclaimed himself the highest Being—but without God or gods! "I have created myself," announced the son of the earth. He launched an attack against his dependency, seized possession of himself for himself, proclaimed himself an individual, forgot his mortality, his insignificance, the accident of his living. It was his flight from the community, from economic association, from the diocese, from traditional good and traditional evil, from the mob. Working upon himself, giving form to his mind and his body, seemed to him as important as winning a battle, writing a book, discovering a new country, or erecting a church. That which was hateful to the pious—the ego—was magnified to gigantic stature. The Pope himself deserted the Christians, became a Greek, and claimed the title, *Il Formoso,* the well-formed man. Man as an individual owed concretely to Florence his entrance into the world.

This transformation in man's individual importance became conspicuous under Cosimo di Medici. It began with Niccolo Niccolini, who drew from the treasures of three continents to lay the foundation of the great libraries of Europe; with Pico della Mirandola, the author of *The Dignity of Man;* with Marsilio Ficino, who restored the harmonies of Plato to the West. This revolt of the aristocracy, which was to upset all traditional thought, reached its climax under Lorenzo di Medici. The individual, entirely by his own efforts, climbed to the loftiest of earthly heights. A free man's soul was worth more than the souls of all those others who could not achieve sovereignty of the spirit. That individual was called, in the same epoch and in the same city: Leonardo da Vinci, Michelangelo, Ariosto, Guicciardini and Niccolo Machiavelli.

CHAPTER II

MACHIAVELLI STUDIES POWER

THROUGH the darkness of the centuries there stands out Cosimo's grandson and heir—Lorenzo di Medici. He rides through a silver-shimmering olive wood accompanied by his huntsmen and friends. Suddenly he draws rein, lightly touches Marsilio Ficino on the shoulder and asks, "What do you think is the meaning of happiness?"—"The spirit?"—"No, the will!" Lorenzo answers.

He believed in will—that all-resolving word to the gifted wolves of the Renaissance—because he was driven by a sense of boundless energy. It seemed to Lorenzo that everything which in nature, in storms and mists, thunder and snow, raged to no end, was captured, bound, and shaped by the individual will in man. Therefore his ideal did not lie within the scope of human potentialities; only the infinite appeared perfect to him. And where he suspected a spirit similar to his own in the endowment of an individual, where he suspected that another man also held this higher aspiration, he felt he must give help. Because of this he was delighted by every talented youth. The conscience of this man of perplexing contrasts, who dedicated verses to the violet and set an unsuspecting city afire, who celebrated chastity in enthusiastic litanies and died in his fortieth year because of his still more enthusiastic love for the handmaids of Venus, was active only in its solicitude for the talented and extraordinary men of his time.

Lorenzo could not only perceive every spark of genuine

PAINTING BY VASARI

LORENZO DI MEDICI

"Intended to smother all political opposition in color, light, and song."

PAINTING BY SANTI DI TITO

MACHIAVELLI

"Remained always a modest paramour of Power."

talent in his circle, but he was sensitive also to the weaknesses of the humanists around him. His ironic attitude toward himself and his basic aloofness from his own friends revealed them to him.

Whoever philosophized, poetized, painted, sculptured or was occupied with mathematics or philology in Florence gathered around Lorenzo. His home in the Via Larga, palace, library, and museum all in one, was open to all. Only the façade, the name, the aureole suggested the Prince. Within, there prevailed a free and easy intercourse. No etiquette recalled the ruler, no master of ceremonies regulated propriety. Every day another of the fifty guests presided at the table: the mathematician, Paolo Toscanelli, whose maps were to show Columbus the way across the sea; Sandro Botticelli; Michelangelo; the poet and philologist, Poliziano; the poet, Luigi Pulci; the philosophers, Marsilio Ficino or Pico della Mirandola. Lorenzo brought together famous men and beginners and created friendships among the first minds of Italy. His half-royal, half-bourgeois home outshone the courts of the Peninsula and became the cynosure of humanists in all countries.

These people lost their awareness of Lorenzo's generosity, for it became a habit. He gave his friends the gift which could not be repaid since nature herself had endowed him with it: the impulses of his broad, all-embracing and always self-contradictory soul. He aroused them by his fortune; for destiny had bestowed upon this man the gift of seducing all. He made himself the master of every difficulty, every hostile force. When Florence was engaged in an unsuccessful war with Naples, he rode into the enemy camp and convinced the king of the advantages of an alliance with the Tuscan Republic. No enemy dagger, no trap, no intrigue was able to reach him. It seemed as if the very stars espoused Lorenzo's cause. Pope Sixtus IV died, as Lorenzo had hoped, on the right day. His successor, Innocent, became his best friend. The Holy Father elevated Lorenzo's fourteen-year-old son, the later Pope Leo X, to the rank of cardinal. Alliances and friendships of the Powers of Europe fell to him. When he traveled, the winds were favorable, and never were his festivals troubled by bad weather. All accidents joined for his benefit; blind nature was kind to him. When his flatterers called him a son of Apollo they were, to be sure, flattering, but they were not lying.

Lorenzo no longer ruled the city as had Cosimo, from a room in the bank. The commercial enterprises of his family did not interest him; anything resembling a balance sheet bored him. Educated like a prince, surrounded by flatterers from his youth, always accompanied by sparkling young men, assailed with pleas for annuities from the potentates and men of letters of all Italy, he came to believe that the wealth at his disposal was the natural attribute of a ruler. Nothing must suffer for lack of money, and everything purchasable had to become Medicean. The choicest stables, the finest hunting grounds, the rarest gems, the costliest collections and the most magnificent gardens of Tuscany came into his possession. The merchant mind of his forefathers, who despite all their munificence had governed their expenditures by their income—this new morality of an evolving society was completely lacking in him. Extravagant and luxurious living, which stood in contrast to the economical habits of his forebears and to the newly proclaimed maxims of thrift, was the natural element of Lorenzo and his circle. Education for the bourgeois mode of life, which had been firmly established in the Italian cities, was interrupted.

Lorenzo consumed one of the greatest inheritances in Europe not only to satisfy his whims, but also to win over the Florentines. Luxury and extravagance became for him a personal necessity. During his carnival processions, the whole city became a stage. Leopards and panthers, hundreds of splendidly gowned women, servants in silk and satin, thousands of dogs and countless hunting hawks made their appearance in these pleasure-spectacles. Magnificence in everything was to convince all levels of the population that the Medici dispensed happiness and fortune to the whole Republic. Lorenzo intended to smother all political opposition in color, light, and song.

Every commercial enterprise of the city was infected by Lorenzo's character. Trade in commodities became more and more neglected and pure exchange of money was increasingly practised. Speculation in money obviously involved more risk, but it was more profitable than the long process by which a raw material became first a manufactured product and then, finally, money. Simple exchange attracted those with much capital. Petty and grand usury, always at home in Florence, increasingly supplanted and suppressed trade.

The money so swiftly earned deserted its owners with equal speed. Money was allowed no time, given no chance, to increase. General skepticism was so strong that there was no longer any respect for the sanctity of gold. Money, seized in the name of the Lorentian pleasure-mania, was spent in the maddest luxury and was not allowed to become capital. With old and young it was the style to take one's pleasure on a sumptuous scale, to let emotion and color flow in the grand manner, to make every family festival a public celebration, and to spend one's fortune, whether inherited or the fruit of usury, on clothes, banquets, gaming, and women. If money was invested it was only as barren capital, in order to build palaces. Building exalted these men and enhanced their splendor. The little men took pride in the edifices of the great; architecture was part of the general festival which was Lorenzo's regime. He supported it by example and by law. A decree of the Signory proclaimed freedom from taxation to all who "built on land where as yet no house has stood, nor the beginning of one".

The ruling Medici claimed the doctrine of complete

freedom from care. He did not approve of worry about the future. In his carnival songs he constantly called upon the citizens to enjoy themselves from one morning to the next. To him, and to all men of his circle, the thought of educating the Florentines seemed absurd. Since he recognized corruption as an important instrument of rule, he strove to give it a broad basis. All were to enjoy it.

His firm, however, was no longer able to supply the sums necessary for him and his rule. The foundations of all the Medicean enterprises had been severely shaken in the course of half a century. One after another of the ninety foreign branches of his bank closed their doors. His business representatives, released from direct control, imitated Lorenzo's negligence and assisted in the failure of the firm by inaccuracy or scarcely concealed thievery.

The more the ready money in his foreign enterprises was endangered, the greater were the funds he withdrew from the business. With them he built his palaces and bought land. Never had the Medici possessed so many estates as now in the period of the decline of their business talents. Lorenzo was neither merchant nor banker, but the august owner of large landed estates, *latifundia,* throughout Tuscany. And in order to save his firm from a crushing and disgraceful bankruptcy, the city was forced to aid it financially.

Through the course of their century-long labors, his family had encompassed Power with gold in order to capture Power; now the city was to pay ransom for the kidnaping. Within a short time the finances of Florence were as unstable as those of the firm of Medici.

In the art of appropriation Lorenzo had no weaknesses and made no exceptions. He found means to direct into his coffers even the thinnest trickle of gold which flowed to the Republic. Nor did he ever lack a formula for making each predatory act seem lawful, and here only was his reign ungracious and unsmiling. This humanist, who constantly declared that a man who did not know his Plato was neither a citizen nor a human being, had the city of Volterra pillaged in order to possess himself of its neighboring rich mines. It was the first destruction of an Italian city in centuries.

He forced priests who were administering the portions of poor young women to deliver the funds to him. He had his own men at the customs and salt bureaus, and in all the administrative offices of the city. In return for a small commission they plundered for the benefit of the Medici. Even the notaries contributed percentages of their receipts and no contract was closed without Lorenzo's taking part of the profits in arbitrary taxes.

The splendor of a reign that promised pleasure to all became a dearly bought enchantment.

He continued, however, to receive the applause of the little men. By means of his very taxation policy he broadened the basis of his rule. For he held in check the struggle of the poor against the rich. It is easier to hide the truth from the many than from the few, concealing reality beneath hopes. In the hands of Lorenzo, property taxes became a popular tool, the ever-fresh source of new revenue and the instrument of his exceptional cunning. The taxation system functioned as a torture-wheel, crushing gold instead of useless blood out of the victims. The people of Florence always paid enthusiastic tribute to the ruling family whenever their rich enemies were impoverished by the even richer rulers.

Lorenzo was careful not to remind the little man of the finances of the Republic by direct taxes. The common Florentine was not to know that it was he, for the most part, who paid for all the magnificence. The income-tax scale had fifteen levels; those in the lowest level paid four per cent, those in the top level thirty-four. Still, all this was according to law and, had it been applied impartially, would have guaranteed some stability. Illegality, however, was the order of the day. New imposts, new progressive levies on income were invoked against enemies or former friends. Lorenzo denounced lagging taxpayers publicly as rapacious oligarchs. He could deprive anyone of his property; through his control of the Signory he could have any wealthy man newly assessed. The fiscal authorities replaced the police. They supplanted the Medicean bank as the organ of Lorenzo's rule.

By means of property taxes, Lorenzo tried to free himself from his own party, from the rich families which had given him power, that is, from the stato. Whoever among the wealthy was not blindly obedient to him, whoever struck at the arbitrary, clandestine discipline of the stato, must be reduced to beggary. To further his absolute, personal supremacy Lorenzo not only worked with his own stato against Florence, but with the populace against the stato. Lorenzo attacked the most important, the sole unassailable law, the unwritten code of supreme authority: he abused the regulations of internal diplomacy. In his innermost circle he felt that he needed no dissimulation, that he could appear unmasked. He was impatient and gruff, expected his desires to be understood and obeyed when he snapped his fingers, and demanded subservience. Lorenzo treated the highest and wealthiest lords of Florence superciliously; he patronized them, regulated their marital affairs and their amours, daily threatened them with additional taxation, and forbade the linkage of too powerful families by marriage. He preferred the less wealthy; he even preferred men who did not belong to that peculiar institution, the stato; and he eliminated from the stato those who were most esteemed.

The strongest members of the stato, the Pazzi and the Salvati, he simply expelled from positions of authority. He attempted to ruin financially the commercial and banking firm of the Pazzi, which in the last half century had had higher balances than his bank.

The men of the stato, however, were not thralls. Nor did they need the Medici's money. They could neither be led nor corrupted nor intimidated. They could not be deceived by fables about Fatherland, Liberty, and Constitution. They were merchants with money and an indebted following not only within the Republic, but with extensive connections throughout Italy. Theirs was the gratitude of cardinals, the favor of the Holy Father, and the friendship of Venice, Milan, and Naples.

And it was from the ranks of his peers that danger arose for Lorenzo and his less important brother, Giuliano. Rich, youthful Francesco Pazzi, as a result of a hint from Lorenzo, was being specially persecuted by the authorities. The subordinate bureaus plagued him daily with their officious malice. They called him to account for alleged obscurity in his tax statements; they repeatedly made him wait for hours and would then discover new openings for chicanery. What the small organizations began, the great one completed: the Signory passed an inheritance law which was actually directed solely against the house of Pazzi. Nevertheless, Francesco avoided open enmity with Lorenzo. Their deep mutual hatred showed itself externally in suave friendliness at the frequent banquets.

But Francesco Pazzi could not long endure the humiliating situation into which the Medici had forced him. He had many relatives and a large number of young friends in Florence who were indebted to him as their patron and who were ready to venture for his sake into the baptismal waters of rebellion.

His following in Rome was even more important. His house arranged the affairs of the Vatican and credited to the Holy See the huge sums which the Medici refused to advance to Pope Sixtus IV.

Around the throne of Christendom there now formed an opposition to Lorenzo, a *fronde* of those driven out of the stato of Florence. Francesco's allies were: his kinsman and head of the house, Jacobi Pazzi; the archbishop of Pisa,

Francesco Salvati; and the intimate of the Pope, Cardinal Rafaelo di Riaro. "Holy Father," said one of the conspirators to Sixtus, "the precondition of our victory in Florence is the death of Lorenzo, Giuliano, and perhaps of others." "I do not desire at any cost the death of those two," answered the Prince of Christendom. "I cannot give my consent to that. Lorenzo is a rascal indeed, but I do not desire his death. I desire only a change in the stato."—"Good," was the reply, "we shall try our best. But if Lorenzo should die, the Holy Father will forgive us?" "Ah," replied the tormented priest, "thou art a beast. I desire a change in the stato."

The Holy Father left the council room and his friends decided upon the murder of the Medici. A papal army was already at the border of Tuscany in order to enter the city as soon as the overthrow had been completed.

The chiefs of the conspiracy were back in Florence, urging haste. Too much time had already been wasted. On the morning of the day before Easter the friends met. The prominent men in bank and Church not only supported the attempt, but were themselves ready to strike down their victim. The moment was at hand; their treachery must be swift and efficient. Their hatred for Lorenzo was so strong that they could not assign the task to any common assassin. They meant to win power with their own daggers. In pressing haste, but with attention to the smallest detail, the plan of the attack was once more discussed. Lorenzo and Giuliano were to die immediately and the Florentines then either persuaded or driven to liberty.

The confederates separated. Some went to the church to commit the murder, others to the city to join their armed forces and occupy the Signory, the palace of the Medici, and the bridges over the Arno.

With a few friends, Francesco Pazzi entered the already overcrowded cathedral. Lorenzo was standing before the altar in the front row, with the glow of the Easter tapers upon him. The two who were to murder him—two priests—wormed their way through the crowd to his side. Francesco's eyes sought for his victim, Giuliano Medici. Someone whispered softly to him that Giuliano was not there. For a moment he was terrified, thinking that the plot had been discovered. But he swiftly regained his composure, left the church and hurried to the Medici's palace. Here he was received immediately. In the house of his enemy, by a remarkable effort of will, he lost all of his apprehension and became pleasant and suave. In splendid spirits, he told the somewhat astonished Guiliano that he had to come to accompany him to church. If Giuliano had perhaps remained in his room because he was troubled by dark forebodings, he now went gladly, as if freed from a danger. On the way to the cathedral they joked merrily. Francesco even embraced his victim to learn whether he was wearing a cuirass beneath his garments. They entered the church on time.

Giuliano made his way to his brother so that they might receive the holy wafer from Cardinal Riaro together. This moment, when the two Medici kneeling before the priest bent their heads to the ground, was the one for which the conspirators had been waiting. Francesco's dagger struck Giuliano in the nape of the neck. He sank to the ground. Francesco fell into a maddened rage and with his short sword began to hack furiously at the dying man. Lorenzo, however, had only been lightly grazed by the thrusts of the two priests; he was down for but a moment. A splendid fencer, he defended himself valiantly with his sword and then, covered by two attendants, he escaped behind the bars of the sacristy.

When the words of Cardinal Riaro, who had been reading mass, were interrupted by the noise and cries of the fight, the kneeling people in the church thought at first that the dome had collapsed or that the cathedral was burning. Panic for a moment protected the struggling men at the altar from the interference of the congregation; but suddenly the people understood the murder scene. They surged wildly forward, intent on killing the Cardinal. The clerics screened his flight behind the iron gate. The sacristy saved di Riaro as it had Lorenzo.

Not only in the cathedral, however, but in the city also, the people, especially the Lesser Guilds, rose in defense of the Medici. Archbishop Salvati, with a small troop of armed men, had succeeded in making his way into the Signory. But the gonfaloniere, a loyal adherent of Lorenzo, was not taken unawares. He called the watch and the servants of the palace. They threw those who had already forced an entrance out of the windows on to the piazza. In the space of seconds a noose was flung about the neck of the archbishop and he was left dangling between earth and sky. Near him, suspended from the same balcony, hung many of his companions. All the conspirators were already in the hands of the mob, and every prisoner was slain. Within forty-eight hours of the attack on Lorenzo's life, seventy followers of the Pazzi were killed out of hand by the mob.

Francesco Pazzi, seized by the rabble, still dared to cry, "Popolo e libertà". A thousand hands reached for him to tear him to pieces. Naked, bleeding from many wounds, he was dragged through the streets to be hanged beside Salvati from the window of the Signory. Francesco uttered not the slightest sound of complaint. Icily he stared at his torturers. His relative, the gray-haired Jacobi Pazzi, was killed in the street by the people. Against him, as the head of the family, the mob fury mounted to its highest pitch. They dragged his body through every street in Florence. "When they finally arrived at the entrance to his house," an eyewitness recounts, "they fastened the rope to the curved molding, drew the corpse high and screamed in laughing chorus, 'Go ahead and knock!' "

The name Pazzi became a synonym for oppression. This family and their name seemed to the Florentines the only obstacle in the way of happiness.

With the approval of the government, there grew out of the defense of the Medici an uprising of the people. Within this movement all the contradictions in the Republic flared up. Lorenzo knew well how to use the sum of these contradictions to his own advantage.

And the entire history of this city: the struggle of all ranks to push their way upward into the sphere of the rulers; the constant hatred among the various factions, which spread from the assembly place before the Signory through every quarter and into every house; the decline of the patrician nobility into small groups which slashed at one another —all these factors joined to create a feeling of abhorrence for the wealthy, rebellious enemies of the Medici.

Real murder without restraint did not begin, however, until the guilty conspirators and all the friends of the Pazzi and the Salvati had paid the penalty. Then the innocent began to suffer. For thirty nights the Republic was a land without mercy. When evening darkened the city fear choked every sound. In the piazza the avengers gathered. Newly recruited police and vigilantes watched for suspects. Everyone trembled who, in accustomed freedom, had ever ventured an ugly word against Lorenzo, his father, or his grandfather. It was known that all these former doubters disapproved of the attack in the cathedral; it was known, too, that many republicans would use the attempted assassination as a pretext to join openly with the ruling family; nevertheless the authorities acted as if every non-Medicean was a murderer.

Lorenzo skillfully removed the bars which were always necessary to hold in check the hatreds that arose from social contradictions. In Florence, such revolutionary energies dwelt in the guilds. The favorite road led from the guild to the chamber of the Signory, where enemies could be denounced anonymously. Violent emotions festered within the corporations. And since these enmities could not discharge themselves within the corporation, they overflowed into the street. From the guilds came the crowds of desperate men who fired the houses of their enemies and murdered the women and children of opponents. Within the guilds, the unofficial privilege of the Florentines—the right to make civil war—was the greatest pride of the native-born.

Lorenzo had wanted to liquidate this chronic strife. Now, however, he did not oppose it. Thus he won the grateful support of the little men, and at the same time disposed of his prominent enemies and the many wealthy citizens who saw in him the end of liberty for Florence.

This task Lorenzo performed without issuing edicts. For a time his palace became an armed camp. Those who were really shocked by the murders, and all flatterers, met in his home in order, as they put it, to give over to him and to the city their weapons and their property. Lorenzo, in mourning, wearing black, merely complained, in the midst of all this gracious attention, of the general excess of misfortune. It was not necessary for him to name his enemies; he knew that the people were murdering as he desired! He remained silent. If a plea for aid made its way through to him, he spoke of his lack of influence under the law.

For real Power demands the opportunity to wash its hands in innocence.

At the end of these days of murder, Lorenzo justified himself and the deeds of his furious followers before the authorities of the city, sitting in solemn session: "What zeal . . . What loyalty to avenge my brother. Not only can I not refrain from rejoicing therein, but I must count it to my honor and my fame . . . Where even thieves and murderers find refuge, in church, the Medici are delivered over to assassins . . . There can be no exoneration for the Pazzi;

if they had felt enmity, they were perfectly free to attack us . . . They have, however, confused private enmity with public affairs . . . Always I shall acknowledge you as my Fathers, always shall I be willing and ready to carry out your commands. I shall not hesitate, should you order me, to terminate with my own death this struggle that began with the death of my brother. . . ."

From the defeat of the Pazzi to the death of Lorenzo, in 1492, Florence experienced a decade and a half of inner peace. The sovereignty for which the Medici had striven had been attained.

Yet no accusation pained Lorenzo more deeply than the charge that he wished to violate or even to correct the Constitution of the Republic. He constantly reminded the people of his family's struggle against oligarchy, and always sought to remain close to the Lesser Guilds. He proclaimed himself the friend of the little man, made public speeches about the common people, and complained to cobblers and tailors of his heavy burdens. It was one of his political inventions to slap in brotherly fashion the *miserabili* cheerfully on the back.

Lorenzo even permitted the citizens the pleasure of holding elections, and the greater satisfaction of being themselves elected. But those whose names were drawn from the urn were his followers. He established a secret system of influencing the elections.

Until his time elections were managed by a purely technical commission, which often arbitrarily set aside these laws designed to determine eligibility. The names of the eligibles were thrown into a closed sack. A man from the Signory drew a name out of it and then the name was placed on the ballot.

Under Lorenzo, the board of elections was made up of his own creatures, and the closed sack became an open one. Lorenzo's hand replaced the hand of chance.

This sleight of hand, however, was not enough for

Lorenzo. It seemed to him too narrow a basis of legality.

He allowed the numerous boards and officials to continue and even gave them splendid new names. But under the ever-popular pretext of ordering finances, he subordinated all these institutions to a new tribunal: the Council of Seventy. In the Council of Seventy there was room only for the friends of the Medici, only for those who in the course of decades had proved their loyalty as members of one or another of the public commissions.

The magistracies, the Signory as court of last appeal, in fact, the whole ruling personnel had—until the reign of Lorenzo—been renewed every second, third, or sixth month. Within the framework of a custom such as this, no bureaucracy could arise. The Medici needed now, in place of people of rank, a firmly entrenched officialdom. For only the mechanical device of a bureaucracy could weld the small group of rulers to the great mass of the ruled; could subordinate the many to those who controlled the state. Only by means of austere, soulless offices and grottos of tiny desks; through the vanity of insignificant clerks; through apparently meaningless formalities, could the inwardly free man, who was not bound to a community or group, be kneaded, molded, trodden down, de-anarchized, and disciplined. This bureaucracy was largely composed of Florentines with legal training. Among them was Bernardo Machiavelli.

For two centuries his ancestors had held high offices in the Republic. Sixteen of them had been justices of the peace and fifty of them priors. His forefathers had always been on the side of those populani who welcomed periods of rebellion in order to break into the ruling clique. The Machiavellis had long been involved in politics and for them the intricacies of Power held few secrets. Their insight into shifts of fortune, the constant ups and downs which characterized the history of this Republic, kept alert their interest in all paths that might lead into the Signory. They too might become rulers some day.

Such firm family traditions protected the city from the despotisms of most of the other Italian cities. In Florence, fools were not permitted to come to power, as in Milan, where a ruler spoke to his subjects only when separated from them by a fence; or as in Ferrara, where bloodhounds were let loose upon the citizens for amusement; or as in Naples, where a private cemetery for murdered opponents was established so that the ruler might stroll in it at his leisure. To be sure, the Florentines could not find any secure basis for freedom; but they recognized it as the concomitant of culture and as the highest virtue. The traditions of liberty in these Florentine families, who were always as ready to use their daggers as a steer its horns, acted as a check upon vicious authority. The struggle of their ancestors for freedom carried on under the eternal risk of exile, imprisonment, confiscation of property, or even death, seemed to the citizens of the Medicean period too cruel and too expensive.

Lorenzo preferred to place the children of these very families in official positions. Thus he emphasized the common republican tradition. The names of these well-known populani made his position legitimate and smoothed the path to sole rule. The Medici planned to attain all their goals by subterfuge. They were successful in this method because the forces of evolution—all the objective elements which were not apparent to the eye, but which were nevertheless operating steadily—worked for them. In the end, it was easier to administer the growing city by excluding the citizens from participation than by allowing their voluntary activity in the city's institutions. It became, indeed, a necessity.

The necessary personnel—legally trained and with a reputation for holding popular sympathies—was not difficult to find. For these old families were impoverished. They did not understand how new wealth was made; they had forgotten how to take advantage of crises.

Bernardo Machiavelli was one of those who could no longer live solely on his inheritance. His wife, like himself of an old Florentine populani family, possessed only the dream, but not the means of patrician splendor. Four children were born to him, two sons and two daughters. Unsupported by any income, his patrimony swiftly dried up. Poor at figures and understanding nothing of business, he was yet able to estimate the time which still separated him from utter bankruptcy. To leave the city, however, withdraw to his tiny estate, become a tiller of the soil—that was unthinkable to this learned student of law.

Florence left open to him only the path to the bureaucracy. He became a discontented treasury official. A little man, defeated by his troubles, Bernardo never forgot to be cautious. As consulting tax attorney, he knew very well the function of the treasury as a gold mine for the Medici; but fear kept his mouth closed.

Only at home did he become talkative. But even within his own four walls he would say no more about politics than was permitted by the authorities. Before his wife and his children, his otherwise skillfully concealed bitterness raged out against the priests. He brought the anticlerical phrases and the antipriestly superstitions of the Florentine streets to the evening meal. Each time he began his wife trembled anew, suffered for the faith of her children. She wanted her second-born son, Niccolo[1] to become a clergyman and tried to save him from Bernardo's tongue. She composed hymns to the Holy Virgin for her child. But the son took after his father. Already Niccolo grinningly delighted in the peppery coarseness of Bernardo's unchristian rancor. The witticisms of his disgruntled father were the sole words of enchantment this child, who grew up without fairy tales, ever heard.

[1] Niccolo Machiavelli was born in Florence on May 3, 1469.

Not far from the Ponte Vecchio, in the narrow street which later bore the name Via Guicciardini, stood the small three-story house which Bernardo had inherited from his ancestors and in which the very modest career of Niccolo Machiavelli began. He spent the entire day in the street. The wild life of these Florentine children was squeezed into the narrow space between the façades of the tall houses. They accompanied events in the Republic as a shouting, jubilant chorus; they were more cruel, more vicious, more thievish than the adults. They begged threateningly at the carnivals; during the Pazzi uprising they played mockingly with corpses; they formed the merciless moral police of Savonarola, and later joyfully plundered his monastery. As a child Niccolo familiarized himself for the rest of his life with the street. In his eyes it lost all mystery and all idealization. He acquired its impulses along with its speech. His memory and his love of the factual drove him to seize upon the realities of the little people with his eyes, his mouth, and his nose. The streets of Florence buried themselves deeply in Niccolo's consciousness; in his mind the topography of the whole city lived. He was spiritually one of its charter inhabitants.

Children of other officials and patricians were already reading Greek, or were apprenticed to one of the Greater Guilds. They were studying music, sculpture, or painting. But Niccolo was learning to swear, learning the proverbs of the walls and house-fronts and latrines. He remained without artistic talents—an exception in artistic Florence. Pictures, statues, melodies did not interest him. Art bored him. And when later he became acquainted with Michelangelo and Raphael, their aims concerned him no more than a wind that might happen to be blowing in some distant land.

Niccolo still allowed himself, like every forceful young man, the luxury of indecisiveness. He followed the call of the easy roads which led to no goals. Those who feel great strength within them are, at the beginning of their conscious existences, untroubled. The germs of many talents left him no time at all to speculate upon his career. Usually, only the ordinary know exactly what they want to become.

Bernardo, however, must have grown daily more and more worried about his adolescent son. The first-born, Toto, about six years older than Niccolo, was nothing but a supercargo in the miserable family boat. He had already proved his worthlessness. The younger brother remained the sole hope. And he wanted, nevertheless, to take his chances. Niccolo decided not to study law, which would have opened to him the safe path into the bureaucracy. The atmosphere of the city, saturated with Latin phrases and Roman allusions, fired him with the general humanistic fever. Knowledge of law was commonplace within officialdom. It led from desk to desk, from rung to rung, within the hierarchy. As a humanist, on the other hand, one might remain an unemployed intellectual; but one might also attain to something extraordinary, gain fame over night. Writing a successful poem, an excellent translation, a classically formed oration could advance one further than plodding the even road of law. Those who sat around Lorenzo in the seats of power were humanists, not jurists.

Niccolo Machiavelli was but fifteen years old when Dante's statue in the church of San Giovanni was being crowned.[1] His works and Petrarch's were being joyfully commemorated because they had been written in Italian—the language which up to then, as Lorenzo observed, had only been sinned against. The stream, however, which flowed from the union of correct Latin with the noises of the piazza carried the youth along. This stream nourished Niccolo's innate disposition toward the unrefined, the harsh, and the turbulent. Like every Florentine who was not totally uneducated, he learned Latin as he learned to read and write. His interest in the classics, however, was not literary. He sought more

[1] 163 years after Dante's death, 110 after the death of Petrarch.

concrete knowledge: facts, dates, events in Roman history. He too felt that an illustration drawn from classical antiquity was an analogy applicable to all times.

This mixture of the classic and the modern, that is, the Italian, became the base of his intellectual alloy, the very substance of his whole being.

At this time, as an unknown wanderer through the streets of Florence (neither his contemporaries nor later research ever unearthed any information about his youth), he built his powers of offense and defense. Those powers were to form the new humanism. For through Machiavelli humanism was directed into political channels. Up to the time of Cosimo, the early humanists had been primarily intellectuals who, incidentally, often worked for rich men as private secretaries and occasionally became rich men themselves. But now humanists became essentially politicians. Machiavelli, Guicciardini, Vettori, Aretorino, Leo X, had some literary interests, but these were subsidiary to politics.

Among these humanists, Niccolo was one of the most poorly educated. His contemporaries did not account him a scholar. "Machiavelli," wrote the contemporary historian of Florence, Varchi, "is no man of letters, rather, a man without literary culture."

He merely emphasized the new trends. He transformed these trends into a new intellectual attitude.

From time to time it appeared as if culture would collapse of its own weight. An intellectual Hercules seemed necessary to clean out the libraries. Unknown to them and independent of them, Niccolo Machiavelli completed what Lorenzo, Pico della Mirandola, and Marsilio Ficino had begun in this direction. It was precisely the genius of this self-tutored youth that enabled him to do this. Humanism stood in need of a man with his particular defects, with his lack of religious imagination, with his secularism, subtlety, and lack of sensitivity. It needed a man who was temperamentally incapable of understanding pure theory, pure philology, love of books for their own sake, and conventionality.

Since the power of ruling others had now become a good in itself, practical men sought to acquire this power. The struggle involved every conceivable form of force, treachery, and violence. As various and yet as monotonous as the passing of the days, this lust for Power manifested itself in the men of the Renaissance. It was as inseparable from them as the weight of their bodies.

Niccolo Machiavelli's intellectual contribution did not ban morality from the political intercourse of nations, classes, and social groups. He did not exercise the enormous and satanic powers ascribed to him. He did not transform the world from a pacific to a military paradise. Before, during, and after Machiavelli's time, not only the tyrant and the dictator, but the politician in general and the demagogue in particular, has had to be a talented dissembler, a ready opportunist, a master in the field of human weakness, an accountant of forgotten sins, a prompter of vanities, a skillful juggler with ideals, a lover of cunning, and a worshipper of force.

Niccolo Machiavelli merely formulated in words those elements in the statesman's craft which for centuries had been recognized and practised. It is this formulation which gave his name to an eternal impulse, an eternal fact. The heroes of his age were deaf and blind to the rationalizations by which Power could justify itself. Machiavelli saw the spirit of violence in their conduct and praised it as natural to the elect, the resolute, and the fortunate men. He was in a position to see those factors clearly because his age was trampling into the dust all medieval concepts of sanctity. For although that trait which posterity has called Machiavellism is eternal, baseness in politics had always been accompanied by a bad conscience until the end of the fifteenth century. Far as it was from reality, the Christian ideal, like all accepted ideals, nevertheless had exercised an influence upon men's actions.

Nowhere, however, was the gulf between good and evil, between Heaven and Hell, so consciously and decisively spanned as it was in the Republic of the Medici.

Florence became a city of skeptics. People remained neutral to ideals and ironical toward traditional concepts of morality. The moral universe held not the slightest interest for them. They were convinced that all ideas might just as easily be false as true. In this belief they felt themselves free and superior. The chroniclers complain of the lackadaisical attitude of many rich Florentines. Neither outbursts of enthusiasm nor pessimistic prophesies could shatter their apathy. Heaven was a hollow word to them, and earth charged with opportunities for malice and ruthlessness. A compound of valor, venality, and adroitness characterized their way of living and their relationships to other men. It became the custom among them to praise acts which in other times were done only in secret. It did not wound their dignity to live without the halo cast by honesty, family, love, church, and courage. They felt that they could do without the veil which had always hidden deeds and emotions; and they did not shudder to view naked their own hearts and those of others.

Politics were purified of all moral ballast. To live in this world, without perfectionist ideals, without poetics, without fictions, without accepting any abstractions,—this was the realistic political aim of the Florentine.

"Speculation on supernatural matters, or on anything which cannot be seen," wrote Machiavelli's friend, Guicciardini, "is purest idiocy." And Vettori, whose life was always closely associated with Niccolo's, declared it ridiculous to desire to foster trouble in the State because of ideals. To be more than merely flexible, to desire more than immediate profit from favorable or unfavorable circumstances, was to his mind striving for unrealities. The intelligence and clarity of vision of the political man of Florence were in the service of practical, attainable things.

The sole reality remained for them, however, the individual alone. Michelangelo believed that the depiction of trees, meadows, harbors, and streets should be left to the lesser talents because the true subject of painting was the human body. Similarly, Florentine politicos looked upon the individual as the sole object of their art.

This common intellectual peculiarity, which was limited to no political system, was possessed by Niccolo Machiavelli long before personal misfortune forced him to take up the pen. He was free of dogmatism and all the baggage of traditional authority. He longed for direct, personal experience. Often in his life he was to find himself in a dependent position. In his own words, he was to "follow in the footsteps of many a man who wore a finer cloak." Yet he never lost his independence of thought. This youth, who had still won no position in Florence and was still waiting for his appointment to office, was born an objectivist in politics.

The interests of the men who were his masters did not in the least affect his gift for truth. He wrote as if he were expounding a geometrical proposition instead of political doctrines which always cloak deeds in words. Enamored of logic as he was, he was still careful not to assign reason too important a role on the political stage. His major premise taught him that whenever reason was opposed to human emotions it could easily be put to flight. The passions of the individual were for him the determining element in politics. It was his task to describe the effects algebraically; to take their measure once and for all and to establish their reciprocal relationships.

The struggle raging in the world, the unrest throbbing in men's minds, and the bitterness that despoils towns and cities, all grow alike, he felt, out of the individual. The world in general is impelled by exactly the same passions that move individual men in particular. Through the centuries men have lived in a perpetual state of warfare. Their existence is a constant, noisy disharmony. In misfortune men are cast down without measure; but of fortune too they soon grow weary. When their luck is good they swell with vanity and pride, and point to their virtue as the cause. They become unendurable to their neighbors. In misfortune they are despicable and can be bought for a song. But fortunate or unfortunate they are driven by a burning passion, a profound thirst for life which keeps them ever ready to struggle. If they do not have to fight, then they fight because they are ambitious. Ambition never deserts them, no matter to what heights they may climb. Victors never remain satisfied for long. Their desire for gain is insatiable and greater than their opportunities for acquisition. Discontent is the supreme determinant, the eternal cause of action; one part of mankind desires to have more than it possesses, the other fears to lose what it already has. Thus arise enmity, war, the ruin of one country and the elevation of another. Withal, these plunderers are simple-minded. To a large extent they obey the needs of the moment. They are like "small birds of prey, so mastered by the lust for their spoil that they do not observe the larger bird hovering near them to rob them of their lives". Neither the experience of their forebears, nor reason, can save them from destruction; for they are sluggish, they live from hand to mouth, they believe that nothing can happen which has not as yet happened, and almost always they follow paths which were cut by others. Their lives are counterfeits.

"Their baseness," Machiavelli writes, "can neither be conquered by time nor ameliorated by kindness."

"When some villainy remains for a time unknown, this is only because of some unknown reason which does not come to light until the baseness comes out in the open. Time, the mother of wisdom, discloses all contemptible actions."

Knowledge of evil is as old as thinking man, and the

struggle against it as old as religion. Machiavelli was the first to declare the renunciation of this conflict. Indeed, he made it a fundamental principle. But he by no means transformed evil into good. He did not pervert morality; never was he hypocritical. Evil was to him an unalterable reality, like death, the sea, and the four seasons. Evil was not only part of existence; it was the impelling force in the world. Not to recognize it was foolish and unrealistic. All the hymns that men sing to the Good are products of either the optimistic or the hypocritical make-up of the individual. They are a form of toying with make-believe and with the ought-to-be. Mulling over the ought-to-be is flight from observation of fact, mere dreaming in a paradise of indolence. "For there is," Machiavelli writes, "a very great difference between the way men live and the way they *ought* to live, and he who clings to what should be instead of to what is works rather for his destruction than for his sustenance. A man who always and everywhere would act according to a perfect standard of goodness must, among so many who are not good, eventually be undone."

In the three fundamentals of his thinking, *necessità, virtù, fortuna,* Machiavelli discovered to the world the new reality of Power. The world was no longer to consist of many pious souls counting their tithes; no more was it to be molded within a general idea of the Christian community. There would be no more crusades; but rather, strictly delineated territories and fortresses, rationally working systems of government and commands functioning like clockwork. He disclosed what since his time has been a permanent demand: the need of nations for *armi propri,* for their own weapons.

The man who does evil does only that which nature forces him to do: the inborn elements of his body and soul mold him. Necessità—compulsion—is the mother of all things. Machiavelli wanted the political man to reckon with this compulsion of nature as the sailor calculates the wind and the architect estimates the stresses of a building. He felt that nature is the sum of reality, and only when a man understood her chaotic variety could he be practically and directly effective. His thinking expressed the attitude toward life of those Florentines who had invented eyeglasses, built roads and dyed linen superbly, and who now, with their newly-acquired impiety, believed they could control man as they had regulated the flow of the Arno. To Machiavelli the feeling that there was no God who had created the world was so matter-of-course that he no longer emphasized it. As far as he was concerned, therefore, there was neither morality nor immorality in the workshop of existence, only emotions, which were determinable forces. Bloodthirstiness, cunning, excess, ingratitude, much hatred, some love, a modicum of respect for tradition, latent passions for innovation and change, daring, lust for gold, ennui, desire for fame, ambition, envy, hunger, vainglory, fear of the present and dread of the future—these to him, were the motives that drive men. With untiring patience he combined the elements in this game of passions. It was necessary merely to juggle them in order to attain political goals.

Powerful and decisive men, men aflame with the fire of virtù—the virtue of rulers—know reality and rejoice in it. They know, he writes, that "nature has placed riches in the world to be won rather by depradation than by industry, rather by evil than by good device; they observe the works of men and see that all who gain great riches and great power have reached their goals by deception or by violence. Then, in order to obliterate the memory of the unscrupulous nature of their acquisition, they obscure what they have seized by cunning or superior might, with the name of honest profit."

Not all, however, are destined to reach this goal. For it is not simply a question of a lottery of violence, in which any ordinary bandit draws a lot. That man alone enters the ring as one of the elect who is bold only when it is worthwhile, only when the supreme stake, Power, is at hazard. This man, by virtue of his *grandezza del animo* and his *fortezza del corpo* is the emancipated bearer of the entire future. This chosen soul, at once impelled and consumed by virtù, must be almost ideally cool-headed. He knows that relationships are constantly shifting; he understands new circumstances and adjusts himself to them immediately; he does not cling to the method which yesterday brought him partial success; he alters his previous judgments with lightning speed. Yet despite this fine flexibility, he preserves in every situation in life his original pride, as if fate had no power over him; and despite every caution he is always engaged in action. For it is only in direct activity that he is able to discover the vast total of political truths which he would never learn by pure observation and without experience. This man, graced by the virtue of rulers, will above all be possessed of ruthless cunning. For the quality of his virtù—his especial talent for Power—must triumph over an inimical and ever malicious fate, fortuna. It is a struggle of natural forces. The results are in the balance and the forces are equal. On the one side, the man without God striving to attain the highest worldly goals; and on the other side, fortune, also unguided by divinity.

The conflict with fortuna is the struggle of man against his own limitations: the impossibility of knowing the morrow precisely or of fathoming all the forces that govern the present. The individual arms himself with will, purpose, and industry. But the constant element of fortuna tips the balance very easily on those occasions when man can do nothing and knows nothing. In a thousand forms she manifests herself, in a thousand ways she tries to harass and hinder. She can also lure and magically make the difficult seem easy. Out of the darkness, fortuna strikes down the star seeker, and when she is bent upon malice, she casts her lightning bolts from a clear sky. She sometimes lets the hero gain the threshold of success only to snatch the ground from under his feet so that he plunges into dark chaos.

Against the wild and sudden torrents of fate, the man of virtù must construct breakwaters and dykes. Then he will be able to hold the floods within bounds. Fortuna governs only half of our activities. But fortuna crushes men who are inspired by no virtù; those who are weak-willed and powerless and thus unable to gather and discipline the forces of nature, the passions. The virtù of the great individual, on the other hand, seizes the chaotic passions of ordinary men and uses them to attain and preserve this rule.

The man inspired by virtù has at his disposal, in reality, only the imperfect material of human beings. He shapes by his intellect or by compulsion—necessità—"the faithful serfs who," as Machiavelli writes, "will always remain serfs, the honest people who will always remain poor, the disloyal and impudent men who want to slough off all compulsion, the dishonest, the rapacious, and the beggars." His virtù is able to utilize the egoism of confused individuals and relate it to an historical purpose. He raises the masses by necessity into realms where they may even perform heroic exploits. By the virtù which once made Persia, Carthage, and Rome great, he ennobles these animals who must be ruled. "Thus it is said with justice," Machiavelli writes, "that hunger and poverty make men industrious; law alone makes them good."

This rare virtù was the Power which Machiavelli's imagination envisioned. Philip II of Spain, Pope Julius II, Louis XII and Francis I of France, Emperor Charles V, and every ruler of the future had something of Machiavelli's virtù.

In the narrow area of the Florentine Republic at the close of the Middle Ages the spirit of the centuries to come was manifested in many different ways. A man who lived in Florence was an early development of the Italian and the modern European in general. Consequently it is understandable that the thoughts of the not yet thirty-year-old Machiavelli anticipated the great contradictions which were growing among the cities, nations, and territories of the Continent.

CHAPTER III

God and Power

THE INTERNAL wranglings within Tuscany remained of minor importance. The disputing groups had limited goals. But the external relationships of Florence had an effect upon the whole of Europe.

The territory of the Republic was no larger than the State of Connecticut. The population of Florence did not exceed ninety thousand; that of the whole country, with its eight hundred walled towns and its twelve thousand unwalled communities, not more than five hundred thousand. Nevertheless, Florence made itself the channel through which flowed all the streams of growth in the Republic. From the windows of the Signory the illusions and realities of a changing Europe could be observed. An alert ear, like Machiavelli's, could listen to the fundamental motifs of political events. Hence, Florence's streets, animated by the many conflicting elements of the Occident, awakened in one day of their existence more interest than a millenium of the life of the Russian or Mongolian steppes.

Florence, which for centuries had been slowly but decisively influencing the whole continent, was being shattered by world events. Foreign needs had linked themselves with Tuscan affairs. The Florentine money market had been the aide of the centralized monarchy of France. Now the might of this monarchy spilled out over Florence and over Italy.

Each of the four great States—Spain, England, the empire of the Hapsburgs, and France—felt that its unity lent it superiority against the others. The warlike impulse which sprang from this feeling fed the flame of battle for many centuries and drew Charles VIII from France to Italy, and to Florence.

Before Charles VIII began his invasion in order to protect claims to the crown of Naples, he sent emissaries to the more important cities of Italy. Florence, because of its money, its geographical situation, and its authority, was the key position which must be secured without violence, if possible, under the guise of friendship. Lorenzo's son and heir, Pietro Medici,[1] the characterless ruler of Florence, was more athlete than statesman. He played ball for hours at a time, publicly measured himself against professional wrestlers, sported with his friends and relatives, drank a great deal, and often was not to be seen for days because he had locked himself up with his women, preferring this occupation to all others. Yet this man *refused* to furnish assistance to Charles in his campaign. The son of the great Lorenzo was a half fool, but for once he wished to follow the right course. His refusal had no national motives; no one in the whole of Italy had such motives. Pietro merely feared that Charles' campaign would involve him in entanglements with the neighbors of Florence. He wanted beyond all else his peace and quiet.

The question of what stand to take with Charles VIII threw the factions and the passions of the upper Five Hundred of Florence into a turmoil. The everyday conversation of the opposition among the leading populani dealt solely with matters of foreign policy.

All were for France. "In our hearts bloom the lilies," declared one Florentine.

The great puzzle of foreign policy—the question of

[1] The son of Cosimo was known as Piero the Gouty. Lorenzo's son was known as Piero or Pietro and to avoid confusion is designated here as Pietro.

Florence's relationship to Charles' campaign—trickled out of the palaces into the homes of the common people. The multitude had no exact information, but they lived in a general state of expectancy, breathing an atmosphere of adventure and drama.

Only one man, the Dominican monk, Girolamo Savonarola, in the monastery of San Marco, grasped the import of these events.

In long white nights of prayer he struggled for certainty. God would not help him, however, until he had learned to look upon earthly things as of no importance and to fill his days with the contemplation of God. With his spirit starkly intent upon salvation, in sweet ecstasy and incessant hymns, he had visions. God revealed Himself to him.

Girolamo Savonarola acquired the certainty of a prophet. His will, shaped in the cell of the monastery of San Marco, became a center of magnetic force, an activating power. He was the instrument of devotion. "I am like the hail," he cried, "which striketh all who are uncovered."

Savonarola mocked the petty calculations which the political experts and the masters of the famous Florentine combinazione wove about the expected invasion. He alone in this city of philosophers, money-changers, and keen critics, recognized the truth: that this march of Charles was to heap one monstrous misfortune atop the other! Savonarola broke through the veil of whispered rumor and announced the French expedition in prophesies thundered out with apocalyptic phrases. He frightened the people, filled them with dread. "O, Italia," he cried, "horror upon horror shall crash down upon thee: the horror of war upon famine, the horror of pestilence upon war, and one truthful report shall drive forth the one before it. Scarcely shall one rumor have announced a barbarian army, when first this and then another shall appear. A rumor from the west, a rumor from the east, rumor upon rumor from all directions . . . The priests shall lose their offices, princes shall clothe themselves in hairshirts, and the nations shall be ground to dust by misfortune."

For the preacher of such disaster, the expected calamity was inevitable. It would be useless for human energies to oppose it. He called upon the numbed Florentines before his pulpit not to take up weapons against the invasion, but to abhor their sins and those of others.

The hundredfold death which was now to begin was a needful revolutionary work of God. The Almighty was destroying in judgment this seat of the Church, this Italy, corrupted by crimes without number. The people of Florence began to say, "A prophet is among us."

Pietro Medici and all the other miserable puppets of Tuscan politics were, he said, but contemptible targets. The chief enemy sat in Rome and was "a painted doll, a voluptuous, shameless whore, worse than a brute". He had bought with gold the succession to the throne of Saint Peter. His name was Borgia and he called himself Alexander VI. The whole earth must rise against this Lord of the World, against this betrayer enthroned upon the seat of Solomon, who for money opened the gates of the temple, for money gave the sacraments, for money distributed the highest offices, for money forgave every sin and for money set the bells of all the churches ringing. Savonarola imbued the tiny Tuscan Republic with moral fervor and invoked it to world revolt. His pulpit was to be the Mount of Renewal, and far beyond the limits of San Marco was to unite all the devout who wept at the condition of the Church; was "to strengthen in their zeal all soldiers of Christ in every village and hamlet, in every city and castle, in Germany, in France, and in Spain. For they all whisper to me their readiness," he declared.

He was conscience, burning fiercely in defense of its faith. He sought the direct power necessary to injure his adversary. "Take from them their goods, O Lord," he prayed; "take all that they possess."

He knew that his visions—the armed saints, the arrows raining from heaven, the black crosses in Rome which obscured everything, and the golden ones in Jerusalem which shed light everywhere—could be but symbols of the military might of the laity. In his imagination, the whole world was arming against Rome. "Heaven and earth, good men and angels, indeed, even evil men" were on the march; and Charles of France was but the first of this host.

Sermon and cell had never sufficed this monk. He had a full knowledge of secular things, even though he spoke only in symbols. His Dominicans brought messages back and forth. He knew that Charles VIII was surrounded by men hostile to the Borgia. The untiring enemy of Alexander VI, Cardinal della Rovere—later Pope Julius II—was in the entourage of Charles of France.

Impelled by infinite hopes, Savonarola cried, "O, sword, sword, thou shalt restore order everywhere."

The city seemed no longer to belong to anyone. For six decades the Medici had done their work well and fulfilled the law of dictatorship: they had rid themselves of every leader of the opposition. Their opponents were either dead or in exile. A dictator's own indispensability is proved and consolidated by the destruction of all successors. Florence was Medicean only because there was no one to proclaim the fall of the family.

In a few days Charles VIII would be in Florence at the head of his 3,600 lancers, 6,000 Breton archers, his 6,000 crossbowmen, 8,000 Swiss and countless light artillery, surrounded by uprooted feudal grandees from France, Spain, and England, and by numberless unknightly knights and Italian emigrants. Coming from Lyons through Grenoble, he had crossed the Alps at the pass of Mont Gènevre, plundered Rapallo, and in Turin, Asti, Casale, and Piacenza had held magnificent celebrations. Now he was already encamped with his army on Tuscan soil, a few hours from Florence—in *Pisa!*

Florence was alluringly helpless in the face of the royal troops. The city felt as if it were captive, no longer capable of any decision. Excitement seized the people and drove them out of their houses. Curses and shrieks recalled the long past, pre-Medicean days of revolt. Boisterous groups gathered menacingly before the houses of well-known members of the Medici family. Tens of thousands of the men of the Lesser Guilds wound through the streets to stand patiently for hours in the piazza before the Signory, waiting for news. The troops of Pietro were at the city gates. Sentinels did not dare leave their guardhouses. The crowd, rich and poor, made pilgrimages to the church of San Marco.

Savonarola's voice was the first in a half century to cry out against the Medici. His words might at any moment lead to deeds.

In the midst of the crushing throng of pilgrims stood Niccolo Machiavelli. The monk, however, could not affect this man's mind any more than could the suddenly blazing faith of the Florentines. Niccolo remained cold, and all the pious words he was hearing buzzed annoyingly in his ear. What did this monk really want? Why was he worrying about the secular affairs of Florence? Machiavelli had the impression that the vultures and rogues of the Church wanted to rob him of his fatherland. Not that he was an adherent of Pietro Medici; he had nothing but contempt for that human parcel of frailty. Machiavelli had always pictured the man of Power, the heroic protagonist of the virtue of rulers, very differently.

It seemed extremely improbable to him that in impious Florence a priest should lift himself into the sphere of Power. This friar, however, was a fact. With his impassioned orations, he was the victorious child of the times.

Savonarola remained the single great surprise in Machiavelli's life. Neither change, nor victories and defeats, neither assassins like Baglioni of Perugia, nor city tyrants like Hercules of Este, were able to astonish him. But the surprise he experienced on seeing this monk paralyzed him. He was near enough to see him clearly, yet he did not comprehend him. Machiavelli was blind to the genius of faith, as he was blind to Leonardo da Vinci and Raphael. Had Savonarola not been a priest, Niccolo would have attempted to come close to him, as all his life he had sought to be near the powerful, not in order to flatter them or to share their rule, but to observe. He remained always a modest paramour of Power; but he always had to feel it with his hands, work for it, behind the scenes if there were no other way. His preoccupation with Power formed his whole existence. Power was the food, he wrote, "which is meet only for me, for which I was born."

He could not, however, come close to a priest who was no pope but merely an innovator, and who argued for absolute faith instead of for the great virtue of action. He hated the frock with all the strength of his prejudiced imagination.

The world would have been much better off, Machiavelli thought, without monks. Or at the most it should have but one monk. The one would enable him to satisfy his desire for all kinds of experience, even the disagreeable experiences which monks inevitably brought.

And what was this friar going to do with the power thousands of hands were offering him? Savonarola answered by condemning the long since deceased Cosimo Medici. "When Cosimo said to you," he preached, "that men cannot rule with the Lord's Prayer, never forget that those are the words of a tyrant, used to cast our city under the yoke and lead it away from God." Cosimo's dictum, however, was nothing more than the essence of the spirit of Machiavelli, and Savonarola was preaching against an adversary unknown to him.

But perhaps there was hidden behind all these other-worldly phrases a profound and cunning recognition of the things of this world; perhaps the monk sensed the absolute nature of Power; perhaps the white frock of the Dominican was but a veil to conceal bold designs to rule? "For he who reads the Bible with understanding," Machiavelli wrote, "will perceive that Moses had to kill many men in order to win assent to his pious laws and regulations."

But now that he was in a position of power, the monk, who always in the past had breathed fire, used all his influnce to pacify the Florentines. He suddenly grew mild; he over-looked material things, because he saw other blessings. With the utmost impressiveness, he instructed the masses to be merciful when they were waiting eagerly for a sign from him to destroy. "O, Lord, thou who hast died for us, forgive, forgive . . . Florentines! Give alms, pray, and be as one!"

He did not desire a revolt in Florence. He trusted only Charles of France and not the sinister glances of those who wanted to burn everything Medicean. Historians, even his enemies, declare that with a wave of his hand he could in those days have destroyed the old rule and seized Power for himself.

Savonarola invoked Power as the scourge of God; but he could neither weld nor wield it. The core of sinfulness in Power, even when used for good, repelled him. His inner, higher world rejected it. Let others burden their souls with Power. His conscience could not endure it.

Niccolo Machiavelli perceived instantly this angelic strength and political weakness. This monk, he felt, was putting his trust in faithful masses who tomorrow might lose their faith. This monk was putting his trust in Florence, the city of moods and swiftly changing whims. This monk was not utilizing his advantage to arm himself so that he might compel the devout to greater devoutness and force the unbelievers to believe. *Savonarola understood nothing about Power!* He had nothing in common with Moses, Cyrus, Theseus, or Romulus, who realized that if they themselves remained defenseless they could not long hold their people in subjection. The monk was for Machiavelli a prime example of the sinner against opportunity! "Savonarola does not know," he wrote, "that time cannot be waited on, that fortune changes, and that evil cannot be appeased by kindness."

Savonarola, for all his transcendent aims, had no organization, no armed forces of his own. He wanted to retain supremacy without a coat of mail. And since he saw everywhere the necessity for Power, observed that words and faith dissolved into nothingness without it, he compromised and worked with borrowed Power.

Now, with the crisis at its zenith, the ancient Medicean Signory, the old stato of rich populani, was to be the force to free the country from Pietro Medici. He believed that only the Signory was in a position to banish Pietro because it was the sole political body. The revolt against the Medici was to arise out of the core of existing power.

The eminent populani agreed with Savonarola in the opinion that Pietro had plunged them and the city into misfortune. For if he had not acted in opposition to the King of France, if he had instead made an ally of the king, Florence would now be in league with the victorious army on Italian soil. Nearly a hundred of the first men of the city were invited to a conference by the Signory. Despite their anti-Medicean feelings, individuals still stammered when they wanted to speak rebelliously. If the benefits they had received, or their fear of the consequences, or their love of the dynasty, did not keep them silent, then the custom of sixty years interfered with their finding the saving word. But finally Piero Caponi, the foremost diplomat under Lorenzo and Pietro, loosed the tongues of all. "Pietro di Medici is no longer capable of leading us," he cried. "It is time that we emerged forever from the government of children." On his motion, the citizens of Florence ratified the alliance with Charles, which in the existing situation meant that they flatly capitulated. They believed that sacrificing Pietro would save as much as possible. But Pietro was a step ahead of them in capitulating.

He declared with swift decision, "I have neither money nor power nor influence enough to offer resistance." And he, who a few weeks before had been the boastful enemy of Charles, was the first to ride to greet him. Pietro Medici presented him with all the fortresses of Tuscany, with every mountain pass his father had made impregnable, with the port of Livorno, with Pisa, and with all the future taxes of Florence. With every word he gave and when he was through he knelt before the foreign monarch. In return for this surrender, Pietro asked only permission to be the right hand of the French against Tuscany. Essentially, he wanted the alliance against Florence which the Signory had firmly decided to obtain and use against him. Charles VIII looked upon Pietro's surrender with favor. Encouraged by this support, Pietro left the French camp and returned to Florence to restore his authority. He had lost the frivolity which had characterized him. Power meant something to him.

Pietro Medici entered Florence on the evening of the 8th of November, 1494. He sensed immediately that the whole atmosphere of the city had become hostile to him. Power slipped from him, as in a dream one loses the strength to use a weapon. An eyewitness wrote, "Pietro was fearfully isolated. One friend deserted him in this direction, another in that." Nothing was of avail any longer; neither violence, nor money, nor promises. His brother, Giuliano, later Pope Leo X, tried to win the suburbs by distributing money, but even gold was no longer accepted from the Medici! The condottiere of the city, Pietro's own brother-in-law, in reply to

Pietro's command to march against the Signory, said that he had sworn loyalty to the Republic, not to the house of Medici. From eight o'clock in the evening of the 9th of November, the republican oaths, which for sixty years had meant nothing, became important. Suddenly the cry rose, "Popolo e libertà!" In the entire city the Medici found but a single man crying: "Palle!"[1] In a moment the bells of the Signory were ringing for the Republic and stirring the emotions of the people. Not even violence was any longer necessary against the Medici, and no one's skin was even scratched by a dagger. The stato no longer dreaded the little men who marched through the dark city with kindled torches bearing the flag of the Signory. The troops cried, "Popolo e libertà!" and guarded against the vengeance of plunderers. Suddenly the rule of the Medici seemed to be an impossible, undignified, unendurable tyranny. It seemed so not only to the enemies of the Medici, the eternally intriguing lords, but to all. Illustrious men and common men, newly rich and hereditarily rich, newly poor and traditionally poor, now turned against the Medici. All who had shared in the power of the Medici and all who had looked upon that power as a matter of course could now no longer tolerate it. Pietro's own cousins were ashamed of the name Medici and wanted in the future to be called populani. The closest, best-known friends of Lorenzo and Pietro formed a procession and shouted for the Republic in the piazza in front of the Signory. The Signory had to fend off these new friends with a company of lancers.

A sixty-year-old sovereignty, which had radiated enough splendor to last humanity for centuries, was ended here in the space of four hours. At eight o'clock in the evening Pietro had tried to make his way into the Signory. His former associates, the *signori,* had refused him admittance. At midnight he rode secretly and in disguise out of the city toward Bologna.

[1] Palle—Balls were the cognizance in the Medicean coat-of-arms.

"I would never," said the ruler of Bologna, Bentivoglio, to the exiled Pietro Medici, "have abandoned supreme power in so fugitive a manner. Rather would I have let myself be hacked to bits while I still held a weapon." Bentivoglio was still entrenched in good fortune, and moreover had faith in his severity and his shrewdness. He could not conceive of the kind of spiritual earthquake which creates new values for the mass of the people. Against these the individual, whether he be a despot in power or a truth seeker at his desk, is helpless. But Bentivoglio was soon to experience it. Only a few years after his proud statement he had to flee from Bologna without a struggle, as his present guest had fled from Florence.

The earthquake which had destroyed Pietro's supremacy upset the Florentines. They were prepared to chance everything for the city they had freed from the Medici; prepared even to take up arms against Charles of France. The king and his soldiers, who had been received with rejoicing by the Florentines after the expulsion of Pietro, now demanded his restoration. The surprised Signory did not hesitate. It called the prominent citizens of the city and prepared every detail of the resistance. They planned a barricade battle without compare, a battle which would use the hundred narrow by-streets against the unmobile French army.

The bitterness of the Florentines made this decision easier for the Signory. The soldiers quartered in their houses were an oppressive burden; they were looked upon as an inundation of plunderers. Each man had the enemy in his own home; each felt himself threatened and wanted to defend himself. Rumors of looting ran through the city. When foreign soldiers caroused through the streets, stores were closed, goods concealed, and houses locked. At night the soldiers cut down citizens and the citizens murdered belated soldiers who lost their way. In the dark alleys of the *borgo ognisanti* quarter of the city a street battle was already raging. Frightened by the noise, the Swiss guards thought the king was in danger. They formed ranks and were about to storm the guarded Signory when, at the last moment, the king's trumpets signaled the Swiss to retire to their quarters.

Surprised by the firm determination of the Florentines, who a few short weeks ago had celebrated him as a deliverer, and intimidated by the threatening attitude of the city, Charles was ready to be conciliatory. The fact that the king did not know what he wanted made him even easier to sway. He cloaked his hesitancy in all the romantic hues of the Orient and Occident. He saw himself as Lancelot, as Tristram, as Charlemagne. He pictured himself as the king of Christendom, converting the whole world. One moment he wanted to restore Pietro Medici from chivalrous reasons of legitimacy; the next, to establish an eternal friendship with the Signory. First he saw as his task the reform of the Church and the purification of the papacy; then he wanted to conclude an alliance with Alexander VI. The basic reason for his vacillation was not merely his temperament, which was so easily responsive to fame and pleasure, but the inconsistency of his policies in general. He wished to make the French Church independent of the Pope, and at the same time to renew the universalizing tendencies of Rome by his own coronation as Emperor of the World. On the royal flags there shone, next to the French coat-of-arms, the words, "God's will" and "Emissary of God". His proclamation, dated in Florence, and printed in German, French, and Latin, vowed that his only aim was to unite Christendom and to free it from the menace of the Turks. He claimed he intended to conquer no territories.

The King of France met here in Florence the prophet of the diseased Church and wounded mankind. Savonarola had announced and lauded him. Now Savonarola urged the monarch to march on to Rome. He told the king that the reform of the Church would fill the sea and the earth, yea, even the heavenly regions with the name of Charles. He showed him the immediate, imperative duty of holding a council directed against Borgia. And he promised proofs of the Pope's monstrous crimes. Never had Savonarola felt himself so near to his goal. He would show Rome as he saw it to the world gathered in council!

Savonarolo lived in the hearts of many men before they had even seen him, and after they had once heard him they never forgot him. In the Republic, in all Italy, and throughout Europe were tens of thousands of little Savonarolas; and in Florence Girolamo spoke, wept and cursed for them all. Ideals of dignity, faith, and purity; ideals which could have their source only in the Church, were Savonarola's message to Charles.

The moral condition of the world; the opposition which, a decade before the theses of Luther in Wittenberg, was fermenting in all countries; the army, ready to pounce upon Rome; the twenty-four-year-old king—all these factors lent incomparable significance to the meetings and discussions of the Florentines.

The other European sovereigns, who as rulers were obligated to carry out reforms, were no more devout than Charles. But they were more restricted temperamentally, and therefore politically more dependable. Above all, they had the most important factions of their countries behind them. All France was laughing or raging at the war. The French looked upon the Italian campaign as a puerile repetition of the crusades of the twelfth century. They derided the king's knights, who saw nothing but a career of glory, adventure, and pillage. The appearance of syphilis is commonly dated from the campaign. The French called it the Italian, and the Italians the French disease.

Savonarola could not have found a more ineffective or untrustworthy secular arm than Charles. The king would have been willing to begin thirty crusades and to end every one of them in the first conquered city that offered him women, banquets, and spoils. Reform became in his hands a means of extortion by which he forced Borgia to make easier for him the conquest of Naples.

Arguments altogether different from Savonarola's prompted the king to make peace with Florence and withdraw from Tuscany. He was encamped in Florence without money. Twice already he had been on the point of cutting his campaign short for this reason. The French cities were refusing to support the war with as much as a single gold piece. Pietro Medici, the monarch's protegé, had been impoverished by his exile. He was begging throughout Italy for arms and money. The Signory, on the other hand, was enabled by the corporation of rich populani to pay immediately. They gave the king 120,000 gulden for peace and departure, and Charles not only left Florence but granted to the Florentines the right to enjoy the same privileges as Frenchmen in trading with his kingdom.

This commercial agreement was the sole point in the peace treaty which was lived up to by both sides. These trade privileges remained the material foundation of the Republic. Throughout the chaotic conditions which were now beginning, Florence had an assured zone of trade. Despite future French defeats, Florence was to be staunchly faithful to France. Her own economy required that she remain dependable. Charles VIII of France deserved the title the Signory bestowed upon him: "Restorer and Protector of Florentine Liberty".

The Florentine people—the great mass of the uninitiated —believed, however, that Charles' departure was the work of their prophet. He alone, by his piety, had saved Charles from the path of darkness. Savonarola himself lived in the same belief. It seemed to him now that everything was combining to aid the cause of world reform. He blessed the army marching off to Rome as the host of the devout.

The revolution in Florence daily broadened and deepened after Charles' withdrawal. Now distress was growing oppressive. The public debt, guaranteed at three per cent, was yielding only half of that; the Signory was paying in notes that had only a third of their nominal value. Bonds, the favorite investment of small savers and heirs of minor estates—which under Cosimo were the pride of the Republic—had fallen to their lowest point. The opposition could revive the religious ties which before the new material hardships had been considerably weakened.

The fermenting, anti-Medicean, antioligarchic morality was seeking a will. The prophet gave it. "O Florence," Savonarola cried, "thou art nought but flesh with eyes. The days of thy songs and dances are forever gone. Cleanse thy streets and thy places with streams of tears. Cursed be the useless books, cursed be vain beauty. Cursed be false science, cursed be the sinners in the fruit of their bodies and their fields, in the toil of their houses and their cities. Cursed be pleasure, cursed be all who live in pleasure and from pleasure."

The multitude who knew neither Latin nor Greek, who either worked laboriously or did nothing laboriously, who went to sleep regularly and arose early—the common people—could more easily endure a thirty years' war than thirty years of moral nihilism. And they intended now to take vengeance on the immorality of the Medici.

The interest in the classics, which for more than a century had been reshaping the emotions and processes of life, remained both within and without the Church a movement of aristocratic minds. Where the Renaissance touched the mass of the people, and it did so only on the fringes, it remained merely an uninspired paraphrase. Humanists could not hold popular assemblies, as did the disciples of Savonarola. The Renaissance was an individual, not a collective, experience. It was an intellectual mountain, there for all;

but the ordinary man and above all, many men at one time, could not climb it. Nor had the Renaissance promulgated equality of the rights of man. Rather inequality. It proclaimed that *each man* had the right to be more than his neighbor: not only the Pope, or the king, or the rich man, or the aristocrat. Like every intellectual movement, it demanded personal effort. The Renaissance believed that fortune was not attainable by the magic wand of principle. Spirit was, in general, hostile to hard and fast principles. If it made use of them, it was only out of curiosity to become transiently acquainted with *this* limitation, with *this* mode of living also. Perhaps only the highest genius had an intellectual right to principles—as for example, a man like Savonarola, who was being inwardly consumed. He remains the sole man of principle in one of the highest epochs of the human spirit, when all other representative men were profoundly unprincipled. To their hunger for life and knowledge, principle seemed like a prison, like a lifelong enchainment to a point of view. Such a condition was proper only for reformers and counterreformers.

On this account, also, the Renaissance only widened the gap between the cultured and the uncultured. The classic attitude toward life, the attitude of the Renaissance, was harmful to men and thereby to religion. The emphasis on strength made the cultured man consider all laws and religious traditions as restrictions for the great masses, mummery for the weak and unmanly. Pope Borgia, with his worldly appetites, for he too was motivated by these new forces, was not at all different from the condottiere, Malatesta, who had inscribed on his shield: "Foe of God, Mercy, and Humanity".

The masses, however, remained pious. For them, the protecting walls of convention still had strength and meaning. Even if the common man was no more moral than his superiors in his daily life, he still clung to the old Christian customs on weekdays and to the old Christian ideals on Sundays. He had to, for he lacked the material means to move in the spheres which were beyond recognized good and evil! If vice prevailed among the people, it was in secret, concealed through decency, neither praised nor poetized. And all those pious souls for whom the expulsion of the Medici meant the beginning of Justice; all who were lured and encouraged by the sound of the word Liberty, and wanted more than merely the stato without the Medici, came to the monk ready for political revolution.

His sermons became altogether political and wholeheartedly favored a democratic constitution. They embodied the sentiments of the populace. Savonarola was now unconstitutional master of the city as Lorenzo had once been. As Cosimo had once ruled the city from his counting house, the monk now reigned from his monastery cell. To him came the severe, surly populani who would shortly be speaking in the Signory and on the piazza against tyrannous power. The priest became the head of the radical party.

"Italy's wicked sovereigns," he proclaimed, "have been sent us as punishment . . . Their palaces and courts are refuges for criminals . . . houses of all the monsters of the earth for their boundless concupiscence. There they live unabashed, sucking out the blood of the people. There fawning philosophers invent new glories, and the poets trump up genealogies for their masters . . . But what is worst, in this Babylon, in this city of fools and godless men, priests are seen in alliance with the Evil One. . . ."

After Charles' withdrawal, Savonarola, at the zenith of his power, drew down upon Florence the enmity of the Pope, of Italy, and of all the independent powers of Europe.

Tuscany became the theater of war. Now the peaceful days, the firm, secure conditions of long decades, were at an end. The subject cities of the Florentines, Pisa at their head, revolted against the Signory. It was easy for them to find allies among the imperial, Venetian, Milanese, or papal condottieri. Florence seemed outlawed on her own Tuscan soil. The noble, stricken city was at once merciful and audacious. Despite her strict laws, Florence opened her gates to the peasants driven out of Tuscan villages. Savonarola even insisted that the refugees be given shelter in the houses of the well-to-do. With empty purse, Florence made war against poverty, against the external foe, and against the men of little faith. The people were in desperate straits. Florence was dying; Florence was pestilent; Florence no longer sold linen and brocade; she was avoided by the world and by the merchants and bankers of Europe. In the houses of Florence the children died like animals because they did not have a crust of bread; the diseased lay on the piazzas; in the streets men collapsed from weakness; women by the thousand lamented before the Signory; Florence's sole nourishment, sole hope, sole munition, was faith.

Savonarola wrote to his brother, "Our monks and the men and women of the common people, when they breathe out their spirits and commend their souls to the Savior, seem to be falling asleep, not dying; so that those remaining in life do not merely not fear death, but rather, long for it."

Pietro Medici thought at this time that to regain his mastery he had only to tap at the gates of this city, which three years ago had disdainfully cast him out. His secret friends proclaimed that he wished to distribute bread, declared that the monk and the revolution had dried up the fruitful plains of Tuscany and that he, Pietro, would restore Lorenzo's times, with nourishing, if earthly food. But the starving city forgot its hunger when it heard the word Medici. Pietro and those in league with him were beaten back by the Florentines. "And if the whole world has been on the march for Medici," a chronicler writes, "they would not have compelled us." After the victory the city forgot its prayers to breathe freely and to celebrate.

Savonarola warned the Florentines, "You must not let yourselves so easily be overcome by joy and sorrow. Do not put off practical measures! Keep your martial spirit alert with all your might!"

At the peak of a three-year-long crisis, the monk was as incisive as the crisis itself. Now, at last, he declared, the struggle was beginning against the universal peril of Roman sinfulness and for universal reform. He trembled with dread lest the Florentines would no longer be able to follow him after the victory over their immediate opponent and he prayed in the cathedral before the multitude, "Open up, O Lord, the hearts of this people, that they may understand the things that live in me and that thou hast revealed and commanded unto me!"

But the Lord did not hear his prayer, for the monk thought the influence of God on politics too direct. Savonarola was to the people of Florence merely a vow which they had taken while in the greatest anguish, a vow of pious reaction against the Medici, which they forgot once the emergency was past. The great love of the Florentines for their prophet concealed from the very beginning a fundamental misunderstanding which suddenly became apparent to all who saw clearly. Unfriendly external forces, days of common distress, and immediate political aims were only temporarily able to dispel this lack of understanding.

The Florentines understood by piety, faith, and Christianity, not Savonarola's struggle against the entire world, nor the golden era of triumphant, apostolic purity, but the fight for Liberty and the Republic. Savonarola was to them a moral impulse, the coiled spring of direct action against the Medici. He personified for them the heavenly blessing, the divine guarantee of their urban-democratic aspirations. For the monk, however, Republic, Constitution, Freedom, and Democracy were only a means to the end of universal reform.

This faith in universal reform alone drove Savonarola to political activity. Florence was to become the model republic. By the example of its orderliness and freedom, its regulated finances, its codified laws, and its charity, it was to convert the nations to God. Florence was to prove to the world that the Bible could and must be the scripture of the Constitution also. Since he linked his distant aims directly with practical exigencies, the Florentines went along a little way.

Savonarola had fulfilled his obligation to fight the public danger and act as the source of energy; now he himself became a danger. Intercepted letters convinced the Pope, Alexander, of the international significance of the monk. He saw that San Marco hid a dangerous conspiracy against him which was constantly being fed anew. And in order to split Florence from Savonarola, *he himself* split with all the enemies of the Republic, even dropping Pietro Medici. In return he demanded the surrender of the monk.

Since Pietro Medici no longer existed, his enemy, Savonarola, was no longer needed.

For a year Rome and the Signory haggled over the head of the friar. Alexander was ready to support the Republic against all her enemies and to permit her to tax the ecclesiastical estates which lay in her territory. But if the monk were not delivered up to him, he threatened to proclaim an interdict against the godless and heretical city.

Alexander VI, who considered Savonarola a rather mediocre fool, and who ordinarily paid tribute to the principle, "Live, and let the others talk", turned against the monk because this friar had leagued himself with the European Powers against the Ecclesiastical State. The Pope was defending his State, not the Dogma. The Holy Father excommunicated the Dominican. To counter the ban of the Pope, Savonarola hurled innumerable curses and monstrous sarcasms.

The bells of the churches of Florence rang against the monk. At the altars the tapers were extinguished as a sign of the papal sorrow for the excommunicate. Official piety, the Church, was crossing swords in Florence with unhierarchic, groping Faith. The followers of the friar were perplexed by this conflict. Their consciences felt burdened. If they listened to the sermons of the excommunicated monk, they made themselves guilty of the same fatal sin as the preacher. The foundations of their habits were threatening to collapse.

The office of the Pope was above his faults. As a man Borgia could err, and unquestionably he was entangled in sin. But as highest priest was he not above error? Had not Caterina, the Saint of Siena, whom all Florence reverenced, said that one must obey the Pope even if he were the Devil incarnate? Many of the faithful continued to revere the monk, but they avoided his sermons. Thus they thought to find the correct path between their consciences and the duty of Christian obedience. Only those continued to come to Savonarola who were firm in their faith, only those for whom the Savior had said, "Believe, and thou hast eaten!"

Savonarola was no longer permitted to enter the great cathedral. He preached in the church of San Marco, calling for a revolt against Borgia and against the impious, undemocratic men within the city.

He, who at the inception of the Republic had advocated pardon to all internal enemies, who more than once had saved them, suddenly wanted to crush all opposition. "O Florence," he threatened, "wilt thou be more gentle of spirit than God? Know then, thy gentleness is madness, thy mildness is cruelty . . . He who wishes to restore a tyrant or a government of the few, him must you put to the block! Strike off his head; even if he be the chief of the greatest family, strike off his head . . . Put your hands to the sword! Make yourselves the terror of evildoers. Justice, signori! Justice, magistrates! Justice, men and women! Let all cry, Justice!"

"Is the Pope more to you than God? A Pope entered as a fox and will die as a dog." His words of annihilation fell on barren soil. Savonarola had no other power in those decisive days than the fire of his faith, and that was no longer capable of igniting the city. He lacked executive power. He could implore, but not command; plead, but not compel. Phrases of terror, unbacked by power, served only to warn his opponents. What Savonarola neglected when he was capable of it, four years before, on the 8th of November, 1494, ferreting out and intimidating his enemies, he now sought to attain by the pressure of the anonymous masses who had remained faithful to him. Since he could not march soldiers in the streets, he organized a parade of the faithful. This, he thought, would offer him new opportunities. Piety was to win him room to act against iniquity, and iniquity would be searched for throughout Florence by children.

Divided into small groups and led by adults, children marched through the entire city, presumably knocking on all doors, but in reality only at the homes of those good citizens who wished to have nothing to do with the Medici but who also hated Savonarola. Intimidated, the householders opened their doors to them. The children demanded everything "accursed", everything which under Lorenzo had served the purposes of a pleasure-seeking, lighthearted, carnival life. They collected mirrors, cosmetics, dice, playing cards, chessboards, bottles of perfume, marble busts of smiling women, portraits of women famous for their beauty, Boccaccio's *Decameron*, books of secular songs, indecent miniatures—all that serves sin, that beautifies and cheers life. In hundreds of sacks these vanities were dragged to the piazza before the Signory. The pious people of the city, called by their opponents "weepers", stood packed together to see the burning of the vanities of men and women whose hearts did not hold the Commandments of God. Hosannas and trumpet blasts resounded. The church bells pealed. Smoke and flames darkened and illuminated the streets and a mighty jubilation rose to the heavens. It was a festival of Faith, celebrated in the same season and at the same place as the carnivals of Lorenzo. Savonarola burned the vain possessions of his enemies because he did not have the power to burn their bodies.

To Machiavelli this new stream of faith, this renaissance of piety outside the Church, must have seemed like a barbarian invasion. He did not see the might latent in the eruption. His city was ugly to him, the streets cold and cheerless; for they all led to the church in which the prophet was praising to the ecstatic mob the blissfulness of death, "We live in this world, my brethren, only to learn how we are to die well."

The universal reform of which the monk spoke seemed to Machiavelli the revival of a subject which one did not talk about aloud because it was fundamentally false and bad: Christianity! To Machiavelli religion was an unfortunate heritage. One accepted it like the other imperfections of this world. He had no desire to fight against Christianity because belief was not in him, because, basically, religion did not concern him. One had to attend church regularly and go to confession, but one talked about religion as little as about death. Talking about religion brought misfortune. At bottom, he felt that Christianity was the most fundamental catastrophe of the continent. For this Savior, with his phrasemongering for slaves, blockheads, invalids, beggars, and cripples, had infected the world with the disease of weakness. "Our religion," he wrote, "has promised blessedness rather to humble than to active men . . . It has made the highest good . . . contempt for earthly things . . . It demands strength in suffering and not in mighty deeds . . . This manner of life seems . . . to have weakened the world . . . and made it the prey of evildoers."

Instead of the vague universal reform of Christianity that the Dominican preached and for which he would have been willing to sacrifice Florence, Machiavelli desired intensely a narrower religion with immediate, practical aims. Religion was to subserve sovereignty, to demonstrate its indispensability as a gendarmerie for the souls of the common people. Ancient Rome, he thought, had the best religion because Power was in command. Religion, like a general, had but one purpose: to win battles. "In the Roman cult," he wrote, "if the fowl ate, the legions fought under good auspices; if the fowl did not eat, the legions avoided battle. But if reason demanded the performance of a particular act, then that act was carried out even under unfavorable auspices. Only the priests turned and interpreted the matter so skillfully that it did not seem to be taking place with the disapproval of their religion."

Machiavelli rejoiced when Savonarola, abusing the books of the clerics, declared "that dogs would no longer eat of them". For in Machiavelli's opinion also, the clergy, at least publicly, should live modestly. Not, however, in order to reform the Church, but because secular power needed the support of the Church in order to preserve a modicum of integrity among the people. Machiavelli wished to simplify the life of the secular official by using the Church. Officials could not check on every oath taken and every tax declaration. The priest must see to the honesty of the little man. "You have to mix a little religion into the matter to make the people obedient," he later wrote, as an official, to a subordinate who had an unpleasant ordinance to carry out.

The Florentines did not share Machiavelli's distaste for Christianity. But he voiced their sentiments when he opposed universal reform. Savonarola appeared to them now as a demagogue and the cause of dissension. "He advances arguments which must make the greatest impression upon people who do not consider further. He represents his followers as the most splendid of men and his opponents as thorough miscreants."

So long as this reformer lived, even though his power was fast waning, the city was threatened by unrest within itself and danger from without.

The Signory could not surrender Savonarola directly to the Pope. That would be contrary to the dignity of the sovereign Republic. Besides, they had no legal charges against him. They had to look for other means. The Signory needed a popular storm, a revolt, a savage attack of the mob against the monk.

They left this task to the sons of rich populani who had been heavily taxed because of the monk in the days of crisis. These golden youths, called by the weepers "evil young blades", were backed up not only by the magistrates but by the prevailing atmosphere. Even Niccolo Machiavelli, despite his impoverished condition, shared the mood of these hot youths. The citizens of Florence, whether rich or poor, had had enough of the manner in which, in Machiavelli's opinion, Savonarola ornamented his lies. They had had enough of frenzied repentance, children policing the city for piety and morals, burning of vanities, foreboding prophesies, and quarreling monks. Florence wanted to sell brocade and live at peace with the whole world; Florence wanted to see the closed taverns again lighted up of evenings. Women wanted to display their forbidden bosoms, finery, and robes again; and the street gamins longed to swear. Now, as if they had triumphantly returned from a long sojourn in the land of piety, the Florentines caroused in the public places.

This hunger for the all-too-earthly became a definite policy pursued by the young insurgents. Their scandalous behavior served not only their own pleasure, but helped reestablish the normal temperature of the Florentine's existence. The golden youths hurled curses at Savonarola, assaulted his weepers, beat his child-police, struck monks from San Marco, spread thousands of rumors, painted up all the walls of the city with attacks on the monk, and at banquets swore vengeance for the six long years of self-denial. They sought Savonarola's life, organized attempts at assassination in the monastery of San Marco, and when these failed, joined with a number of Franciscans in a carefully laid plot against the friar.

Two Franciscans were to challenge Savonarola to a trial by fire. He was to walk through the flames. The Franciscan monks were allegedly ready to do the same. Savonarola said to his monks, "We do not need miraculous signs in order to believe in the truth!" But he was already worn with persecution and allowed himself to be persuaded. His most faithful followers, incited by the enmity of the city, now demanded vigorously of him this great miracle which had been conceived by the "evil blades". A worldly, blasphemous curiosity raged in Florence. Bets were laid on the miracle as if it were a horse race. On the appointed day the partisans and foes of the friar fought in the streets. Each party was afraid that only the representative of its side would enter the fire.

A rain interrupted the brawls as well as the miracle. Savonarola had not satisfied their curiosity; he was considered a deceiver. Only with difficulty did he escape from the threatening mob into his monastery. San Marco was stormed and attempted to defend itself. The rebellion which the Signory needed in order to intervene had finally been whipped up. The friar was taken prisoner.

Inspired by his solitude, Savonarola knelt in a cell of the Florentine prison. With tortured hand he wrote his last book, *Miserere*. The sufferings of humanity weighed upon him. His ear heard the poor, the oppressed, the weepers, and the moaners crying for assistance, and his eye saw that none hastened to their aid. With all the passion of injured mercy he hated individualism and its diabolic ruthlessness. Savonarola looked into the souls of the great men of his century as did no other, and he shuddered at their unchristian blindness and their icy heartlessness. "He whom it pleases not to murder his neighbor," he lamented, "he who does not sow rebellion and dissension, is no man to them." The joint papal-Florentine court which was sitting in judgment upon him was Evil itself, a ravening wolf which a thousand thousand times, and yet another thousand times had lain in wait to lead astray and devour, and now was about to destroy him also. "Can a man resist alone the superior might of the enemy?" he asked. "Can he be stronger than Evil which everywhere gushes forth from within?"

To go down to defeat in this struggle is the highest glory that can be given to a Christian. "Yes," he prayed, "grant me the martyr's death and let me die for Thee as Thou hast died for me."

It is rather because of its saints than because of its popes that Catholicism has survived the centuries. Catholicism conquers time by letting itself be invaded, even conquered by it. Eternity, religion, love, mercy—not intellectual concepts, but ecstasies—live on in the Church through her saints and her prophets. They attack the cold progress of necessity in human and political intercourse. Pope Borgia was the transitory, Savonarola the eternal element of the Church.

Savonarola was condemned to be hanged and then burned. At the place of execution[1] the crowd stood closely pressed, as they had formerly stood for his sermons in the cathedral. But now he no longer lived in their hearts as he had for the past five years; now the scream went up from thousands of throats, "Prophet, thy hour has come. Perform thy miracles!"

"And a few days after they had burned him publicly," a chronicler who remained faithful to the monk relates, "the

[1] May 23, 1498.

PAINTING BY FRA BARTOLOMEO

SAVONAROLA

"I am like the hail, which striketh all who are uncovered."

PAINTING BY FIFTEENTH
CENTURY FLORENTINE PAINTER

The execution of Savonarola on the Piazza della Signoria in Florence.

Florentines made a swine of cardboard and dragged the swine through the streets shouting again and again, 'This swine of a friar! This swine of a friar!'—and such like abuse of stupid people."

The hatred for the Medici remained active even after Savonarola's death; it was the most profound and universal feeling in Florence. A voluntary readiness to sacrifice personal comfort in order to spy against the Medici, to run to the piazza before the Signory and to use their weapons, seized the people of Florence, long unaccustomed to fighting though they were. For nearly thirty years this feeling remained the spiritual foundation and characteristic trait of the Republic. Rule without the Medici meant liberty not only for the corporation of rich populani who actually exercised control, but for all classes. For although, to be sure, all were not permitted to share in the government, yet all were permitted to speak freely. The Florentines loved their city not merely because they were born in it, but because they believed that it was fundamentally free. Their desire for freedom was the form of their patriotism to the city. Above and beyond his victory and defeat, Savonarola had left this desire as a heritage to the Florentines. "The sole form of State appropriate for us," he had said, "is a republic on a broad, legal basis. Woe to thee, Florence, if thou should'st ever again give thyself an overlord."

The preamble to the new Florentine Magna Charta of 1494, which shaped the life of the last thirty-three years of Florentine independence, proclaimed, "The present constitutional reform has as its aim the liberty of this flourishing people. It is our wish that not only we, but our children also shall enjoy this most holy of blessings, liberty, and that none shall ever dare to usurp sole authority and subjugate our free citizens!"

Savonarola, though prone to mysticism, was informed by a trait of intense realism. He did not demand holiness of every Christian. He declared that piety could not permeate the entire man, that there would always be some part of man inclining to worldly things. As a theologian he took these material conditions into account and did not lose himself in demagogic phrases about equality or poverty. Theology, which has always been a barricade against the impressionistic mental wanderings of the healthy human mind in matters of belief, was a primary element in Savonarola's political constitution. Theology kept him from becoming a suspicious, ecstatic monk striving to destroy the secular and ecclesiastical hierarchy. He was a disciple of Thomas Aquinas and no heretic. He recognized the authority of the Pope; he merely claimed that the Curia was superior to the Holy Father. Up to this time it had been permissible to debate this question freely. He did not want to split the Church—outside of Catholicism humanity had no meaning for him. He did not revolt against any particular dogma and from the purely theological point of view he was not at all a forerunner of Luther. He was no anabaptist, no equalizer, nor did he want to divide Florence among the Florentines. Savonarola spoke only for equality for those who were entitled to it. Those entitled to it did not comprise all the inhabitants of the Republic; only the long-established citizens whose ancestors had held some office in Florence were to vote and to participate in the councils.

The plebs, he said, cannot be allowed to permeate everywhere; if the mob overflows the dikes, tyranny will soon prevail. The better classes, those destined to rule, were in his eyes but a tenth of those who had the right to political equality. This aristocracy must be imbued with charity. Compassion was to him the prime obligation of rulers.

The permanent forum of the politically privileged was the Great Council which Savonarola introduced. This Great Council of fully franchised citizens abolished the noisy gatherings of the people, the Parliament, as they were called, which had formed in front of the palace of the Signory. The popular assembly of the Italian communities had always been the breeding place of tyranny. Savonarola thought the little man had to be prevented from selling his freedom for a mess of pottage.

And this Great Council found in Machiavelli its warmest defender. Unsympathetic as he was toward the monk, still he was warmly enthusiastic for most of the political institutions that Savonarola introduced. "The citizenry of Florence will never be satisfied," Machiavelli wrote, "unless the portals to the Great Council are opened to them."

The whole realistic school of Florentine political men, the atheists and heathens, were inspired by the establishment of the Great Council. Nothing pleased them more than this institution of their devout opponent. For liberal-minded men there exist neither devout nor sinful souls. Only the zealot engaged in direct action believes in clear-cut, struggling forces of heathens and Christians, of suppressed and suppressors, poor and rich, educated and uneducated, patricians and plebeians, populani and aristocrats, Lesser and Greater Guilds, bourgeois and proletarians. "All human experience, whether perceived or not, is to be found in the interrelationship between the individual and the group."

Savonarola was also a Platonist, like his Medicean, aristocratic, and heathen opponents. With Plato, he defined the beautiful as the soul, as the idea of the good, and using Plato, he fought everything the educated ruling Florentine praised and considered noble. He felt that devout souls shared in the beauty of God. Beauty was the reflection of divinity in material things.

Bosom friends of Lorenzo, men from the Medicean academies, came to Savonarola. For the deserters of the aristocracy always lead rebellions against their class, and Power ever needs fresh spiritual forces to maintain it. Power without spirit is but dead weight. But spirit misleads Power. Misled by spirit, Lorenzo Medici and the Platonic academy opened the gates of the Republic to the enemy, Girolamo Savonarola. If with one hand Savonarola burned manuscripts, with the other he saved the Medicean library. Botticelli, Michelangelo, and Raphael saw in him an eternal and ideal figure, and even if Savonarola had visions, still he was not a fool. His opponents, the disciples of absolute realism, with Niccolo Machiavelli at their head, had delusions of their own. "Before the march of Charles VIII," Machiavelli writes, "warriors fighting in the air above Arezzo were seen and heard. The air can be filled with fighting specters who look into the future and warn men out of pity for them."

Savonarola had wanted to help bring about the victory of the idea of God. Mankind knows only *one* force equal to religion—*Power!* A higher ideal than God or Power the sons of earth have never borne in their hearts. Savonarola professed divine ideals, but understood little of Power. His opposite pole, Machiavelli, the personified pattern of the future, could not visualize God, but he understood Power. There was no contradiction between God and Power. But if Power did not recognize God, then it floundered like a man half-blind; it lost itself in the wide field of human values. As the Dominican, Campanella, said of Machiavelli, it was like "the worm in the intestines of a man which can have no conception of the whole of its abode." Machiavelli, who hated the ideal as a lapse into the boundless realms of speculation, as a form of non-being, resisted all patterns of perfection as Savonarola resisted all worldly things. Yet both fell victim to the object of their hatred. Machiavelli was, in this country of so many ruthless, absolute, but nevertheless ephemeral men of violence, the first technician of Power. After taking apart and putting together the spirit of Power countless times, he found his way to higher goals. He formulated, without intending to, almost without realizing it, the ideal of virtù, the virtue of rulers. He had hopes of extending the rule of Florence to the very frontiers of Italy. When toward the end of his life he invoked the Italians to struggle against their enemies with the cry, "Kill the Spaniards, for they are only voices, not whole men!" he was neither the technician of Power nor the specialist in sovereignty, but a prophet.

In his heavenly fire, Savonarola forged for the Florentines their earthly liberty. Machiavelli formed the first beginnings of a national army of Florentines, and the spirit of the immolated Savonarola supported the enterprise. Here, in Florence, God came together with Power; for while God had never yet prevented a single battle, yet without belief there would be no fields of glory.

II

IN OFFICE

CHAPTER IV

The Chancery, Life, and Politics

WHEN SAVONAROLA died, Niccolo Machiavelli was twenty-nine years old and without means of support. He hoped that the current, everywhere running against the friar, would vouchsafe him too a lucrative shelter close to the center of Power. The madness of revolution was past and Niccolo felt himself destined for the sober reality, for the new commonplaces, which it had created.

He succeeded in being selected from among four applicants, and his selection was confirmed by the Signory. He was appointed to the Second Chancery of the "Ten of Liberty" as secretary. On the 15th of July, 1498, he took over his post and at once paid a visit to his superior, Marcello Virgilio, head of the First Chancery of the Signory to which his own, the Second, was subordinate.

Virgilio, the real secretary of Florence, who was about six years older than Niccolo, was his friend. It was largely to him that Niccolo owed his position. The Secretary and First Chancellor of the Republic had spoken for him everywhere and told the Signory about the marvelous talents of his protegé. A comradeship of long standing bound the two of them. Together they had caroused through many nights, together studied literature, and together cursed at Savonarola.

Their natures, however, were completely different. Marcello Virgilio was fond of pretty speeches and was affected with all the vanities of those later humanists who lacked the vital spark of their predecessors. In his leisure hours he was a professor of Greek and Roman literature, and therefore looked upon his official position with condescension. The office of Chancellor pleased him only because it lent him dignity, because his artificial elegance stood in need of an official background. Rhetoric was most important to him, for in its broad, tiresome stream it left sufficient room for scholarly quotations. Marcello Virgilio was a conventional person who considered every new idea in literature an act of disrespect to Virgil and any initiative in office an imposition on the Signory.

The Florentine Constitution made an effort to keep power from the bureaucrats of the city, and Virgilio felt quite comfortable in his secondary position. He was an accommodating official for the comfort loving, swiftly changing superiors whom the Great Council elected. An altogether different kind of worker was his friend Niccolo. In his chancery, Machiavelli forgot literature and poverty, forgot the vanities of his personal life. The moment he first entered the office it seemed to him like the realization of something he had long dreamed of. He immediately fell in love with the documents he handled. He devoured them as if they contained the most fascinating tales. Every detail in a report interested him. "It is necessary to observe even the smallest matters," he wrote to a friend, "because great things arise out of small and because one can see the men behind things even in trivialities."

As Secretary of the Second Chancery, Niccolo had more than sufficient opportunity to rummage about in realities. For the Ten of Liberty of the Second Chancery sorted the reports of ambassadors, answered their questions, engaged and paid the secret agents operating outside of Tuscany. They dealt with native condottieri, bought shipments of saltpeter, inspected fortresses, and examined bills presented to the city. All documents having to do with the daily life of the Republic and not pertaining directly to higher politics, Machiavelli had before his eyes and in his hands from morning till evening.

These papers satisfied his ambition; they were his laboratory in which he analyzed droplets of events in order to draw conclusions about the whole of the political world. He never dreamed of leaving his desk to make his way upward into the sphere of the rulers. For knowledge about Power, not Power itself, was his driving passion.

As secretary Niccolo was not permitted to make any decisions. Officially he could neither help determine policies nor advise about them. His position was subordinate according to the spirit and the letter of the law, technically administrative rather than political. Only the imagination of posterity has given him the imposing but likewise unimportant position of Marcello Virgilio, that of Chancellor of the Republic. Decisions were made, where they were not made by the Signory, by the Ten of Liberty, who guided the Second Chancery. These Ten formed a sort of cabinet of technical advisors. They had indefinite, irregular tasks in connection with foreign affairs and war. Machiavelli enjoyed that advantage over the Ten which officials always enjoy over ministers; they remain while their Excellencies depart. The Ten were elected for only a few months. But Machiavelli held his office for fourteen years.

For fourteen years he hurried daily at the same hour in the early morning up a narrow staircase of the Council Hall, where a large, unpleasant, badly furnished—and in winter badly heated—room awaited him. If his clerks were not yet there, if they were cutting the office as they had cut school when they were children, or if they were pretending to be ill or engaged in duties elsewhere, then he copied the reports for the signori himself, inspected the records, made use of seal and stamp, and wrote hundreds of addresses. When the latecomers finally arrived, ate their breakfasts, slipped on their cuffs, scratched themselves with their quills and finally cast a first, unfriendly glare at their tasks, Niccolo always beamed. He would apologize for having come too early; for he did not want to wound his subordinates by his zeal. He knew that their malice, once awakened, was more difficult to soothe than the severity of his superiors. Niccolo did not want an atmosphere of hostility around him. In democratic Florence, every clerk was a fully franchised citizen who might become dangerous. Everyone had a relative in one or another influential position. In his function as an official, he ingratiated himself with his colleagues and subordinates. He let the others fool around as they liked. When the clerks abandoned their work to play cards for hours he would sit undisturbed over his documents. "I cannot send the permits today," one of his letters from the Second Chancery reads, "because Andreas, who was supposed to prepare them, played tric-trac all day long."

A rough atmosphere united these clerks with and against one another. It was the intimacy of petty folk who had to see each other all day long and who no longer had any secrets from one another. People who become thoroughly familiar with each other, in offices, in prisons, or in marriage, lose their mutual respect. Without pretense and a minimum of lies, communal life is like a stable or a madhouse.

The clerks' poverty made them grate on one another. They took their meals in the chancery. In the morning before Niccolo came to the Signory, he would go to the market to make purchases. He brought his beans and smoked meat along with him. "My onions," one of the clerks wrote to Machiavelli, who had just left on a journey, "are now in the frying pan on the fire and two colleagues are watching them to see that they do not burn. Come back soon and lick my ass."

These poor clerks were sometimes on the point of tearing each other's eyes out. Rage and hatred seemed to be part of the air of their room—until a thunderstorm cleared the clouds away somewhat. "Antonio has lost his wits again and quarreled with Andreas," a clerk related to Machiavelli. "Andreas stole the march on him with his sabot and beat him on the back terribly. The poor fellow is wearing a saddle because he has not found anything more comfortable."

Each of these eternal sitters, condemned to sit with each other for ten, twenty, or thirty years, had a different idiosyncrasy. Antonio seems to have been dreaded for his readiness to quarrel. "Niccolo, I am in a mess," a clerk writes. "Mr. Antonio has lost his frying pan and blames me. I am supposed to pay him the damages plus interest. I do not know what to do, and I would like to satisfy him."

Their favorite pastime was obscenity. Their crippled imaginations fled from their duties during the long hours in the office and described adventures without number. Each of them told how he had cheated the most expensive courtezans, seduced the most beautiful women of the upper classes, and led the most delectable ladies of Rome, Venice, or Bologna into sin.

Lasciviousness did not have to be forced on Niccolo. With his whole soul he outdid his colleagues. In his tales the Florentine brothels became paradises and Paradise a brothel. These desk-bound souls compensated themselves for their uneventful lives by blaspheming everything respected and cherished by the city.

If mockery of Florence was called for, Niccolo was first among his colleagues. He wrote a description of the Florentines as animals. The smirking sophisticates easily recognized local celebrities under the masks. In the name of all four-footed creatures the sow, in a solemn peroration, arraigns the entire human race.

The position of these Florentine clerks, low as it was, gave them a certain superiority. For they had their own desks, and they could drive rich men to desperation by repeated examination of their tax-reports; they could make men of prominence wait for permits and withhold powder and pay from celebrated generals. These bureaucrats could release a plague of malice against any individual or against the mass of non-officeholders. They were the tiny, ink-stained Saints guarding the vestibule of Power—the indispensable muck of sovereignty! The Great Council, the Standard-bearer of Justice, the Eight of the Guard, the Six of the Board of Trade, the Ten of Liberty and the numerous commissions and subcommissions made decisions and changes. But in the end, they were themselves dependent upon the indolence, indifference, and malice of an anonymous office. For already a man had two lives in Florence, his personal and his documental life. And the life on paper was capable of destroying the individual behind it.

Niccolo enjoyed spending his days and evenings in the company of these clerks. He was extremely friendly with his draftsman, Blasius Buonaccorsi. Blasius eavesdropped for him, opened the letters of strangers, and kept track of intrigues. When Machiavelli was away on some journey in the service of the Signory, Blasius told everyone with unflagging emphasis how hard his friend was working. He pleaded for advances for Niccolo. He was the first to be convinced of Niccolo's importance and he loved him wholeheartedly, speaking of himself and his friend only as "we". Blasius was Machiavelli's priceless alter ego. But Blasius often copied the minutes of the meetings of the Signory inaccurately. Then Machiavelli would draw large letters on the margin of the careless work, "Blasius, you're lying!"

Machiavelli had a singular, inexplicable preference for scurrilous men. He often made friends with maniacs; he would open his soul to them, carouse and share his bread with them. He seemed to prefer weak-minded souls because he liked the verbal freedom of the half-insane and the abnormal. It was as if he wanted to examine the workings of nature's practical jokes. He drew up the statutes of a Society of Pleasure for Fools. Whoever keeps a secret longer than two days, the articles declared, will be chastised; whoever speaks longest without saying anything; whoever says the opposite of what he is feeling; whoever can disguise himself best; and whoever stares stupidly at everyone during mass and succeeds in blocking traffic in such a way that everyone turns to look at him, will be rewarded.

Even non-Florentine politicians made their way into the fool's paradise of his chancery. History had no great tasks for this signorial bureau. No matter how grave danger or distress or joy were, life rapped but gently on this door. What was really interesting here, aside from the question of salary, was the chronicle of the thousand and one scandals of Italy. When Machiavelli read reports of the marriage of Countess Caterina Sforza of Forli and Imola, he wrote, "Either Caterina will have her lover murdered, or her lover will murder her and her eldest son, or else the son, who has shown a quick temper, will murder his mother and her lover." He was the only one who saw therein a chronicle not of scandal, but of Power. He was in suspense to know how this tangle of baseness, guile, and lust would be resolved. He felt that these were real rulers, always ready to stake everything in order to increase the strength of their positions. The creatures of his imagination were becoming real individuals. The petty clerk, Machiavelli, was meeting Machiavellian personages, and with each successive report, with each successive year, these figures approached closer to him.

The Forlian knot was finally untied. Caterina's lover, who was secretly married to her, was attacked and stabbed to death while she was out hunting with him. Rumor claimed that the lady had hired the assassins herself. Her rage was boundless. Her love and her honor had been insulted. "We Sforzas, when we want to kill," she cried, "do not make use of hired knaves; we dispose of our opponents ourselves."

And in order to prove her innocence and her sorrow, the beautiful young widow had fifty gallows erected in Forli and had the houses of the condemned assassins torn down. She became a Fury. Without a husband, she clung even closer to Power; avenged in order to govern, governed in order to take vengeance.

Niccolo respected very highly the courage of this woman who had grown up in the midst of conspiracies, whose father, Galeazzo Sforza, ruler of Milan, had been killed in the cathedral during services, and whose brother had been poisoned by her own uncle. Niccolo felt that the classic Roman virtue lived in her. She gave him an example of the fulfillment of the prime law of sovereignty: to be able to maintain oneself despite the adversity of circumstance. The courage of Caterina was not rhetorical, but her real, perhaps her only virtue. Her city, Forli, rose up against her. Her second husband, like her first, was killed before her eyes and she herself was taken prisoner. With her were her six children, their governesses, her cousins, her mother, and her sister—all weeping despairingly. She demanded quiet and addressed them. "You should not cry and you should not be afraid; worst of all will it be if you show that you are afraid, for then, I tell you outright, you will be killed. Our forefathers were princes of war, great condottieri. They never knew fear and so were able to defy prison, the fire, and treachery. When I was a young girl, my father was murdered. I have not lost my courage; you must be as I. Otherwise I shall deny you all."

This imprisoned woman, who accepted the chance of being murdered as one of the risks of the tyrant's trade, now placed her hopes in cunning and trickery: the methods which Machiavelli later so frequently recommended in the struggle with spiteful destiny. He was able to observe in her actions how the wiles of an intrepid woman could spike the guns of an enemy army.

The *rocca,* in all Italian cities the last bulwark of rulers, was still in loyal hands. The chief of the rebellion demanded that Caterina order the commandant of the rocca to relinquish the keys. She replied that she would gladly do it, but that she knew the fierceness of the commander of the citadel. He would not obey. Unfortunately, he would believe that she was acting under compulsion. They should allow her to enter the rocca, leaving her children behind as hostages.

As soon as she was in the citadel she began to cheer the discouraged men, and commanded an attack upon the city. Her wailing children were brought before the fortress. The enemy threatened to kill them before the eyes of their mother. Caterina climbed up on the battlements of the rocca, lifted her skirt to her navel and shouted to her enemies, "If you should kill my children, I am woman enough to bear others!" Caterina held the citadel; the children were not killed; relief came from the outside and she remained the ruler of Forli and Imola.

Florence had always striven to keep the friendship of Forli, for the easiest road from Venice to Tuscany led through this fortress. Machiavelli was assigned to hire soldiers and buy saltpeter in Forli. His main task, however, was to keep his eyes and ears open and discover, without directly inquiring, whether Caterina approved of the pro-French policy of the Florentines.

In a flattering, ensnaring speech, Niccolo informed the countess in the first audience that was granted him, of how highly she stood in the regard of the Florentines. He spoke to her from his heart, for at this time he believed all the compliments it was necessary for him to make. Caterina, however, merely listened with boredom for a short time and then cut him short. She said, he wrote to the signori, that "the words which she has received from your Excellencies have always satisfied her, but your deeds have constantly displeased her."

She demanded a high price for her soldiers and, in addition, presented old accounts. Finally, however, they came to an agreement.

Meanwhile Machiavelli had not been able to learn anything of her policies. He could not report to Florence any hint as to her attitude. He had never yet met a person whose tongue was so tightly controlled, who let slip no superfluous word.

At the conclusion of his short mission he experienced another surprise. The countess suddenly declared, Niccolo reported, that she had spent the entire night considering and had changed her mind. She did not care about money. What she wanted was a defensive alliance with Tuscany. She wanted Florence to guarantee the integrity of her territory against all threats. "I should not wonder at this, she told me, for the more one sifts a question, the better one understands it. When I heard this shift of position, I could not restrain myself from becoming annoyed and from showing my annoyance openly . . . I could not, however, obtain anything else from her Excellency."

His first important mission, which he had begun with great expectations, had ended, ironically enough at the court of his heroine, with obvious failure.

In his second year in office, in a period when domestic and foreign political relationships were in the melting pot, Niccolo began the succession of diplomatic missions in which he was "feeling out reality". Everything which had previously been fixed which had appeared as the stable heritage of a great past, dissolved and flowed away like water before his eyes. Between the last hours of Lorenzo Medici's life and the first years after the death of Savonarola only a half decade had gone by; yet this recent past, enjoyed by all Florentines, now seemed to them like a fairy tale from ancient times. The life forms of the day before yesterday disappeared completely not only in Tuscany but throughout Italy. Men forget deeply rooted habits and circumstances which once governed their lives as swiftly as they lose their awareness of the dead. They quickly adjust themselves to the new, unwonted course of life. Machiavelli accustomed himself most rapidly to these changes. For to him, the swift changes of fortune, the tragedies involved in building states and in the flight, return, victory, and defeat of new rulers, made up the animated spectacle of political Nature. That which the ordinary man in his sloth endured with unconcern, Machiavelli followed with the eager curiosity of the adventurer in the spirit.

The Tuscans speedily forgot the political balance of power which the four states—Milan, Venice, Naples, and Florence—had tried to preserve in Italy in order to keep the peace of the Peninsula. The invasion of Charles of France, which the Italians themselves had invoked, had destroyed this ideal, unpolitical, many-faceted spiritual unity. It had destroyed, that is, peace, and the balance of power.

The invasion had revealed to the Powers of the world the weakness of a peninsula possessing the finest cities, the most lavishly stocked warehouses and the best manufactured and agricultural products in Europe. The greed of the mighty saw an unprotected Eden filled with almost inexhaustible fruits. The heart of very European warrior beat more swiftly when he heard the names: Florence, Rome, Naples, Milan, Bologna, Siena, Cazale, Asti, Piombino. Every mercenary in France, Spain, England, and Germany, was ready to march to war on credit if the trumpet called on him to cross the Alps. The discovery of Italian booty was closer, more magical, more real, more easily come by for the men of the sixteenth century than the discovery of America.

Italy was not a country, but rather in its variety a continent in itself. It had presented the rest of the world with countless thoughts, emotions, and memories and now supplied humanity with the wars necessary for the transformation of society. In Italy, the no man's land of the century, the quarrel over the boundary between France and Burgundy and the struggle between Spain and France was fought out. The plans of King Charles VIII, Louis XII, Francis I, and of the Emperors Maximilian and Charles V, miscarried on Italian soil. As a result of events in Italy, England was restricted to its island empire and the Ottoman threat was ended.

Peace was not to appear until the second half of the sixteenth century along with a condition of serflike bondage which brought with it disarmament and an almost complete stagnation in the stream of history.

At the beginning of this period, about the year 1500, during Machiavelli's missions, the simple significance of these disastrous tendencies of Italy were not recognized by any individual, whether theoretician or man of action. Everything which posterity was to know as a pattern was seen by the witnesses of the events only piecemeal. For history is nothing more than the painful spectacle of human impotence and blindness. The destruction of the ancient balance of power in Italy affected Florence directly by destroying her position as the intellectual capital of the Peninsula. It caused covert or overt rebellions of her subject cities and territories, and revolution or treason in her small autonomous or half-autonomous neighbors. If the invasion had revealed the weakness of Italy to foreign Powers, it had also shown the individual Italian cities the weakness of their native oppressor.

Leading the revolt was the second largest city of the Republic, which had been subject to and owned by Florence for a century—*Pisa!* Pisa felt that with the loss of its liberties it had also lost its history. This had previously happened to Amalfi, Genoa, Siena, Lucca, and Pistoia, and it afterward happened to the city which Pisa hated, Florence itself. For Italian cities without independence, or inner freedom, life had no meaning. For centuries Italy had possessed the loftiest of human dignities; loss of liberty meant death from shame. Without liberty the cities became mere shadows of their former substance.

Pisa's revolt was like a strange uprising of a museum where memories are transmuted into will and action. The cathedral, the baptistery, the leaning tower, and the Campo Santo, suddenly became fortresses. Armed men, women, and children stood fast before the walls of the city. For ten years Florence was separated from Pisa, geographically distant but a few hours' ride, by an enmity which was the source of frequent furious attacks. So stubborn was this struggle that it sought to alter nature. For years the Florentines worked to divert the Arno river from Pisa. Pisa was a wound which drained their energies and wealth. The prolonged conflict, the tragic game of patience, became the chronic weakness of Florence. This endlessly dragging, desultory warfare, with its petty battles and half victories, constantly made mock of the hopes of the Florentines, blinded them to clearheaded, farsighted policies. Anyone who promised to take Pisa by surprise, any adventurer who revealed alleged Pisan secrets, and any European ruler who would grant diplomatic aid, could receive money from the usually stingy Signory. Because of Pisa, Florence became the laughing stock of half of Europe. Pisa was the gateway for all enemies of Florence, and Pisa was in league with everyone against Florence. Florence organized campaigns to devastate the villages in Pisan territory. Pisa pleaded in Paris, Madrid, Vienna, and Rome for permission to belong to Spain, the Empire, France, or the Pope, so long as it might escape its bondage to Florence.

By its rebellion Pisa weakened the resistance of the unguarded frontiers of Tuscany. It strengthened the numerous petty rulers in the territory bordering on Tuscany, the completely anarchic, papal Romagna. Now that the balance of power in Italy was no more, these rulers, who fomented disorder and confusion and rented out their soldiers and their condottieri, felt more powerful than ever before. The prices of the lords of Piombino and Urbino, of the Vitellis, the Riaros, the Orsinis and the Baglionis, rose with their demand. For Florence needed them in its war against Pisa, and the foreign Powers, Spain, France, and the Empire, needed them no less.

The moderate, governing populani of Florence were enthusiastically pro-French. All good republicans in Tuscany were adherents of the French. In the eyes of the Signory Machiavelli had proved himself to be of the same mind during his first important mission to Caterina Sforza. And in the unwritten index of trustworthy men which the members of the ruling clique always bore in their memories, Niccolo was noted down as dependable and unequivocal.

Niccolo, who was always glad to return from his missions and hurry back to his habitual daily activities, found a jubilant Florence when he arrived from Forli. In the evenings the homes were illuminated, and the Arno gleamed like a steel sword in the glow of torches. The Florentines were celebrating the victory of the French in Lombardy, the victory of Louis XII, successor of Charles VIII. In league with Venice, the king had taken Milan and was ready—for a great deal of money—to send assistance to the besiegers of Pisa.

Machiavelli was hurt by this vain rejoicing over foreign triumphs. In the festival of the city he heard only the melody of Florentine dependence. He himself felt as limited as the Republic. "Our situation is such," he wrote, "that the success of the French in Italy can rob us of half our territory, but their failure can destroy us entirely." Had he been in a position to make decisions, however, he would probably have pursued no different policies. For the essential weakness of Florence was not rooted in individual men, but in the radical turn that Italian and European conditions had taken. He was never able to forget that alliances between the strong and weak were merely forms of dependence for the less powerful State. This certainty led him to make repeated mental surveys of the impotence of Florence. He could not celebrate weakness with rejoicing and splendor as the Florentines were now doing.

Nor could Niccolo chain himself to France as dogmatically as the rulers of the Republic; for the wars in Italy were still in progress. By adhering to France without reserve, Florence sacrificed the advantage to be got from maneuvering between opposing forces. For Florence, too, the policies which Alexander VI pursued in the Ecclesiastical State would have been correct. "We are for France," the Pope had declared, "and will continue to fight on her side against Spain. But if the military position of France becomes insecure, it is our duty to think of our own possessions. If God permits the Spaniards to grow strong, then it were a great sin to desire other than God's will."

Florence had foregone her opportunities of making her own choice. She was too weak to watch for the more powerful side; she permitted the needs of foreign politics to dictate the content of her own foreign policies. And even when the city followed the proper course, Machiavelli wrote, she did so under compulsion and not from conviction.

This weakness of Florence was Niccolo's besetting thought; it transformed him into a melancholic. His bitterness, however, did not disturb him in his practical, daily tasks. It seemed as if he were confronted with this curse of national weakness in every document of the Military Administration, in every report that arrived from foreign lands. Thus this doubting, melancholy, cynical man had a positive side in the performance of his duties. He believed that the petty tasks to which everyone is subjected had to be done thoroughly.

But as he guarded himself against censuring his colleagues in the office, so also he was careful not to trumpet his gloomy forebodings abroad. It would have been contrary to his nature to have come out openly as a reformer of Florentine politics. He could give voice to his sentiments only in private among those who could understand him. Only when he was in his own circle, protected by friendship and the trust of the powerful, was he able to develop an unsuspected tenacity in defense of his opinions. Only behind the scenes, under cover of documents and of the law, did he attempt to make room for the forces of change to work. But had the Holy Ghost come to him and said, "Go upon the piazza and shout thy complaint of the weakness of Florence into the face of the world," Niccolo would have replied, "Your Divine Excellency, that is not part of my duties. I have my hands full as it is. I am a clerk. Let your Worship speak with Savonarola."

Hence, Machiavelli did not interfere in the optimistic game the Signory was playing with Louis XII. Existing conditions were alone enough to wreck the Florentines' hopes.

The dearly bought French auxiliaries who were encamped before Pisa in order to make an assault upon the city were daily growing more friendly to the Pisans and more hostile to the Florentines. The Pisans found paths to the hearts and the purses of these eight thousand Gascons and Swiss. The soldiers did not think of war, but of an easy life at the expense of Florence. The Signory sent two commissioners, with Machiavelli as assistant, to the besieging army. The commissioners reported the insatiable hunger and the unrestrained arrogance of the mercenaries. The more urgently the delegates of the Signory demanded a battle, the more violently the troops cried out for additional pay. The army became a mob, mutinied, and took one of the commissioners prisoner. Niccolo and a commissioner named della Casa escaped and rode to Florence to report the disaster. The army besieging Pisa no longer existed.

Florence felt that it had been betrayed. The Florentines accused Machiavelli's Second Chancery of having wasted enormous sums of money on a fiasco. The Ten of Liberty were everywhere called "Spendthrift Ten." The Florentines wanted to have nothing more to do with the Ten. They organized an electoral strike. When the term of magistracy of the Ten was up, they refused to elect new magistrates. Florence could neither continue the war nor conclude peace. In the streets and piazzas the citizens spoke angrily against the authorities. In the midst of this excitement, which seemed to be preparing the way for revolt, the Signory was further frightened by a letter from the King of France. Louis took the mutinous troops at Pisa under his protection and claimed that Florence had given them neither pay nor provisions.

In order that the events at Pisa be described to the king, the Signory sent witnesses of the mutiny in all haste to France—della Casa and, as his assistant, Machiavelli.

Niccolo left Florence reluctantly. The Signory granted him only half the travel expenses with which it provided della Casa. But double that sum would not have been enough for him. Machiavelli could not live with an account book in his hand. In Florence his disordered financial circumstances caused him no embarrassment because they had become accepted through habit. The local innkeepers, caterers and friends lent him money. He knew women whose affections cost nothing. He could often win at gambling. In Florence he drew the interest on his kind of poverty—an untroubled spirit and the consolation of a miracle that never came but never remained wholly beyond the bounds of possibility. In a foreign country, however, these perquisites ended. Poverty quickly became bitterest distress. He sensed, before his departure, the difficulties of this first trip to France—a complex diplomatic mission, very limited powers, pressing haste, and worry about his daily needs. His curiosity to see a non-Italian country for the first time was dashed by his anxiety about the Florentine affairs he carried in his baggage. Niccolo, who thrice in his life was sent to the King of France, twice to Germany to the Emperor Maximilian, and twice to Rome to the Pope, always departed in the same disgruntled mood as on his first mission.

But once he was on his way, he forgot his complaints and became absorbed in his mission. In ten days della Casa and Machiavelli reached Lyons. The king, however, was no longer in the city. The two Florentines journeyed after him. In Nevers on the Loire they caught up to the court of Louis XII, the first monarch of Christendom. The authority of this king was unquestioned. In France itself it sprang out of the growing unity of the country and out of his efforts to put an end to arbitrary will by means of the lawfulness of Power. In Europe his position rested on his succession of victories in Lombardy, on his triumphs in Milan and Genoa, and on his alliances with Scotland, Denmark, Venice, Spain, and with German princes. Up to this time Louis had had only good fortune. He sat on his throne as the ambitious son of the Continent, but he did not surrender himself to wild plans as had his predecessor, Charles VIII.

Louis was the Umpire of Italy. In private, Cesare Borgia had given him the nickname, "Lord of the Italian shop". No ruler in Italy felt secure unless he were under Louis' protection. On that account, his court seemed like a constantly moving Italian congress. One third of his entourage consisted of Italians. Every Italian Power came there as a pleader. Venice pleaded for assistance against the Turks; Ferrara and Bologna entreated for protection against the Pope; the Pope asked for a free hand against Florence, Ferrara and Bologna. The second- and third-rate sovereigns of Italy, as well as those who had been defeated and exiled, sent representatives.

For many of the Italian rulers the instinct for intrigue was all that remained to them of Power. They flattered their way to the throne and to the prime minister, Cardinal d'Amboise. They undertook to study carefully the desires, foibles, and vices of the king's retinue. The Italians, with their reputation for superior manners and higher culture, sought to guide the still somewhat crude French society. And they swiftly conquered the first houses of the kingdom. Especially, they won the hearts of the ladies who now began to appear at court for the first time, and to experience, in Italian books, Italian fashions, and Italian music, the pleasures of a world new to them.

The Italians surrounding the throne worked primarily against one another. If a man had three enemies, he made peace with the first, settled a truce with the second, and attacked the third. To all of them it seemed an ideal bargain to receive territories or concessions in exchange for empty promises, declarations of friendship, or compliments. None let it be seen that he was at the limit of his powers, and if someone told him so, he smiled as at a successful joke. The methods and modes of expression of this whole hive of powerless Italians buzzing about the crown were imitated by all the cabinets and courts of Europe. The procedure was called diplomacy.

On the slippery floor of this court, in this atmosphere where intrigue was a matter of course, where every straight path seemed a cunning trick and every crooked path a tour de force of political art, della Casa and Machiavelli made a somewhat awkward and provincial impression.

They were, however, by no means naïve souls or fanatics about truth. Machiavelli claimed that he did not fear to match his wits with the most hardened of liars, that he knew how to conceal truth so skillfully that no one could ever find it. But the distress of Tuscany troubled the two Florentines so deeply; they were so filled with shame over Pisa, that they could not keep silent.

They lacked the essential tool of Italian diplomacy, time. But they hoped they might touch the honor of His Majesty and obligate him to help Tuscany by describing the true course of events at Pisa. Louis, however, heard them listlessly and with unconcealed annoyance. He had just finished his afternoon meal and had not yet taken his siesta. Cardinal d'Amboise interrupted the Florentines with the remark that they had not fulfilled their treaty obligations, had not given the troops sufficient pay and fare. Niccolo tried to prove that the opposite was true; he had all the scenes of the mutiny clearly in mind. But the monarch broke in upon him gruffly. D'Amboise placated the King and declared that the past should be left to rest in peace. The Pisan enterprise absolutely must not be abandoned, for France's prestige was at stake. Overjoyed, the Florentines replied that such was also the desire of the Signory. But the King demanded that the Florentines continue, as provided in the treaty, to support the besieging army. Niccolo and della Casa answered that this was out of the question; the treasury of the city was empty and the citizens in a rebellious temper. Let the king first conquer Pisa; then the Signory would pay everything down to the last centesimo.

Louis, d'Amboise, and the French and Italians in their company were furious at this demand. They threatened the Florentines with the return of Pietro Medici, who like a fearful specter still haunted the Republic. They threatened them with the Pope; they threatened them with Tuscany's neighbors. "The French appreciate," Machiavelli reported in total despair to the Signory, "only the man who is either armed or ready to pay. They look down upon your Excellencies as if you were the Lords of Nowhere."

The tension between Louis and the Signory was the sensation of the court. Florence became the prey of diplomatic gossip. It was rumored that battle-scarred Pisa itself, that Siena, or the Pope, or Venice, was willing to give Louis the money which Florence refused to contribute. Intrigues, centering around the king, sprang up like weeds. Della Casa and Machiavelli ran from one courtier to another denying falsehoods. They were constantly discovering new threads which might become dangerous hangman's nooses for Tuscany if they were not instantly severed.

In this hard, unfriendly environment, della Casa fell ill and had himself taken to Paris. Machiavelli remained alone. From the first he had done the major part of the work. He had written the reports to Florence. Now, however, he was not only without assistance, but isolated. One Florentine partisan after the other grew first apologetic, then indifferent, and finally hostile. Not only was he personally impoverished, not only had he been living for weeks by borrowing, but the Signory sent him no money to smother the wrangling and the meanness of the many petty courtiers. Florence still had a single supporter, but he too, Machiavelli wrote, would soon be lost "if we do not try to keep his friendship by other means than mere phrases". We have no intriguers here, he complained. How are we to win out when we are unwilling to pay the price?

Machiavelli knew the paths which led to the king's ear, and it would have been easy for him to traverse them had he had the means. How gladly he would have played the role of a master of intrigue and disposed of one enemy after the other! He wanted to appear straightforward, and he seemed hypocritical. He would have liked to have seemed important, and he seemed secondary.

The court left Nevers, journeyed to Melun, Blois, Nantes and Tours. Niccolo limped along after the king. He had become a burden to himself. He sensed grasping hands reaching out for Florence, sensed that the enemies about him were on the point of becoming armies and were seeking to choke off all sources whereby he could send the Signory precise information.

He felt responsible for all the unpleasant aspects of his mission. His pride in his ambition and his belief in his own abilities were wounded. But from the depths of his despair, one hope began to ripen in him. Since the normal methods of diplomacy were denied him, he would triumph over the tricks of negotiation with the help of truth! Cardinal d'Amboise was the most important mind at this court. To him he would reveal Italy in all its nakedness. Why should not reality be as alluring as appearance? D'Amboise was a clever man so he would attempt to discuss politics with him as two mathematicians would talk about mathematics. But it would have to be at a distance from the court. They must talk away from these cringing courtiers, away from these rooms where the walls had ears and indiscretion was the rule.

Niccolo had learned that d'Amboise would be away on a journey for some time. He inquired after the road the Cardinal would travel, rode toward him and met with him in the village. It was late in the evening; he did not want to trouble him at night. The next morning, after an all night vigil, he surprised his Eminence. He disregarded inessentials, disregarded propriety, disregarded his own position and began his monologue in a firm, quiet voice. Plunging into the heart of his subject, he told the astonished cardinal, "It is to your disadvantage to destroy us Florentines. For as things go at present, we are weak. *We* are not the king's enemies, but those strong Powers which are trying to unite all Italy under their scepters—Venice and Rome. Venice does so because she is rich and protected by the sea; the Pope, because the ambition of his son, Cesare, knows no bounds. If you destroy us, we shall be swallowed up either by Venice or Rome. You will be making the mighty mightier and the weak even weaker and thus you will be aiding your future enemies. It would be to the king's advantage, however, to pursue precisely the opposite course. He should weaken the mighty and flatter the weak. You can depend upon us, not because we love you or are grateful to you, but because it is to our own best interest to be loyal. And the king can rely upon such selfish motives. You are threatening our present government of populani with annihilation, although you have no more dependable support in all Italy. The populani are with you because of their commercial interests, because of their fear of the Medici, because of their party tradition and because of their instinct for self-preservation. If you realize this, you will see that it is contrary to your interests to break with us because of a few thousand ducats more or less. You will aid me in my modest mission! Thus you will raise the esteem in which we are held and make it possible for us to give you money. We are a peaceful, commercial republic. We need credit, but if you loose the hounds, both great and small, against us and permit slander to be hurled at us, you render us incapable of procuring the required sums. We will pay, but consider that our signori fear the piazza, the taxpayers. It is on this account that they are parsimonious. We live in a republic in which no single one among us has the power himself of deciding. All decisions are drawn-out affairs."

The Cardinal, the mightiest minister in Europe, replied that Machiavelli well understood the art of argument. He was glad to listen to such speech, and there was much that was correct in what Machiavelli had said. But on the question of money His Majesty would negotiate no further. His Majesty heard all sorts of things from Italy, but he believed only "what he could hold in his hands."

After this conversation, in which he had succeeded somewhat in shaking d'Amboise's conviction that the Florentines were unwilling to pay, it seemed to Machiavelli that opposition dissolved. He no longer had difficulty getting the information he needed for his reports. Aside, perhaps, from any direct, diplomatic success, Niccolo had acquired confidence in himself. To be sure, Florence had to pay, but it had won its best ally in d'Amboise.

Niccolo continued to hold frequent conversations with the Cardinal, who received him graciously and listened to him patiently. It seemed as if he were forgetting his restricted mission in order to discuss politics in general. He was in his element. For the first time in the center of the world stage, he was engaged in tense, exciting conversations with its star actor, instead of with his own clerk, Blasius. Niccolo did not, however, forget his mission. He expanded it upon his own responsibility and sensed at once the possibility of doing work over and beyond his assignment.

"I am making an effort," he wrote, "to appear to be in every way a man of loyalty and good faith." In all honesty, he gave the Cardinal advice. D'Amboise was yet to learn the wisdom of Machiavelli's pessimistic predictions on French policies in Italy. Above all, however, Machiavelli was eager to discover the position of France in regard to the Pope's son, Cesare Borgia. For the major danger to Florence was the threat of Rome. Cesare Borgia was conquering city after city around Tuscany. His military power, his fame, and his swiftness were apparently about to upset the boundaries of Italy. Using Cesare Borgia as a club, the French would have been able to extort the very lifeblood from Florence. Machiavelli probed into the question. Did the French have as fraternal and devout intentions toward the Pope as they claimed? Or were they as hostile as they did not declare, but as French interests demanded that they be? Neither friendship nor hostility was actually the case. Niccolo found out a great deal about d'Amboise. He learned to know his character, the laws that governed his actions, and the imperious esssence of his nature. Niccolo discovered d'Amboise's ambition. Here purely individual aspirations came before the political interests of France. D'Amboise wanted to become Pope! To this end he acted as a benefactor of the Church by permitting Cesare Borgia and the Holy See to conquer territories. But this concession was only a conditional one. Neither Louis nor d'Amboise would permit the Vatican to become the head of the most powerful State in Italy. Rome would become that, however, if Cesare succeeded in overrunning Florence. Machiavelli reported to the Signory, that d'Amboise's love for the Pope ceased at the borders of Tuscany. This assurance, which Machiavelli read in d'Amboise's eyes, was vitally important information for Florence. It formed the foundation of its policies in the years to come. In the light of these successes, which Niccolo alone, perhaps, was able fully to estimate, he saw deeply into the affairs of the court.

He sent to the Signory the first of his classic reports, in which all the opponents of Florence can be heard thinking aloud, and in which one day is as clearly differentiated on paper from the next as they were in reality. He had found his native style and terseness. In these reports he was extremely reticent in passing judgment. He pictured the flux of politics and the shifts of dispositions as if he could measure them with a yardstick and weigh them in a scale. He imparted only the quintessence of his many conversations. He listened to the gossip and rumors and then sat at his desk for nights sifting them. Often but a single sentence passed this rigid censorship. If he had nothing new to say, he was silent, despite all warnings from Florence. "If circumstances remain unaltered," Niccolo wrote to the Signory, "I shall say nothing, for I report nothing but the truth."

In these reports, Machiavellism is the maximum human degree of truthfulness. Mankind is eternally being infatuated with idle fancies, fictions, and chimeras, with the glorification of its spiritual and material disabilities. But Machiavelli's legations will always be looked upon as models of sheer reality and truth. The only times on his missions when he played the fox, when he was "diplomatic", were when he surreptitiously gave the Signory advice. To do this he had to pretend extreme humility. For his job was merely to make reports, to communicate the facts "barely and plainly", and leave it to the Signory to evaluate them. He dared not show initiative, nor betray any desire to act independently. His proposals had to be skillfully concealed. If, nevertheless, he did speak out, which was a rarity, he would immediately remark, as if to reassure the Signory, that he was a dunce. He laid stress on the uncertainty of his judgment, or he put his recommendations into the mouths of people of recognized importance. Thus he wrote the Signory from the court of Louis XII that a very important personage had assured him most emphatically and for the last time that, whether as friend or foe, Florence would have to pay.

The Florentines had long ago decided, in principle, to send a plenipotentiary with the necessary credits. Machiavelli now began deliberately to blow the trumpet of disaster in order that the decision be made with all haste. He was well acquainted with the negligence and dawdling of bureaucracies. "If it were possible, your Excellencies should provide your ambassador with wings," Niccolo wrote. "Consider how swiftly time passes and remember that in the present situation one cannot make too much haste to overcome such swift and changeful perils."

The long awaited ambassador finally arrived. Machiavelli's first mission in France was ended.

CHAPTER V

Machiavelli Meets the Master of Intrigue

CHRIST died on the Cross; a drop of his blood would have sufficed, but he poured forth a stream. In addition to Christ's sacrifice, there are the immaculacy of the Virgin, the sufferings of the martyrs, the deeds of the Saints and of the righteous, and all those works that are beyond what is required of an individual. Mankind possesses thus a store of devoutness in Heaven. God's Mercy permits sinners to partake of this store. And the Pope alone holds the key to this source of salvation.

This was the doctrine of the Catholic Church. Out of this ecclesiastically indisputable and humanly comforting concept, Pope Alexander made a gigantic business. The idea of a unity of the human race embracing both the pious and the sinful became a commercial and industrial enterprise. The two hundred thousand pilgrims in Rome in the Jubilee year, 1500, were Alexander's best customers. They were patrons who had purchased indulgences directly from Rome instead of through a middleman, that is, through one of the Churches in the various countries. Long before Alexander, the centralized administration of the Church, to a large extent in league with the bankers of Florence, had been a powerful force in changing the secular world. The Apostolic Church was a pioneer in bringing about the new financial order. It was called the "Mother of Money". This very contact with the commodity of money lent impetus to the bold, but disciplined and calculating Vatican organization. Alexander, on the other hand, became an incalculable force through contact with money. He felt himself rejuvenated by it. He saw in money his own eternal life. It made him dizzy, turned him into a murderer. Most of the crimes attributed to him are pure inventions, but he actually committed a great many on account of money. He did not, of course, consider them crimes. He thought as did his contemporary, Christopher Columbus, that gold is heavenly bliss.

Alexander's passion for gold was surpassed only by his love for his children. He loved them with maternal tenderness and with the resolution, the unscrupulousness of a completely amoral man. Emotions which in most men are incompatible existed side by side, yet harmoniously, in Alexander. He embraced his dancing girls in the presence of his children. He could be most deeply moved by the Holy Mary, and would in the same moment sell the crucifix to the highest bidder. He was always ready to pardon, and his hatred knew no bounds. His impulses were anarchic, at first sight remote from politics. His interests were as personal as if the whole world were his handkerchief, yet he wielded with skill the successful power of the Papal State.

His worst enemies, the Orsini, against whom Alexander, in alliance with the Colonnesi, was warring, were to learn this well. "The Orsini must be disposed of at once," said the Holy Father. "It is necessary to destroy the entire house. We must take everything from them: we must spare neither their women nor their little children." And this declaration did not remain an empty threat. "Your Excellency knows," the Holy Father said to the Venetian ambassador, "that we Borgias already have our hands reddened with the blood of the Orsini. We have already gone so far that we are in duty bound to get all the Orsini in our power in order that they may do us no harm."

After the Orsini had been destroyed, he had to get rid of his allies, the Colonnesi. Therein Alexander demonstrated his political skill. After a joint victory he would assassinate his comrades-in-arms while their friendship was still flourishing. To be sure, this method was not Alexander's invention, but his money and his abilities afforded him the opportunity of being a virtuoso in deceit. His skill at dissimulation was remarkable. The ambassador of Venice has painted the falseness of his mind as the artist, Pinturicchio, painted his countenance. "If he desires to betray us," the Venetian relates, "then I see how the falsehood first begins to form slowly around his lips. Once he has spoken it, he begins to talk more rapidly and warmly. Suddenly his breast seems to open and the words come directly from his heart and no longer from his lips. His features glow; he surrenders completely to himself; he is permeated by what he is saying. The Pope tells me that he would like to take his soul in his hands and present it to our Republic for us to guard it."

When the fate of his house appeared to grow clouded, he became acrid and sentimentally excited. "Friend," he addressed the Venetian ambassador, "express yourself freely and openly to me. In this chamber there are only God, you and I." But he was also capable of giving way to rage. When he did he would curse like a fishwife in the language of his forebears —Spanish!

The froth, the license, and savagery of Alexander were checked and chained in his son, Cesare, Gonfaloniere and Captain-general of the Holy Roman Church. Cesare was free of vices. He was no voluptuary, and if now and then he took his pleasure, he nevertheless was always more than a common sensualist. For nothing in his make-up was uncalculated and he permitted no human weakness to interfere with the attainment of his goals. For Cesare, Power was concrete and unambiguous. It was a momentous mark which he aimed at without emotion. He wanted to possess it as he possessed his horse. A cool, balanced sense of order characterized the mind of this twenty-five year old youth, this son of Fortune, as the Italians called him. He had a sure command of cunning, dissimulation, cruelty and generosity.

Alexander was magnificent at deceit, but his son was a wizard. He discovered the subtly enchanting music of perfidy and clothed his betrayals in bright and luring colors. He inveigled men into disaster as if he were destiny striking them blind in order to achieve its purpose. The Standard-bearer of the Church did not chaffer with the ambassadors in the Vatican as did his father. He was the personification of youthful deceit in action.

In the field he betrayed his allies before, during, and after battle. No victim was fair prey if Cesare had not previously been his ally. A chronicler wrote, "He has completely transformed war into a succession of betrayals." He had been the friend and ally of Duke Guidobald of Urbino, one of the strongest rulers in the Romagna, who was in a position to become the center of the opposition against Rome. They made presents to each other of brocade, horses, and jewelry, and called themselves Italy's best brothers. Cesare borrowed Guidobald's artillery for a campaign against Camerino. One evening Guidobald was sitting at dinner in the garden of his palace. A breathless messenger reported that Cesare's cavalry had turned hostile and was riding madly through the country. The next report informed him that Cesare, in an unbelievably swift night-march, had changed his objective. The borrowed artillery was now directed against Guidobald's own city. Guidobald had barely time to flee the country in disguise. Only then, after having first taken Urbino, did Cesare turn his borrowed weapons against Camerino. He besieged it, invited the ruler of the city to discuss terms, and after signing a generous treaty had him strangled together with his sons.

Faenza, which for months had offered resistance to the papal troops, finally capitulated. Cesare promised to grant the defenders honorable withdrawal. The Prince of Faenza,

Astore Manfredi, whose forefathers had ruled the city for two hundred years, was to be permitted to leave the country unhindered. Cesare, however, had acted so humanely toward the conquered city that Manfredi felt obligated to express his gratitude toward him. The victor received the defeated prince in all splendor. As a sign of his friendliness, he freed the prisoners without collecting ransom, provided the starved city with victuals and forbade his soldiers to enter it. Manfredi, a melancholy youth of seventeen years, looked up to the victor as the lord of all goodness. He pleaded to be allowed to remain in the company of Cesare. A pact of friendship was closed. Cesare invited Manfredi and his brothers to be his guests in Rome. When they arrived in the city they were taken to the Castel Sant' Angelo. A few days later their bodies were found on the shore of the Tiber.

There was only one ruler in the Romagna who put no trust in anything Cesare said. She was Caterina Sforza. She did not fear him, but her followers did. Her frightened men betrayed her and opened the gates of Caterina's last fortress. Behind a wall shattered by artillery she continued to fight. A number of French officers in Cesare's entourage cut down her retainers and after a hard struggle took her prisoner. She was forced to ride to Rome with Cesare. The Pope poured imprecations on the woman, called her "accursed, vile, sinful viper", and would have had her murdered. The French, however, considered her their prisoner and prevented the murder. They declared that women were not killed in their country and took her to the safe asylum of Florence. Cesare bemoaned this loss, for he wanted not only the lands of his enemies but their heads as well. With the agility of a cat he sprang after them, and if he did not always capture them, he never lost their trail. He always kept his eye on them. Until his predecessor in power was buried, a conquered territory seemed to him only half his possession.

Cesare outwitted every city and every tyrant in a different manner. In one place he played godfather to the successor to the throne; in another he dulled the alertness of his enemies by breves from the Vatican. He would join with the burghers against the princes. He would appear as a deliverer from oppressive taxes; or promise to cancel debts; or provide cheap grain; or he would simply buy off the garrison.

Before Borgia began his work, Rome had been the most restive city in Italy. Two great families, the Orsini and the Colonnesi, had controlled the Vatican.

And outside the walls of the eternal city, in the Romagna, which stretched across the Apennines to the Adriatic Sea and the plain of the Po, the impotence of the papacy had really begun. The Romagna was politically, with few exceptions, the wildest territory in Italy. It was a jungle of despots where the petty, local rulers were as vicious as their subjects. Threatening beggars, highwayman knights, and unruly, homeless peasants rivaled their traditional masters in pillaging. Within every tiny peasant village there dwelt the same spirit of determined defiance to everyone as in the castles of the barons. In the Romagna, the great vassals of the Church, the Baglioni in Perugia, the Sforzas in Pesaro, the Malatestas in Rimini, the Manfredi in Faenza and the Bentivoglios in Bologna, fought one another and united with anyone to make war upon the Pope. The Pope's sovereignty was purely theoretical. He received his tribute both rarely and irregularly.

Europe was in a state of transition where all traditions and mystic concepts were being tested for the real Power that was in them. The right and glory of existence were granted to the warrior alone. In this new Europe, surrounded by these rapacious feudal princes, the papacy had to be militant and warlike in order to survive.

Cesare fulfilled this need. He was an administrative device, for the Popes mounted their thrones as old men. Their age deprived them of the flexibility necessary to thread their way successfully through the labyrinth of the Romagna. Cesare had the youthful energy needed to establish the secular power of the Church. For in the decisive years, he and not his father was the ruler of the eternal city. Alexander administered Christendom merely as the source of financial support for his son.

After four years, the results of Cesare's labors were unveiled. It was then revealed that no Pope had ever been as powerful a secular prince as Alexander VI. True, his successor to the throne of Peter cursed the memory of the Borgias. Nevertheless, these Borgias had given the Church a gift which lasted for three centuries. The walls of her cities, and the valleys, rivers, and hills of her territories remained. They had liberated the Church from the dread of being driven out of her own land. Father and son had won new successes for the papacy. In Rome, the Colonnesi and Orsini had been broken. The baronial houses had been humbled and subordinated. The rulers of ecclesiastical territories—the lords of Urbino, Faenza, Rimini, Camerino, Perugia, Imola, Forli, Pesaro and Piombino—had either been expelled or murdered. And never before had the College of Cardinals and the Curia been such willing tools in the hand of the Pope.

The Borgia now owned the hereditary estate of the Church, which had never been precisely bounded. Cesare, however, was not the man to set limits to it voluntarily. He was impelled to go forward. The more easily he advanced, the more he wanted to advance. In his progress he collided with two neighbors, Venice and Florence. Both countries were protected by their alliance with France. Venice was in a position to defend itself, but Florence was not.

In Tuscany, crises were following one after the other. None of them was met; they piled up on each other. The entire skill of the Signory was devoted to keeping these crises from swamping Florence. Because of this situation, Cesare thought he could conquer Florence without striking a blow. The French were opposed, but Cesare intended to bargain with them only after they were faced with a fait accompli. And he especially wanted to measure the degree of resistance within Florence by direct contact. At the moment he was in the field on the borders of Tuscany and had to return to Rome. So for the time being he merely demanded the right of passage for himself and his troops. He wished to march from the territory of Bologna straight across the Republic, thus going through Piombino to reach Rome.

On his return from France, Niccolo found the city in the midst of this new life-and-death problem. True, he was able to report to the Signory that the sympathies of Louis and d'Amboise were on the side of the Republic, but the king was far away and Cesare was at the border. Icy panic settled on Tuscany over night like a sudden frost. The streets leading to Florence were clogged with fleeing peasants, hastily laden carts, and worn animals. In the city itself, a chronicler writes, "People are not working, especially not in silk, and the needy are in the main starving and wailing." The Signory was as perplexed as the man in the street. It neither granted nor forbade the right of passage. But scarcely had Cesare set foot on the soil of the Republic when the Signory concluded a treaty with him.

From the very beginning, Machiavelli had been opposed to the policies of the Signory. Since we are not in a position to block Cesare's passage, he argued, it would be more prudent and better for our reputation to grant the permission requested without reservation.

Cesare's troops plundered the territories they marched through. Niccolo's Second Chancery tried to protect the population by organizing an ordered evacuation. Florence was put on an emergency footing. Machiavelli was commanded to take charge of the guards of the city. In those leaderless days of confusion one task after the other was imposed on him.

Niccolo was frequently sent to Pistoia, to Arezzo, and to the borders of the Republic in the district of the Val di Chiana, where disorder and turmoil were prevalent. The inhabitants of the small villages in this low country had to be kept down, for the peasants, shielded by the general insecurity, were stealing the harvests and seizing the lands of others. They no longer wished to be subject to Florentine law. In these districts the fire of civil war was beginning to flame.

Cesare's passage finally came to an end. His troops were no longer on Tuscan soil and he himself was in Rome. He had left as a legacy the revolt in Arezzo and in the Val di Chiana. One of his condottieri, Vitellozzo Vitelli, a bitter enemy of Florence because his brother had been beheaded by the Signory for high treason, had incited these territories to rebellion. Cesare did not trust Vitellozzo, but he had no objection to his keeping Tuscany on edge. The unrest was doing a good job for Borgia. Cesare was able to inform the Signory and Louis that he no longer had any control over Vitellozzo. Vitellozzo remained on Tuscan soil in the rebellious territory. He would have liked best to take Florence by surprise in a night attack with a few hundred men. Cesare advised him to curb his inclinations toward insurrection. "Even if your coup is successful," he asked him, "how will you be able to maintain yourself?" Vitellozzo replied unconcernedly, "Always begin. The middle and the end look after themselves!"

The enemies of the Florentines, the followers of the Medici, and all who had ever been harmed by the Signory, crept out of their hiding holes and went over to Vitellozzo. Even the exiled Pietro Medici and some of the Orsini were with him. The rebellious provinces declared themselves wholly for the Medici. The peasant communities did this in many cases only to protect their crops from the small robber bands of Vitellozzo and his friends. Florence sent troops. The worried Republic saw itself faced with the prospect of prolonged guerrilla warfare. Tiny Tuscany now had two fronts in its own territory: Pisa and the Val di Chiana.

The frightened city shook with indignation against Cesare. For decades Tuscany had enjoyed internal security. Nowhere in Italy had fewer murders and fewer robberies occurred. In Florence titles of ownerships had seemed secure because ordinarily only economic crises, not naked violence, had made property change hands. Now all the channels of trade leading to Venice and Rome were being threatened by Borgia's confederates. In the midst of peace there prevailed the uncertainty of wartime. The ears of the Florentines rang with the atrocity stories that came out of Arezzo, the Val di Chiana, the area near Pisa, and its border territories. And the Pisans began to take the offensive. They could not strike at the troops of the Signory, but their expeditions could and did destroy crops and set villages afire. One chronicler wrote, "We see in a circle all around us nothing but fire."

Cesare seemed to be the source of all these evils. The Florentines looked upon him as a blackmailer. Alexander's son called himself "Cesare Borgia of France, by God's Grace Duke of the Romagna, Valence and Urbino, Prince of Andres, Lord of Piombino, Gonfaloniere and Captain-general of the Holy Roman Church". But the Florentines called him quite bluntly the bandit! They were astonished at a world which tolerated him and waited expectantly for the lightning of God to strike him down. They compared the words of the Savior with the deeds of the Vatican. The chroniclers lost all restraint. "Borgia has within him an infinite cruelty," one of them wrote, "more than has ever before been seen or heard of. He throws everything out of joint." "I know not whether I am capable of writing down the wickedness of Cesare," another wrote, "for I tremble from fear of God even in listening to tales of it." The former followers of Savonarola, even moderate citizens, trusting in the righteousness of their cause, wished to break off all relations with Rome and refuse to deal with Cesare. The head of the military might of the Church was, to be sure, an alarming foe, but of inferior rank. "We must feel ashamed to be Florentines," a wealthy apothecary wrote, "since we enter into a compromise with someone who is not worth three *quattrini.*" The people suspected that the Signory was disposed to conclude a disgraceful truce with the bellicose son of the Pope. At night the doors and houses of those who had had dealings with Cesare in his passage through Tuscany were chalked with gallows and nooses. This hollow, impotent indignation affected the officials of the Republic also. They had had the task of officially confirming the destruction wrought by Cesare during his march through the Republic and now the Signory overburdened them with work concerning the rebellious provinces. Even Machiavelli was indignant about Cesare. The letters his superiors ordered him to write to the commissioners in the rebellious regions are full of moral revulsion "at the countless infamies of Cesare that have descended upon us, torn the flesh of half our country, and brought us to the brink of famine."

As a Florentine who loved his city, enjoyed its noisy peacefulness, and saw with its eyes, Niccolo was horrified by this man who was menacing and strangling his native land. He shared the uncertainty and timidity of his friends, neighbors, and fellow bureaucrats. But Niccolo did not allow himself to be ruled by his emotion. Under orders from the Signory, he had ridden all through the endangered districts, spoken with the peasants, soldiers, and mayors. He had inspected the guards on the walls of towns and examined the account books of communities. Niccolo had repeatedly seen how weak Florence was, and he was seeking the law that governed this weakness.

Why had war been so beneficial to Rome and disastrous to Florence? In Tuscany it had released antagonisms among the various territories and they had broken out with unsuspected savagery. It had torn open forgotten wounds, given birth to unbridled violence in sleepy villages and busy market places, and had menaced the entire structure the Florentines had built up in their own territory. Why had the mere specter of battle worked so destructively in Tuscany?

In the ecclesiastical lands, on the other hand, the battles and violence centering around Rome had brought about the unity of a huge, wild region with famous cities and rich ports. Machiavelli, whose mind was open to all the aspects of Power, could not answer with the simple formula of the Florentines: because Cesare is a scoundrel! Niccolo, who was always filled with enthusiasm for all forms of action and courage, observed for four long years the process by which gold, steel, and deceit were changing the great area which began at the mouth of the Tiber and ended in the plain of the Po. He studied the new chemistry, the new technique of violence.

Cesare did not merely murder. Once he had achieved a victory he consolidated his conquest without direct violence. In contrast to his predecessors, he did not desire merely to rob his subjects: he wanted to keep them in check. His crimes were committed coolly and he kept excellent order. He simplified the judicial and administrative system, provided credit agencies, tore down old sections of cities, and promised to build new ones. He discussed with Leonardo da Vinci, the foremost engineer of the age, the draining of the swampy districts of the Romagna. The demagogic methods of Cesare did not need so many or such devious bypaths as those which Lorenzo Medici had applied in Florence.

Cesare's demagogy acted stroke by stroke; it was a succession of stunning surprises. It accompanied rather than followed his infamous acts. Cesare had his most loyal bailiffs beheaded, after their work was done, and delivered up their corpses to the jeers of the mob. They had been horribly cruel, to be sure, but it was Cesare who had commanded their cruelty. He constantly emphasized the rights of the Church and the legitimacy of his measures, seeking to make himself popular with the masses in every possible way. He took into his service the associates and mercenaries of the rulers he had expelled. He made them gifts far greater than any wages they could get from the famous condottieri of the Romagna. He had about him a whole circle composed of masterless soldiery.

Niccolo awaited every act of Vatican treachery in feverish suspense. The Duke was his intellectual property. His own logic and that of Cesare were the same: to be bold and adventurous and to keep away from all doctrines, dogmas, and fictions. Watching Cesare, Niccolo became aware of the problems which were to occupy him throughout his life. His approach to problems was neither theoretical nor artificial.

At this time the chapters of his book were taking shape in his head, but only pure chance was to dictate the time he was to write them down. The nontheoretical Niccolo, free of all prejudices, observed the Romagna, and what he saw there led him to ask himself many questions. How and why is Power lost? How is it seized and retained? How does violence become Power, Power sovereignty, and sovereignty a State? How is the State defended, how expanded? How must the prince who has come into sovereignty by crime conduct himself, and what are the military duties of the prince? Is it better to rule by cruelty or by clemency? Must a prince keep his word?

The very weakness of Florence lent such questions as these an incisive gravity. He could make no compromise between what already existed and what ought to be. For Florence was practically powerless. As a patriotic Florentine he had the same feeling toward Borgia that the Prussian officers such as Scharnhorst, who brought about reforms in Germany, had toward Napoleon. They attacked and admired him at one and the same time. With Napoleon as their model they fought battles against Napoleon.

When Niccolo, tired out by his daily tasks, put his thoughts in order at night and analyzed the problems of the Signory, he devised schemes which might have been edicts of Cesare. He combined his theory with Cesare's practise. In regard to Arezzo, where he often stayed as government commissioner, he wrote, that a rebellious city could be won over either by benevolence or by destruction, according to circumstances and the character of the rebelling populace.

"There have always been men who served and others who commanded; and men who served unwillingly and others who served willingly; and men who revolted repeatedly and were repeatedly subdued." The Aretines served unwillingly and the Signory had not been benevolent toward them, but had punished them. It had punished but not destroyed, thus creating a continual source of rebellion in Arezzo. The Florentines had been greedy for Power without knowing how to use it. Their subjects marked this well.

The correct course should have been, "either to win men by kindliness or to remove them from the world. For they can revenge lighter injuries, but not graver." Florence lacked the strength to be cruel. She was not humanitarian, she was weak. According to Machiavelli, only men new to Power possessed the courage to attack ruthlessly and the determination to use the Terror.

It was self-evident to Cesare's admirers that he should murder the princes whom he defeated. To retain a conquered city, the entire family of the former ruler must be exterminated. Not only the prince of a new state, but any newly established system of sovereignty could maintain itself only by liberal use of the block. It is foolish to try to enslave a country without first destroying the men who are willing to be martyrs to liberty, as foolish as it would be to proclaim that freedom had arrived while a tyrant was still living. A man who thinks he can bring about revolutions and organic changes peacefully and without bloodshed does not realize the lust for Power in the minds and hearts of men.

In the first days of all new princedoms, a court must be set up which is not intended to distribute justice. For new sovereignties are hereditary princedoms got by crime and crime sets up patterns which the criminal must follow. The code of Terror is: annihilation of the existing political regime and the seizure of the new one. The unimportant followers and the nonpartisans will—as far as they are needed—come over of themselves. Men new to Power, however, may easily fall victim to their own victory if they allow themselves to be blinded by their own strength. They must not be backward and sentimental in their use of murder and torture. That is, they must not employ cruelty badly.

"By ill-employed cruelties I mean," Machiavelli wrote, "those which increase rather than diminish with time. It is impossible for men to maintain themselves thus." If murder is intelligently committed the new prince can attain his goal with a minimum of victims. The ancient school of pre-Machiavellian tyrants had murdered without the help of demagogy and without theatrical gestures. They had not suborned magistrates to pronounce sentences full of moral indignation. They had worked without applause and without stooping to false accusations. They had not bothered to defame the character of the murdered man. But the new type of murder which is committed in order to secure sovereignty must be the work of a virtuoso in deceit. It is a job for the calculating statesman rather than the executioner.

Sentences should be carried out at one stroke and not spun out over a period of time. The man who becomes so set upon murder that he forgets how to exercise leniency is a bloodthirsty fool whose base acts will never lead to success.

And success alone excuses, justifies, and transmutes all base acts. Executions should be beacons whose light will be visible at a great distance in the surrounding darkness of fear. They must silence the enemies of the new regime. All antagonists, whether persecuted or not, should have vividly in mind the prospect of being tortured, exiled, and beggared.

Machiavelli discovered and formulated the Terror. He called this device of sovereignty "cruel". The man who desired to enjoy his garden, his loves, and his peace, must flee from the savage jungle of public life and remain a private person. Cesare Borgia, however, robbed the Florentines of their privacy and condemned them to live in an atmosphere of violence. Peace was merely a whisper from another world, despite their great longing for it. Cesare not only menaced the Republic itself, but his image was permanently in the mind of every inhabitant of Florence. The Borgia's shadow fell on every conversation of any length, and that is the great triumph of the ruler by violence. Cesare shackled the imaginations of men.

But in Machiavelli's mind Cesare's policy was completely logical. Niccolo saw the fundamental force in politics—egoism—concentrated in one man. This egoism, arising in Cesare from the warlike conditions in the world, became greater than Cesare and expanded into the State. It was, to be sure, still a very crude State. It was not yet able to control its own forces and it gave way to orgies of unrestraint. But the immorality of the individual at its head was an inherent feature of tyranny in the process of becoming the State. Niccolo saw Cesare as the man who shaped events. Borgia was to him the indispensable "prince who can play the simultaneous roles of man and beast".

Suddenly the monotonous voice of daily anxiety was interrupted by a brief sound of joy. A report spread from desk to desk in the chanceries and passed through the huge gate of the Signory. It excited the entire city. Cesare's condottieri, the Orsini, Olivretto, and Vitellozzo Vitelli, had risen up against him. Vitellozzo, Cesare's best soldier, was gathering about him all the independent rulers who were threatened by Borgia. His allies were the Lord of Perugia, Baglioni; the tyrant of Siena, Pandolfo Petrucci, and the ruler of Bologna, Bentivoglio. Besides these, Vitellozzo called from their hiding places and refuges all the rulers whom Borgia had exiled.

They were to meet in the neighborhood of Perugia, in La Magione, for a council of war against Borgia. "The serpent, Cesare, is swallowing us one after the other," was the watchword. Venice and also Florence were asked to send delegates to La Magione. Vitellozzo had just been forced by French threats to leave Florentine soil, but he now proclaimed himself a friend of the Florentines. The Signory had scarcely received his message, when they were sent a second invitation. Cesare asked them to send envoys to Imola. The Signory was in a quandary.

Should they ally themselves with Vitellozzo and the Orsini, who were the friends of the Medici and the plague of Florence? Or should they join the Devil himself, Cesare? If the Signory had been able to act freely, it would immediately have sent representatives to La Magione in order to support the petty bandits against the father of banditry. But Louis of France declared quite plainly that he would not abandon Borgia. The Signory dared not oppose France.

But it also had to consider Florentine public opinion. Cesare was an abomination to the people of Florence. The pros and cons were weighed again and again. The Signory finally decided to deal with Cesare and inform him of all that was known about the conspiracy. The Signory, however, did not want to honor him with an ambassador, so it sent to Imola merely the Secretary of the Second Chancery, Niccolo Machiavelli. His task was to watch Borgia closely, and try to learn his plans while pretending friendship. He was to sign nothing, to commit the Signory to no definite policy, and to protract the negotiations as long as possible.

The Duke received Machiavelli like a long-awaited friend. He did not know that the Florentine envoy had come to him empty-handed and without the power to make treaties or to bargain. He thought, therefore, that he would be able to conclude an alliance promptly. "We have a long common frontier and the same enemies," the Duke said. "Florence has two wounds, Vitellozzo and Pisa. I can heal both."

"What should we do," asked Machiavelli, who wanted to avoid generalities, "if we were attacked by the condottieri, with whom we do not want to conclude an alliance out of love for your Excellency and loyalty to France."

"I would personally rush to your defense," Cesare replied. "In addition I would carry all the costs of the war." Niccolo regarded this all too generous reply as unsatisfactory.

After his second audience, Niccolo became more familiar with Cesare although he was still far from intimate with him. The Pope's son sat before him in black velvet with a heavy golden chain about his neck and cast a fleeting glance at the lean little negotiator with his pale, bony face, sunken cheeks, and large mouth. Cesare saw in him nothing extraordinary, merely another of the clever diplomats Italy was full of. He looked upon Niccolo as a mailbox into which one tossed information. And if a touch of intimacy did arise in the course of a long conversation, it was lost by the next audience. Niccolo tried to capture the nuances in Cesare's words. As always during a mission, he was dissatisfied with himself. For years his mind had been following every act of the Duke's. But now he doubted his ability to reach the innermost core of Borgia. "I do not know," he wrote, "what the Duke in reality secretly desires." Cesare was a splendid speaker. His terse phrases were a delight, but he always stopped just short of the truth. "Cesare is impenetrable,"

Machiavelli reported. "No matter how enthusiastic he may be at heart, neither his voice nor the expression of his countenance change."

The two began to exchange lies about alleged secrets. Machiavelli recounted the many services Florence had rendered Cesare, and Cesare ended the battle of bouquets with the assertion that his condottieri had rebelled only because he had refused to surrender Tuscany to them. Each tried to read in the eyes of the other how much was believed, how much rejected. Since Cesare, in his insecure position, could not offer the Florentines very much for the alliance he desired, he hinted at wonderful prospects. If Florence and Rome, backed by France, were to join forces, who remained in Italy to resist them? But he also tried to arouse the Florentines' appetite for more immediate gains. "Machiavelli, what a fine tidbit this wealthy city of Lucca would be!"

Machiavelli reported to the Signory, however, that Cesare did not take any Italian alliance seriously. For Borgia's ambition, only alliances outside of Italy had any significance. The more importunate Cesare's proposals became, the more emphatically Machiavelli warned the Signory. "He speaks so straightforwardly, so amicably, and so warmly, that it almost seems we need not fear. Nevertheless, because of his past behavior, we must be on guard constantly."

In the course of their conversations, Cesare often attempted to take Niccolo by surprise. "Are you not in league with my craftiest enemy, Petrucci of Siena?" he once asked Machiavelli.

"No," Niccolo rejoined. "The alliance to which your Excellency refers is merely an ancient treaty of neutrality which, moreover, expires this month."

"He seemed to believe me," Niccolo reported. But Cesare did not believe him!

"Machiavelli," he unexpectedly asked at another time, "an Orsini has informed me that two representatives of Florence have offered him an alliance. What do you think of that?"

"I ask your Excellency if the Orsini have never lied to you?"

"More than once," Cesare answered, and their laughter disposed of that question.

The sole responsibility for the enmity between Borgia and Florence was conveniently shifted to the condottieri. Here Machiavelli and Cesare met and outdid one another in moral indignation. No one abhorred treachery, breaches of faith, murder, and violence, so intensely as these two! Cesare referred to the conference of the hostile condottieri in La Magione as "the fraternity of moral bankrupts".

"The condottieri," he declared, "do not seem particularly dangerous to me, and I know them better than anyone else. This Vitellozzo, who enjoys so much renown, cannot boast of a single brave deed. His invariable excuse is the French disease. He knows how to pillage unarmed territories, and he can rob those who do not stand up to him. That is the extent of his ability. I do not desire to boast, but I stand far above such petty villainies. At the moment I am stalemated, but I am the stronger. I tell you, it is a bad year for traitors."

Cesare's optimism was not justified by his situation. For the first time, after an unbroken succession of victories, he now found himself in danger. Vitellozzo and Orsini had destroyed those troops which had remained faithful to him. Confident of escaping punishment, enemies rose up in castles and cities. Rebelling captains seized fortresses. The long arm of Venice extended secret support to everyone revolting against Borgia in the Romagna. Alliances and temporary coalitions were formed overnight. In many places, exiled rulers were at the gates of their former cities. The center of the Romagna, Urbino, had already fallen. Cesare was still in command in Imola, but none of the roads leading to

Imola were safe. Bold determination, combined with a few lucky accidents, might make the Duke the prisoner of his former subjects, tools, allies, and victims.

What was going to happen? The Signory put this question to Machiavelli repeatedly with increasing anxiety. He reported daily but never said more than was justified. "Your Lordships must excuse me and consider that I am dealing with a prince who is an absolute monarch. If I am not to report fantasies and dreams, I must first confirm my knowledge. To do this, time is necessary. I do not waste my time; on the contrary I make good use of it."

Niccolo drew no specific conclusions from Cesare's insecure situation. He thought the defeat was merely the temporary result of a military revolt. Cesare would learn from it to depend upon his own, not upon hired troops. If only he could survive this serious crisis! Luck must intervene here, and he believed that the Duke would be lucky. Was he not the son of the Pope and the ally of the King of France? The authority of this position lent him credit in misfortune.

But aside from this cold reckoning, Machiavelli was carried away by Cesare's genius for action. His reports are succinct, chiseled, enthusiastic descriptions of this virtue. Niccolo was accustomed to sit at his desk weighing his thoughts quietly and unhurriedly. During these tempestuous events in Imola, he felt that he was near a decisive force he had never before known. Cesare commanded everything and debated nothing. A minimum of secretaries and a maximum of effectiveness! Everything took place calmly and in absolute secrecy.

Niccolo was unable to learn anything at all from the secretaries, the army captains or the ministers. It was a womanless court, a camp without gossip. Cesare's liking for secrecy kept everyone about him silent. Machiavelli saw more couriers coming and going in one day than he saw in Florence in a week. Money blotted out past errors and filled the gaps left by defeats. "Without debate or discussion, more money is spent in an eventful week than in another country during two years."

The Duke now began his counterattack. He removed his troops from the territories which were most endangered so that he would undergo no further defeats. The fortresses still in his possession were hurriedly refortified. The trumpets of his recruiting officers outsounded those of the rebels. His reputation as a general saved him. Within two weeks he had thousands of new recruits. Imola became a huge camp. The raw troops were constantly drilled under the command of tried mercenaries and before the eyes of Cesare himself. In order to flatter the people of the Romagna, he kept their countrymen as commanders. "No one knows as well as Cesare," Machiavelli wrote, "how to dissolve a disloyal army and create a new one."

Assistance from the French was also beginning to arrive. Cesare was ready. He rose above the disaster, Machiavelli reported, with "his eyes fixed upon his foes, ready and willing to start a general conflagration." The leaders of the rebellion, a short time before so victorious, seemed paralyzed. They had let precious time slip. They were operating independently, without any unified plan. Niccolo observed that none of them was concerned with the common purpose; each had only his own gain in mind. He saw that the duke enjoyed the advantages of confidence and determination. Borgia was going to separate his many enemies and defeat them singly.

Fear, dissension, suspicion, and treachery invaded the camp of the victorious rebels.

Cesare called Machiavelli to him to witness the sport. He was to report to Florence how the affair was being settled. "Machiavelli," the duke said, "all of them are now my good friends. Each claims he opposed me and deserted my flag only against his will. Yesterday Baglioni sent me assurances of his loyalty from Perugia. Today Orsini summoned up his courage and visited me in person, disguised as a courier. Tomorrow another will come. Vitellozzo writes me ardent letters of submission every day. He would like to heal with words the wounds his dagger has dealt. Oh, they think they can play with me."

"Your Excellency," Niccolo answered, "I have never had doubts of your success. Had I from the beginning expressed my thoughts I could stand before you as a prophet."

That cold, inclement November, Imola heard the passionate confessions of converts. Each tried to forestall his ally by being the first to go over to Cesare. From Perugia, Siena, Camerino—from every center of the revolt—came masked officers and couriers. A number of the converted rebels simultaneously sent messages of peace and attacked Cesare's troops. But none of the condottieri, even those who were still secretly attempting to take Borgia's fortresses, failed to reassure Cesare. The Duke wondered at the apparent naïveté of these generals who were so thoroughly practised in crime. Did it perhaps conceal cunning greater than his?

Cesare was anxious to destroy his enemies completely. He therefore wanted them to trust him implicitly and believe that he trusted them. Hence, instead of simply embracing them as prodigal sons, he said, "Toward you, who believe no empty phrases, I shall employ none. Reconquer Urbino for me. By new deeds the old may be buried, and new faith grows out of joint efforts and common interests."

The peace pact between Cesare and the rebels was the essence of perfection! The insurgents promised to reconquer all of Cesare's former possessions. They themselves were to retain all the territories which they had held before the revolt. A defensive and offensive alliance was concluded between the condottieri and Cesare.

This peace pact worried Niccolo greatly. Had the condottieri and Cesare united against Florence? "Everyone here," he wrote, "speaks of peace, and everywhere are preparations for war." War against whom? He sought to extract definite information from Cesare.

The Duke declared that he had no intentions of attacking Florence, or even of permitting Vitellozzo and Orsini to revive the old game against Tuscany. Then his language suddenly changed, grew more emphatic. "Up to the present," he told the anxious Florentine, "I have been in no very favorable situation. I therefore did not want to make grand promises. Now I am in a secure position and so enough of generalities and meaningless assurances. I do not want amity in general, such as you desire, but in particular, for my immediate aims. I feel that the Signory has imposed upon me. You are my neighbors; I must know whether I dare confer benefits on you." Florence, he went on, would hire the whole world as condottieri, but not him. Why did not Florence give him command of its army and at the same time conclude the long-discussed, long-due alliance. As the price of the alliance he would conquer Pisa and within a short time destroy Vitellozzo.

Machiavelli replied that this was out of the question. For Cesare was no plain condottiere with whom one could sign a contract for hire, but the strongest Power in Italy. Alliances were founded upon armament. How could Florence deliver up its arms to him and simultaneously conclude an alliance? As far as Vitellozzo was concerned, had not the Duke just made a permanent treaty with this man?

This last objection Cesare had his secretary answer. "It is ridiculous to take this peace pact seriously; even infants are laughing at it. Vitellozzo and Orsini are the vipers of Italy. There are a thousand ways to dissolve this treaty. The Signory must send a plenipotentiary, for such matters cannot be settled by written proposals and eternal reference back to Florence."

Machiavelli was frightened and at the end of his patience. He had already stayed two months in Imola and now, suddenly, immense perils loomed. He feared that the Signory, deceived by the inactivity and straits of Cesare, would overlook the nearness of disaster. Niccolo was receiving no instructions. He no longer had anything to say to Cesare, and in addition was no longer granted audiences. "It is frightfully dangerous to be silent with men like this prince," he wrote. He felt, too, that evasion had its limits. He suggested a maneuver to the Signory. Instead of provoking Cesare still further by doing nothing, Florence should act as if it were preparing for war on Borgia's behalf. The matter could be easily turned so as to conceal the purpose of the preparations from Florentine public opinion, and it would not be difficult to exaggerate the extent of the preparations to Cesare. "For he has no means of checking up."

On the eleventh of December, the Duke and his army left Imola. Machiavelli rode along. Neither he nor anyone else in the entire camp knew the goal of the march. Niccolo sought in vain for information. He heard only vague rumors. "Even Cesare's intimates are building castles in the air," he reported to Florence. The army moved forward slowly in an endless procession over narrow, ice-covered roads. The mystery of this march depressed Niccolo terribly. Long hours of silence gave him leisure for gloomy suppositions. Were they marching against Venice or, after all, against Florence? Phrases from conversations with Cesare at Imola made his heart beat more swiftly. If he had not been afraid of appearing a fool he would have put spurs to his horse and ridden to Florence. But what would he have been able to tell the Signory that he had not already written? After ten days the army rested in Cesena. He still did not know which way the duke intended to turn.

In Cesena remarkable events took place with startling suddenness. From here the duke arranged rendezvous with his new-old allies, Vitellozzo, Orsini, and Olivretto. The star performers of La Magione were to conquer the city of Sinigalia for him. He would meet them there to receive their homage. Sinigalia was situated on the Adriatic Sea, in the opposite direction from Tuscany. Niccolo's nightmares vanished. But new mysteries puzzled him and kept him in suspense. Cesare dismissed the French troops which had until now accompanied him—a completely inexplicable act!

The duke was striving to show weakness. His intention seemed mainly to win the confidence of those about Vitellozzo. He threw his troops into a carefully planned state of disorder. He did not provide for their baggage, and soldiers drifted from the army, deserted it in small irregular groups, plundering right and left along the road and deep into the surrounding country. Spies reported everywhere that the papal army was daily growing weaker, that soon it would cease to exist.

From Cesena the duke marched to Fano, fifteen miles from Sinigalia. Here he was informed that Sinigalia had surrendered; only the citadel was still resisting. The duke sent word to Vitellozzo that he would march in with his artillery the following day and immediately storm the fortress. He asked that room be made for his troops by quartering the condottieri's soldiers outside the city. All of them except Olivretto obeyed this request. At the same time he sent fraternal greetings to Vitellozzo, the Orsini, and Olivretto, and invited them to a great celebration in the town hall.

On the bleak morning of December 31, 1503, Cesare's entire army arrived at Sinigalia. Here he had arranged a meeting with his officers, who for weeks had been marching along side roads in small detachments. He had given detailed instructions as to the division and concealment of the various troops. Everything was prepared with mathematical precision. For weeks and months he had planned these movements and the secret had been well kept. Now ten thousand foot

PAINTING BY LORENZO DI CREDI

CATERINA SFORZA
"Avenged in order to govern,
governed in order to take vengeance."

HELIOGRAVURE FROM
PAINTING BY RAPHAEL

CESARE BORGIA

"His terse phrases were a delight, but he always stopped just short of the truth."

soldiers and two thousand cavalry of the papal army stood before the gates of the city. The army marched into Sinigalia while the duke remained with his bodyguard awaiting the condottieri. Paolo Orsini, Duke of Cravina-Orsini, and Vitellozzo came to meet him. As soon as the generals neared, Cesare's escort respectfully moved aside and let them take places close to Cesare. Their welcome was most hearty—except that the ranks had closed around the condottieri!

Cesare saw that Olivretto was missing. He signed to his adjutant, Don Michele. Don Michele rode in all haste to Olivretto who was drilling his troops in the market place and asked him amiably why he did not come to welcome the duke. He suggested that Olivretto order his soldiers to their quarters immediately for otherwise the duke's troops would occupy quarters which did not belong to them. And nothing ought to cloud this splendid day of peace and reconciliation. Olivretto gave the necessary commands and rode with Don Michele to meet the duke. Like the others, Olivretto also was taken prisoner.

A quarter hour after Cesare had seized his condottieri, he entered the town hall with them and there had them put in chains. His soldiers immediately descended savagely upon the quarters of Olivretto's unsuspecting troops. All were overpowered and put to the sword. Machiavelli hastily sent a note to Florence. "The duke, scarcely arrived in the city, has had Orsini, Vitellozzo, and Olivretto arrested and imprisoned. The city is being ravaged. Everything is in confusion. It is now three o'clock in the afternoon and I have not yet found anyone by whom to send these lines. In the next letter I shall send details. In my opinion, the prisoners will no longer be alive tomorrow morning."

Machiavelli's prediction was correct. That same night Vitellozzo and Olivretto, sitting back to back on two chairs, were strangled with the same cord. The two Orsini were murdered a few days afterward.

From his room Niccolo heard the hoof beats of Cesare's guard which was struggling to put a halt to the pillaging by the Borgia's own troops. Screams, trumpet blasts, and smoke made him close the window. He forced himself to overcome his weariness and excitement. His pen soothed him, and he did not put it down until he had described every detail of the day. With thorough coolness he called this thirty-first of December "in every respect rare and remarkable". It was the greatest single act of betrayal he was ever to see. And not only the spirit of it, but the technique of this clearheaded, purposeful treachery, its dexterity and polish, filled him with admiration. Only this final act gave him the explanation for the behavior of Cesare and his army during the past few weeks. Machiavelli felt very close to the duke that night. But the night was not yet over for him. Toward two o'clock in the morning the duke had him summoned. Gone was Cesare's animus toward Florence. He was glowing with happiness and extreme excitement when he received Niccolo.

"Machiavelli," he said, "until now I could not tell you what my intentions were when I asserted that I was a friend of Tuscany. I have freed you of your most dangerous enemies. To get rid of Vitellozzo and Orsini, the Signory would have sacrifice two hundred thousand ducats, but even so the deed would not have been done so smoothly and thoroughly as I have done it." The duke, however, did not dwell long on things of the past. The murder which had taken place but two hours before was already an old story. He intended to leave Sinigalia on the morrow. "I would have left today, for the rocca has surrendered, but I have stayed in order to put a stop to the pillaging." Cesare was already thinking of the next logical steps which must result from his act. To him, until everything was done, nothing was done. He still had two foes: the Duke of Urbino and Pandolfo Petrucci in Siena. The Duke of Urbino, as a matter of fact, had been expelled from his city, but he still lingered as a dangerous specter. At the moment he was in Tuscany. The Signory must surrender him.

Despite the mood of mutual joy uniting Cesare and Machiavelli, Niccolo replied, "Your Excellency, our dignity could not suffer this. Florence will never surrender a refugee."

"Machiavelli, you speak very well," the duke answered, without insisting. "But as far as Petrucci is concerned, we must come to an agreement. Although he himself did not fight against us, Petrucci was the chief of the rebels. He remains a danger. He is clever and wealthy. He will gather together the scattered remnants of our enemies, for it is he who provided Vitellozzo with money to proceed against you. You have the opportunity to avenge yourselves, and he who does not take vengeance while he can deserves to be repeatedly injured. Understand me rightly; Siena is in league with France. I do not want Siena at all; I merely wish to destroy Siena's ruler, Petrucci. The Pope is going to deal with Petrucci and treat him very amicably. That must not mislead the Signory. We intend to lull his suspicions with friendly letters from the Vatican. Meanwhile I shall be proceeding against him. Machiavelli, it is very sweet to dupe Petrucci, that master of deceit."

Not until near morning did Niccolo finally get to bed for a few hours. The army immediately marched on. He shared its life and described its difficulties. This army moved with a rapidity hitherto unknown in Italy. It set up no winter quarters and covered hundreds of miles in a few weeks. Every night, after arduous, day-long rides, Niccolo wrote his reports. He reminded the Signory to felicitate the duke. Cesare was very much set on congratulations. He wanted absolute moral justification of his acts in Sinigalia.

A few hours after the murders he had promptly sent the Italian States and the princes of Europe a description of the events. All the measures the slain condottieri had taken in following his orders were portrayed as cunning attempts at deception. "Pretending to conquer Sinigalia for me, the traitors concentrated their troops and hid them in neighboring castles. The night of my arrival they intended to attack me and the garrison of the rocca at the same time." And not only Machiavelli, but the whole of Europe pretended to believe this story.

Louis of France congratulated Cesare for a deed "worthy of an old Roman". The historian, Giovio, coined the phrase "beautiful deceit". Duchess Isabella Gonzaga, renowned for her piety, sent Cesare a hundred handsome masks for the carnival as token of her admiration. But to Machiavelli's horror, the righteous fathers of the Signory remained primly reserved. True, they ordered him to convey the felicitations of Florence, but they wrote him also to be restrained in expression and above all to emphasize that the Signory assumed the deceased had really been guilty. "Privately, we believe that what has occurred is incompatible with honor and good faith." These instructions seemed totally incomprehensible to Niccolo. He was determined not to carry them out. The next day, however, he was freed from his anxiety. The Signory sent him another letter. Overnight the Ten had deliberated the matter, and Niccolo was now to convey to the duke the great admiration and respectful gratitude of the Florentines for the end he had made of such dangerous foes.

Cesare thanked Machiavelli and explained to him in detail at Niccolo's final audience why it was necessary for him to appear to be what he really was: the restorer of Justice! For the Signory to proclaim this truth publicly was, he said, more important to him than military aid. He desired to introduce peace and freedom into the conquered cities. On that account he had not permitted those whom his enemies had expelled from Perugia to return. For these exiles were striving for rule by force. "And I do not expel one tyrant in order to open the gates to ten others. Because this is my policy, many cities have already risen up in my behalf. If they do not take my word, like the citizens of Siena, then I bring artillery to their walls." Before parting from one another they discussed justice, peace, and the problems of governing a new princedom.

The Signory was still determined not to conclude an alliance with Cesare. In order to cloak their intentions in gestures as friendly as possible, they followed Niccolo's urgent advice and recalled him, sending in his stead an ambassador extraordinary, Jacobi Salvati, a man from one of the first families of the Republic.

In the three and a half months he had spent with Cesare, Machiavelli was able to accomplish little for Florence. But during this time, as never before and never afterward, he had held his hand upon the throbbing heart of Power.

CHAPTER VI

In Rome

SHORTLY before he was sent to Cesare Borgia, Machiavelli had married a Florentine woman, Marietta Ludovico Corsini. When he left, he promised faithfully that he would not be away more than a week, but the week passed and others after it and still Niccolo did not come back. Marietta remembered his promise and held it against him as a debt.

Niccolo did not miss her and he did not write. The only news she had of him came through his friends. Marietta wanted Niccolo and she was bored. Feeling more helpless and impatient every day, her memory of him became distorted until, at the end of the third week, she was sure that he had deserted her. She gave up trying to control her sorrow and her weeping was so persistent that all her friends and neighbors soon knew her troubles. It seemed obvious to them that Niccolo had forgotten his young bride and was enjoying himself at the court of the monster Cesare Borgia, the prince of all vices.

No longer knowing what to do, Marietta walked almost daily to the office of the Second Chancery at the Signory in an effort to get news of her husband. The clerks made a fine show of sympathy and they enjoyed these visits. But when Marietta left the office they also enjoyed their many speculations on the nature of Machiavelli's married life. They were all very curious because they had heard Niccolo tell such lusty tales of amorous adventure. Blasius Buonaccorsi would scream at them to mind their own business.

Blasius was not only Niccolo's friend; he had become Marietta's confidant as well. She poured torrents of troubles on his head. Blasius acted as a go-between, consoling her and serving Niccolo. For he, and not Marietta, provided everything that Machiavelli needed from Florence and could not ask of the Signory; books, clothes, and rumors. And Niccolo had never been backward in asking. "You are most boring with your eternal requests," Blasius wrote him. Blasius had just ordered an expensive edition of Plutarch from Venice for his friend. Immediately thereafter Niccolo asked him to have a suit made up by the most fashionable tailor in the city.

When Marietta learned, through Buonaccorsi's wife Alexandra, of the secret correspondence and the secret expenditures of her husband, she was plunged into despair. Goaded by her grief, she discovered fresh sins every day. Niccolo had her modest dowry at his disposal and was leaving her penniless in Florence. At her expense he was being an unfaithful spendthrift. She wanted to run away, and she left her husband's house. Apparently she intended to console herself with a young Florentine who seemed attractive to her because he enjoyed the advantage of being at hand. Blasius wrote to Niccolo, who refused to take notice of his friend's hint.

Alexandra alone was able to soothe her rage and calm her vengeful thoughts. The two women became the closest of friends. Alexandra, too, had her troubles with Blasius. The two wives kept their heads together all day long and gabbled their anger away. Their favorite topics of conversation were not only the sinful behavior of their husbands, but the affairs of all the families of the Second Chancery. The wives of the clerks became the windmills of the Signory, grinding all rumors exceeding small.

In due course, however, Marietta grew accustomed to her troubles. Fundamentally, she was a loyal, industrious woman who had to learn marital patience against her will.

She was to share far more in the constant cares of her husband than in his rare joys and rebelled against this destiny, which was soon to become a matter of course to her.

Machiavelli's prolonged mission, which caused such dismay to Marietta, had made him a well-known man in signorial circles and in the foremost families. Phrases from his reports, which became public through indiscretion, spoke for him throughout the city. His name suddenly became something to be reckoned with. More and more frequently he was mentioned in connection with Borgia. The curiosity, the stabbing fear, the excitement which Cesare aroused, worked to Niccolo's advantage. The Florentines envied him his ability to remain for two months unharmed with the "monster". He rose, not in rank, but in the esteem of his superiors. The gonfaloniere and the chief of the First Chancery both spoke with enthusiasm of Niccolo's missions. He was generally looked upon as an official who would make quite a career for himself.

This thought, however, infuriated his colleagues. Behind his back there arose a whispering campaign against his achievements. His unoccupied desk excited envy in the office. Whenever the clerks had to prepare documents which Niccolo usually took care of, they trembled for fear they would lose their most sacred possession—their laziness! They attempted to injure Machiavelli by gossip and made an effort to awaken distrust of him in the Council of Ten. Whenever the life of the bureau was stirred by rumors of dismissals or reductions in salaries, they spread lies to the four winds in the hope that Machiavelli would be affected.

Because of this, Buonaccorsi implored him to return. Niccolo would have liked to leave for Florence, but the urgent orders of the Signory fettered him to Cesare. When he did arrive in Florence, however, the intrigues ceased, and all the clerks in his chancery greeted him smilingly. They crowded around him and demanded that he talk, for they thought he knew all of Cesare's secrets.

Machiavelli could tell much about the duke, but those at home knew more about the general political situation. During his absence, the King of France had grown suspicious of Cesare. He was secretly encouraging the formation of a coalition against Rome. With the assistance of Spain and of Emperor Maximilian, Cesare intended to become King of Middle Italy. Louis of France was ready to oppose this ambition with armed force.

Florence felt that it would be saved by the new French armies marching to Italy. The characteristic of this city seemed to be complete infatuation with life. Her optimism robbed her of all political and military memory. But a short time ago, Florence had been in a constant state of alarm. In the brief intervals between one peril and the next, the Florentines wanted to have their fill of the peaceful richness of existence. Without resorting to the demagogy of Lorenzo, and without numbing the intellects of the populace by daily festivals, the Signory succeeded in recreating the splendor of the Medicean period. It sought to prove that the true heritage of Florence, the happiness of her citizens, needed no monarch for protection. Once more, as in the times of Lorenzo, the eye was delighted by monuments, palaces, and festivals. Once more pleasure became a major occupation of the people.

On clear spring nights, the men in power threw open the governmental palaces and invited the citizens in. The whole city became festive. Dwellings were wreathed in flowers and brilliantly lit with torches. Men and women clothed themselves in crimson velvet and purple satin, in damask, silver, and gold. The Signory wanted the citizens to enjoy life all the time, not only at official festivals. It sent silverware, tapestries, and the signorial musicians to important celebrations in the homes of illustrious citizens. Wealth induced the upper bourgeoisie to hold great feasts. When the palace of the Strozzi, which had been building for decades, was completed, the owner gave the citizens a banquet in the gardens of the new estate. A guest wrote, "With each course an animal on a triumphal car or on a huge silver platter was served. And musicians escorted the pages."

Together with representatives from the wool guild, which liberally supported sculpture and painting, the Signory engaged in negotiations to find a place for Michelangelo's *David*. Michelangelo, Sandro Botticelli, Leonardo da Vinci, and Pietro Perugino appeared at the final conference. Up to that time the statue of Judith had always stood before the gates of the Signory. The representative of the city declared that the Judith could not fittingly continue to guard the portals of the government. "For our insignia are the cross and the lily, and it is not fitting that a woman who killed a man should stand there. Perhaps it is for this reason that we have lost Pisa." In Judith's place, Michelangelo's giant was to stand guard. The Signory also assigned work to Leonardo who had just finished the Mona Lisa. He received a commission to cover the walls of the Great Council with murals. That same winter, Raphael came to Florence looking for employment.

The Florentines, although they had their feet on the ground, lived in a realm of culture and hated all the war scares which piled furiously one upon the other in Italy. A moment of apparent calm, therefore, was enough to make them conclude that peace would last forever. Their lack of warlike instincts was the result of their plutocratic, cultural traditions. The rich wool, banking, and cloth guilds, which spent so much money for the adornment of the country, became suddenly miserly when it was a question of defending that same country.

Attacking the Florentine men of wealth, Machiavelli wrote: "Several centuries ago, when the Emperor of Byzantium saw that Constantinople was being threatened by the Turks, he vainly demanded money from the wealthy citizens in order to prepare against the danger. When the siege finally began and the citizens heard the enemy thundering before their walls, they came to the emperor laden with gold. The monarch drove them away, saying: 'Go and die with your money, for you did not care to live without it.' "

Against its will, the Signory was forced to fight against the rich, pacifistic Florentines who were unwilling to pay their share and who tried to shift the burdens of the city onto weaker shoulders. In this struggle, the gonfaloniere, Piero Soderini, found Niccolo his most effective aide. As an administrative functionary, Niccolo was not permitted to speak before the Great Council, but he did compose the gonfaloniere's speeches. Niccolo put the matter of taxation not as a financial problem but as a question of survival which was as fundamental as it was simple. He asked the Florentines bluntly, "Do you or do you not desire the independence of your city?"

He tried to cure his fellow citizens of their political myopia. He wanted to bring them down to earth. "Forget Florence for a while," he said in a speech he wrote for Soderini, "and survey all Italy. You will see only hostile forces. You are dependent upon France and threatened by Venice and the Pope. You trust in your alliance with the French and refuse to arm yourselves. But if you wish France to keep her promises, you must not be a featherweight on the scales of Italy. You must be as strong as you are able to be. Among private persons, laws provide for the observance of deeds and contracts; but among States, only arms decide. We must regard as enemies all who are stronger than we are and all those who are capable of conquering us, even though we be temporarily in league with them. It is not yet three months since the existence of Florence hung on a thread as a consequence of Cesare's threats, his march through our territory, and the uprisings in the provinces. At that time, when you saw burning villages and plundered cities in Tuscany, you were willing to pay all that you had originally refused to pay. Sovereignty rests upon Power and forethought. You must forget neither the one nor the other."

From his desk, Niccolo sought to inspire all the mayors and commissioners of the Republic with the spirit of his speech. He feared a surprise attack, a danger which the general situation of Italy and the impotence of Florence made very real. He knew that such an attack would unquestionably be tragic for Florence.

"Despite all treaties," he wrote to a government official at the frontier, "we must not close our eyes for a moment. Do not forget that the course of events is almost always contrary to expectations."

The fresh disturbances Niccolo was expecting came simultaneously from Rome and Venice. Pope Alexander VI died while his son Cesare was lying ill in bed. At that moment, when everything depended upon the suddenness and boldness of Cesare's decisions, he was groaning helplessly, bathed in perspiration. He observed in his feverish condition how every hour that passed swept away some of his fortresses, territories, power, and renown. "I foresaw everything that could happen on my father's death," he moaned, "except that I would be lying motionless and at death's door myself."

Several days after Alexander's death, Venice attempted to occupy those cities of the Romagna which were situated on its borders and which, as a result of Cesare's work, were subject to the papacy. The Venetians inspired revolts and threw their own troops and condottieri into the struggle.

Florence feared and hated Venice. The Venetians were on the point of seizing Faenza and Rimini, and the envy of the Florentine merchants was so great that they could no longer enjoy the peaceful skies of Tuscany. They saw the hostile forces only because their wares were threatened and with heavy hearts they underwrote loans for their city. The Signory was driven to rapid action by the agitation of the public. Niccolo reigned in his office as a subcommander of the intrigues against Venice. The struggle against the City of the Lagoons had to be carried on surreptitiously, by fomenting local rebellions and discreetly supporting condottieri, because Machiavelli knew that Florence alone did not have at its disposal sufficient means to prevent the invasions of Venice into the Romagna. The Signory, however, wanted at the very least to conquer Forli, the gateway from Venice to Florence—if not by weapons then by money and intrigue. The Florentines had a party in Forli and were bargaining secretly with one of the condottieri.

But the Signory did not want Cesare to learn of this. At the same time it wanted the support and favor of the Forlians against Cesare and Venice. The Signory therefore had to declare itself publicly both against Borgia and for Borgia. The squaring of this circle of lies was not impossible. Each party had to be assured that Florence's public declarations were only for appearance's sake and totally different from her actions. "It is necessary," Machiavelli wrote to the Florentine deputy, "to proceed with extraordinary skill and cloak the deception in such a manner that none of the conflicting parties will remark it."

Florence was the advance guard against Venice. The center of events was Rome. Venice's claim that it was the territorial heir of Borgia could not be decided in the Romagna itself, nor answered by Florence alone. Alexander's successor, the senile Pope Pius III, had left everything hanging in the air during his three-week period of rule. The church conclave was about to go into session and fill once more the throne of Christendom.

Machiavelli was ordered to carry on the work he had been doing against Venice. He was to go to Rome, make reports on the conclave, and place himself at the disposal of Cardinal Soderini, the brother of the Florentine gonfaloniere.

It was the first time Machiavelli had been to Rome. Since Niccolo had first begun to think he had had definite imaginary pictures of classic antiquity, but the ruins were for him merely heaps of moldering stone, the Tiber but a filthy stream, and the roads of the Roman legions no more than muddy paths. The direct contrast between the past and present in this anomalous, half-buried city; the mixture of new and orderly splendor and deserted wilderness which Rome presented, elicited no comment from Niccolo. His contemporaries, Erasmus, Luther, Guicciardini, Ariosto, Aretino, Michelangelo, Leonardo da Vinci, and Raphael, felt in Rome that they were before the altar of nations and epochs. No hue of sky, no monument, no library escaped them. Niccolo, despite long and frequently unoccupied weeks, felt rushed and busy.

The day after his arrival, accompanied by two servants, he rode on a mule along the river bank through the Tiber quarter, passed the Castel Sant' Angelo and went to the residence of the Pope. Here he called on Cardinal Soderini. This cleric, the confidential representative of the Florentines, explained recent events in Rome to Niccolo. The city was seething with unrest and frantic from insecurity and fear. The troops of the condottieri, Baglioni and Alviano, were raging through the streets in wild gangs, as if they had never in their lives received their pay. True, Cesare was still master of the Castel Sant' Angelo, but he was surrounded and sorely beset by the Orsini. The Orsini, thirsting for vengeance, had become mad dogs. Fabiano Orsini had murdered one of Cesare's loyal officers in the open street and washed his mouth and hands in the officer's blood. Frightened by the tumult and fighting, the people barricaded the streets. Stores were closed and necessaries were every day becoming harder to obtain. The cardinals were not yet agreed on Pius' successor, but they had declared jointly that they were unwilling to begin the conclave under pressure from the condottieri. In such circumstances, it was impossible to talk with anyone about Venice's conquests in the Romagna. There was nothing left to do but wait until the new Pope mounted the throne. That might easily take weeks or months.

After visiting Soderini, Machiavelli was received by Cardinal d'Amboise, the minister of Louis XII. D'Amboise, who expected money from the Florentines for an Italian *condotta,* greeted him quite amiably. He and Soderini made things easier for Niccolo. They acclimated him to the Vatican atmosphere, that compound of politics on a grand scale and local gossip which was always difficult for a stranger to breathe. In Rome, ambitious careerists from all countries thought they were upon the threshold of success. One heard here the hum of voices in the great Vanity Fair of Europe. Independently of Soderini and d'Amboise, Niccolo attempted to come to grips with the mass of rumors, to feel out the prevailing temper and locate secret documents. "It is generally rumored," he reported, "that Cardinal Giuliano della Rovere will become Pope. But one must not forget how fickle the intentions of the cardinals are. Ordinarily, they do not vote as they have promised."

This time, however, to the astonishment of all the diplomats and their secret agents, the princes of the Church kept their word. The conclave which elevated Giuliano della Rovere to the throne of Christendom lasted but a few hours. It had been the shortest election in the history of the Church.

The new Pope, sixty-two years of age, who called himself Julius II, had been involved in the most important political events of the past thirty years. He was acquainted with both fortune and misfortune. He had frequently fought as a victor and had as frequently been defeated. "Everything and the opposite" Julius had experienced up to the time of his election. He had reigned as the most powerful ecclesiastic in the Campagna, threatened Rome from Ostia, and had then been forced to flee into exile. He wandered homeless for some time before he became the most influential adviser in the camp of Charles VIII of France. He then led the king's armies to Italy, and backed Savonarola's plans to hold a consilium for the indictment of the Pope. Later he fell into disfavor, only to become once more one of the leading figures in France. Above all, however, della Rovere had led the opposition to Borgia. Julius had used every possible means to inflict injury upon Alexander, but he was flexible enough to pretend to be reconciled with him when the king wanted to make an alliance with Borgia in order to achieve the aims of French politics.

As Cardinal, della Rovere had lived like many other Renaissance princes of the Church, for he loved the beautiful creatures of this world more than its creator. He helped his daughter and nephews become wealthy. He took pleasure in jewels, silver, and the delicacies of the table and was vain about his clothes. He himself attended to his silken bedcovers—a fop at the altar!

Venice, France, Cesare Borgia, Spain, and the emperor helped to bring about his election. They all thought that Julius would be an easy tool to handle. They reasoned that this man, exhausted by a wild and adventurous life, would be content, now that he had arrived at the threshold of old age, to enjoy his pontificate in peace and quiet.

But to judge a man, newly raised to Power, by his past is frequently a blunder. As the holy Augustine once declared, the human soul contains mysteries more profound and wonderful than the vast swell of the sea, the broad courses of the rivers, the immense circle of the oceans and the orbits of the stars. Cardinal Giuliano della Rovere, from the hour of his election, from his first contact with Power, became fired with the vitality of genius. He became the incarnation of the spirit of his century. His attitude toward life combined the creative imagination of Michelangelo with a military vigor which strove to raise the entire world to the level of his desires.

A few days after his election Rome became a city of serenity. Still without any of the instruments of Power, he forced the various factions to make peace. Julius, who did not intimidate the Romans by cruelty or punishment, was proudly called by them "Il Terribile". They respected in him an elemental force which was not to be opposed.

Niccolo heard and sensed this enthusiasm. He exerted pressure to gain an audience with the Holy Father as soon as possible. The common talk about Julius meant little to him. He wanted to analyze the man in his own way. In the first week of the new pontificate, the Holy Father received him.

Niccolo's anticlerical passions, which bordered on the manic, prevented his feeling a trace of timidity in the presence of the tiara. With Julius he did not even have the self-consciousness which all men experience when dealing with a stranger and which had slightly disturbed Machiavelli in the presence of Louis XII and Cesare. Niccolo expatiated upon the danger threatening Florence as long as Venice held part of the Romagna. He assured the Pope that Florence was struggling against this danger as a faithful servant of the Church. He spoke little for Florence and much against Venice. More rapidly than other priests, Julius dismissed the language of pious protestations.

Both immediately turned to hard facts. Their estimates of the Venetian threat to the sovereignty of their lands were in agreement. For the independent territories of the Peninsula, Venice was more dangerous than any non-Italian Power. For when she conquered a city, the victim became her subject and no longer had the privilege of autonomous government. The city was forced to conform economically and politically to the patterns of the conqueror. Ordinarily, however, a foreign Power allowed a vanquished enemy a remnant of local and economic independence.

At this time Spaniards and French were engaged in a struggle in southern Italy. The Ecclesiastical State was very weak. There seemed at the moment to be no power capable of withstanding the Venetians. Would the Republic of the Lagoons bring the entire Peninsula under its sway? Would it grow so strong that a united Italy would arise—at the expense of the other sovereign States of Italy? "The Venetian enterprise," Niccolo said, "will either be a gate opening up every State of Italy to the Venetians, or it will bring about their downfall."

In the hall of state of the Vatican were two men who violently opposed the "Una Italia" for which the critical moment had arrived. These were Machiavelli, the future prophet and eloquent voice of unity, and Julius, the crusader for an Italy freed of foreigners and "barbarians". Thus are the actions of men limited. Machiavelli feared that the Pope would be too weak to oppose successfully the Venetian enterprise. The Holy Father did not have the material means of rule. And, in addition, he was in a dilemma created by the promises he had been compelled to give to secure his election; promises to the Venetians, the Spaniards, the French, and Cesare Borgia.

Machiavelli did not yet know how firmly determined the Pope was to act against Venice. He reported that he had not yet found out enough and for the time being, therefore, he had but a vague idea of Julius' intentions. He urged the Signory to send him exact, detailed reports, gathered on the spot, of the activities of the Venetians. Niccolo had noticed the Pope's quick temper and wanted to drive him into a fury against the common enemy by inflicting a thousand tiny needlepricks. Armed with facts, he aroused Julius to a foaming rage.

Niccolo understood the men he dealt with because, for

the purposes of his task, he became temporarily infatuated with them. This habit lent him a profound sympathy with the cares of others and thus enabled him to see clearly into men. Because of his familiarity with the emotions of the men who were the decisive forces in political life, he was able to judge them with an accuracy and insight not to be found in any political documents. In this manner, also, he understood Julius' mind. He knew the sincerity of the Pope's rages and no longer had doubts about the character of the pontiff. "The Pope's heart beats stormily," he wrote to the Signory. "It drives him violently to action. He is determined to preserve the authority of the Holy See under all circumstances and is filled to the uttermost with ambition and passion for glory."

Association with the Pope gave Niccolo knowledge of the perspectives of world politics. In Rome he learned how distant lands, impelled by their own interest, united and separated again, and how whole peoples moved on toward their vague, indefinite goal. He learned too how the Pope used these movements among men for the preservation of the Ecclesiastical State. Machiavelli reported that the impatient high priest, after the first flush of rage had faded, could patiently nurse his enmity.

The pontiff was no condottiere and had no love for unplanned violence. He wanted to act subtly, being anxious not to appear clearly and openly perjured. He was moderate in all things. He gladly permitted circumstance to work for him, publicized his acts as absolute necessities, and was for the most part impetuous and ruthless only in the final, decisive moment. He disdained the use of poison or the dagger. Instead he attempted to profit by the contradictions of Europe as a sailor tacks with the winds of the seas. Day and night he labored at the coalition which was to develop into the League of Cambrai.

Julius would be able to encircle Venice by using the

antagonistic interests of the various European Powers only if he could convince the Powers of his own defensive intentions. He therefore avoided open provocation. Although he quite openly threatened Venice with a hostile alliance of the entire world, at the same time he pleaded with her to renounce her conquests. "We will never abandon the fortresses of the Romagna which we already occupy," the Venetian ambassador replied to his urgings. "We would sooner sacrifice the last stone in the Republic." "And I," the Pope rejoined, "would sooner surrender the tiara than the Romagna."

These two firm wills formed the two banks through which the stream of Italian politics was to flow for the next few years.

The Pope tried anxiously to prevent Venice from evading the issue. The Venetians claimed that the campaign against the fortresses of the Romagna was aimed not at the States of the Church but against Cesare Borgia, who still held a few cities. "The Pope pretends he is convinced of the truth of these protestations," Niccolo reported.

Cesare, who had helped place the tiara on Julius' brow in return for the promise that he would be continued as military head of the Church, as he had been under his father, received, instead of this appointment, the command to evacuate his fortresses. Weakened by his illness and the blows of fate during recent weeks, he assumed that the promises of others were more dependable than his own and waited impatiently for his nomination to the office of gonfaloniere. While waiting, he conceived a thousand plans and carried out none. Finally, however, he tired of his irresolution and declared himself ready to march immediately through Tuscany to the Romagna to attack the Venetians. The Signory, however, refused to grant him the right of passage. Machiavelli had to convey these grave tidings to the Pope and to Cesare. Niccolo was aware of the Pope's antipathy to the duke, the man who had helped him to Power. Hence he feared that Julius would be glad to have Cesare as far away from Rome as possible and would be glad to burden another city with this dangerous man. Indeed, he had written to Florence hinting as much!

The pontifex received Niccolo, listened good-humoredly to the Signory's reasons, and remained silent. Niccolo continued to talk; the Pope still said nothing. Machiavelli looked about him in astonishment, bothered by the strange feeling that he was speaking in monologue. He had never yet encountered a silence like this. He fell silent himself and looked inquiringly at Julius. Unexpectedly, the Pope nodded approval. Then he dismissed Niccolo with extreme friendliness. "The nod of the Pope's head," Machiavelli reported excitedly to the Signory, "was the sign for me that Julius is in agreement with us." The Pope was seeking someone unbound by promises who would be able to deal Cesare the final blow.

Niccolo hurried from Julius to Cesare, who lived in an adjoining apartment in the Vatican. Machiavelli realized that the duke was helpless. Whether he would be assassinated immediately or would continue to live did not matter. It was obvious to all that he was day by day drifting closer to his end. Only a campaign in the Romagna could have given Cesare the opportunity to regain his position and the Signory had closed this last avenue to recovery. The little Secretary of the Second Chancery held in his hand the verdict against his idol of the year before and the former oppressor of his fatherland.

Cesare thought himself indispensable in the struggle against Venice and received Niccolo pleasantly. The Florentine at once announced the resolution of the Signory. The duke leaped from his chair and shouted at Niccolo every threat that came into his head. He would make an alliance with the devil himself, would rush to Pisa and show all the opponents of the Signory the surest way to victory, would sell himself to the Venetians for a mess of pottage. His words tumbled over one another. Then he stopped threatening and tried to persuade. He spoke for a long time, making only feeble efforts to retain his dignity. Niccolo attempted to pacify him. A feeling of combined pity and embarrassment made this last hour with Cesare seem unbearable to him. Finally, however, he found the right moment to take his departure with propriety.

Cesare's present situation did not destroy the past in Machiavelli's mind. He knew the duke as he had been; sober in excess of good fortune; a decipherer of the mysterious and obscure attributes of Power; a teacher of virtù. He cherished this image in his heart as a monument which he was to reveal to all posterity.

Cesare had become Julius' prisoner, but he escaped to Naples. He was arrested by the Spaniards, who had promised him safe-conduct, and transported to a prison in Spain. He escaped, and died during a skirmish in the thirty-second year of his life as a brave soldier in the service of the King of Navarre.

From Florence, Niccolo received enthusiastic and emotional expressions of gratitude to the Pope. Machiavelli's reports, which reflected nothing of this rejoicing, were disappointing to the Florentines. "You are being laughed at because you will not free yourself of Cesare, and some think that you are hoping he will give you one more tip before the end."

So long as the Florentines were afraid of Cesare, Niccolo could transmit the fruits of experience to the Signory and describe the motives of the duke objectively and in detail. But now none would admit that the panic of the past year had existed. The moral system of the philistines in Florence was reaping its revenge, and Niccolo, in order not to lose his reputation at home completely, wrote against the duke with an assiduity equal to his unwillingness. He declared that the Almighty was exacting retribution from Cesare for his monstrous misdeeds and called him a despoiler of the Church.

All circumstances were uniting to aggravate the difficulties of Niccolo's stay in Rome. Buonaccorsi kept repeating emphatically that this time not only his colleagues at the bureau were intriguing against Niccolo, but even important members of the Council of Ten were letting slip ominous remarks. Machiavelli feared for his position. And at this time, especially, he could not afford to lose it, for Marietta had borne him a son. She wrote tender letters about the boy, whose sole inheritance was his father's smile and his eyes, "black as velvet." The son not only made Niccolo's poverty harder to bear, but also increased his disturbance at being away from home. The more pressing Niccolo's cares became, the more he envied the prelates, ambassadors, and condottieri with whom he was forced to come into contact. He would have liked to live on an equal footing with them. Since he could not, since his wealth and his salary were insufficient, he seemed to himself a cheated beggar. His cry of distress was extremely monotonous. For forty years he wrote the same pleading, begging letters.

Machiavelli could not pay for his lodgings in Rome and wrote to the Signory summing up his insolvency. "I received 33 ducats on my departure. Postage expenses have consumed 13. For 18, I bought a mule; for 39, a suit. That makes 70. My lodgings, with 2 servants and a mule, cost 40 centesimo daily." His rescuer, Buonaccorsi, besieged the treasury of the Second Chancery for his friend's expenses. "Niccolo, I have got money for you," he wrote. "The others can scratch their behinds." But couriers did not depart as regularly as Machiavelli needed money. Buonaccorsi nevertheless managed to find a messenger. "Tomorrow," he wrote, "Michelangelo, the sculptor, will bring you money." But Niccolo's bad luck pursued him. The money did not reach him.

"One of Michelangelo's servants brought the money back to me because the sculptor turned back after he was on the way."

Machiavelli lived in complete retirement in his hostelry. The days passed before him in a threatening procession. "If I remain here any longer," he wrote, "I am afraid I shall have to be carried back in a coffin."

A few short hours were spent in writing and then the rest of the long day was given over to complaints. After his work was done, he kept his pen in his hand and scribbled with bitterness and despair. He sent acquaintances ridiculous obscenities and scabrous, senseless tales. "Your letters," one friend wrote in reply, "have given everyone here a very good time. We all shook with laughter at your jokes and sallies." Then he suddenly fell silent. For days he read Plutarch, did not answer questions or reply to greetings, and wrote only to the Signory. Even his friend Blasius finally felt hurt by this persistent silence. "Niccolo," he wrote, "you probably think of me only when you are sitting on your stool."

His reports on Borgia and Julius and his reflections on Power took color from his mood of distress and despair. Niccolo's thinking processes, however, were not blurred by the complications of his humble, miserable existence. For man "is like a coin upon which the image of God has been stamped."

The journey home, permission for which finally arrived, seemed a liberation to him.

Simultaneously with his return from Rome came the tidings of fresh perils for Florence. In Naples the French had capitulated to the Spaniards under Gonzalo de Cordoba. Four years before, Machiavelli had already predicted this very struggle to Louis' minister. For the sake of a temporary advantage, Louis had thrown open the doors of Italy to Ferdinand. In order to avoid strife, France had offered its enemy great opportunities for expansion. And now Louis was being forced to finish the conflict under far less favorable conditions. A settlement of accounts when two political forces are working at cross-purposes cannot be avoided, Machiavelli wrote, "but only postponed to the advantage of the other side."

Florence's fate depended upon the armistice which the French were discussing with the Spaniards at Lyons. Niccolo was sent to France to describe in detail the dangers of the new situation to the signorial representative at the court of Louis XII. When he arrived in Lyons, the truce between France and Spain had already been signed. Machiavelli returned to Florence with the information that the Republic, as the ally of Louis, was included in the treaty.

CHAPTER VII

The Militia

IN SOUTHERN ITALY, in the fields where Hannibal had once won victory at Cannae, along the swamps and lowlands of the Garigliano, high up among the ridges and passes of Abruzzo, and in the treeless plains of Apulia, knights, foot soldiers, and mercenaries from Andalusia, Castile, the Romagna, German Switzerland, Swabia, Gascony, and the Provence, had refashioned the military profession within the course of a century. The military knowledge of the past was used in combination with newer methods to create countless patterns of attack and defense.

The noblest chevaliers of France fought here. It was as if the dreams of the troubadours were becoming reality on the arid plains of Calabria where warriors licked the morning dew from the grass to quench their thirst. Here fought La Palice, called by friend and foe alike the sparrow hawk of battle; and old Montoison, feeble in peace but in the field like a youth; and Frontaille, who could march a hundred leagues in three days if it meant giving battle. Chief of all was the bold Bayard, whose life was without stain, who knew only fearlessness and courtesy. The French chevaliers knelt down before the armies, said their prayers, kissed the soil, and mounted their steeds to match themselves in tourney with Spanish grandees. Even in large engagements, these knights sensed the sectors of gravest danger and rushed to them. For in them dwelt the guileless dream that they could decide each battle by themselves. These noble, heavily armed guards, with their gilded harness and colorful aigrettes, provided for their own armor and attacked alone without any real relation to the other armed forces, without the support of mass pressure behind them. Here they flourished for the last time before they evolved into modern cavalry!

Besides these noblemen, who served Louis of France for honor and joy rather than for reward, phalanxes of the king's Swiss mercenaries also descended upon Italy. With their short front and deep ranks they formed a mighty torrent sweeping all before them. The momentum of these troops was irresistible. The common men, serfs, and peasants, who comprised this soldiery, preserved their democratic organization with the self-will of free men. They would fight to the last ditch and they gave no quarter. They wanted to be worthy of their hire and the bonuses they received after assault.

These foot soldiers did not compliment their foes as did the knights. To them the Spaniards were "gallows birds", the Germans, "bookworms", and the Italians just "buggers". They themselves were never called anything but "vultures". The Swiss were impatient for direct decision by force of arms, for they longed to go home and save their crops from rotting in the fields in Appenzell, Zurich, St. Gall, and Berne. They frequently forced their captains to give the signal for attack. The Swiss favored a mass formation; they were not lone fighters. Operating in Calabria as instructors, they brought order to the rank and file and introduced those tactics of concerted action in battle which were to be used during the sixteenth century. In each engagement they unfolded new techniques.

These Swiss mercenaries jeered at every inadequate and wasted effort in battle. They had restored the foot soldier to favor after a thousand years of oblivion and had thus created the weapon which the practical, warlike character of the epoch demanded, the European infantry. The Spanish were at a frightful disadvantage before these Swiss and their disciples, the Gascons, and before the light and heavy cavalry which also formed part of the French army.

The Spanish general, Gonzalo de Cordoba, had under his command a few thousand Andalusians and Castilians, who were largely impressed peasants and slum rabble. These people were armed in the most haphazard manner. Some used crossbows, some longbows, others rusty pikes. Whatever they found in the antiquated armories of their homeland they bore in their hands in merry confusion. No rules or regulations determined the allotment of their weapons. They did not know how to use even these ridiculously ineffectual arms and they understood nothing of fighting in battle formation.

Poorly and irregularly paid, poorly shod, poorly clad, without any military reputation whatsoever, they were the classic image of the despised foot soldier. They would have gladly returned to their homes had they not been separated from their native country by the sea. They would have deserted if it were not that the populace slaughtered all marauders. They would even have gone over to the enemy if the enemy had needed such a ragged, demoralized soldiery. Avoided like lepers, like lepers they clung together and were the first to invent the system of quartering without paying. Eager for booty, prone to pillage and rebellion, they plundered not only the populace but their own officers. These soldiers did not even wait for the mighty shock of the orderly Swiss and Gascon formations. At the first sight of hostile lances they ran away as if bewitched.

But when they could not retreat, their instinct for self-preservation drove them to a new method of defense. This defense, born of the military ineptitude of the Spaniards, was the great tactical and strategic idea which Gonzalo extracted from the situation of his army. The new method of fighting adapted to the terrain of Calabria arose from necessity and from the poverty of the Spanish king, who could not afford trained mercenaries. The soldiers hid from the enemy behind a rampart or a trench. A brook, a primitive barricade, a hill, a collection of carts, an irrigation ditch or a sunken road might serve as a place of refuge. The Spaniards made use of every irregularity in the land. The bulwarked front against the attacker was created. Offensive had given rise to defensive.

The attacking phalanxes shattered on the parapets. Their order fell apart. The short front and deep base of the Swiss troops which had annihilated the enemy like a fateful, flowing wave of steel, had suddenly lost its force. The arms of the infuriated pikeman no longer felt the living body of the foe, but the rampart and the trench, an unknown, lifeless obstacle which made mock of every human effort.

And if the Swiss nevertheless overcame this obstacle, invented to meet the violence of their attack, their strength was exhausted. They no longer poured through like a stream in spate. The most they could do, if they were fortunate, was to surmount the barricade in small, disorderly bands. The principle of unity, the pressure of ranks twenty, thirty, seventy or a hundred men deep upon the first rank, was removed. The foremost spears of the phalanx were no longer driven forward by those behind. "The stress from behind" was gone, as the German-Swiss complained.

Behind the ramparts stood cannon and hand arms. They had finally found their place after having made more noise than corpses for over a century. They were defensive and offensive at once; defensive in that they helped sustain the bulwark, offensive in that they fired into the enemy ranks. The cannon stopped the gaps in the bastions. Culverins fired from between carts and batteries were placed behind the ramparts. Out of isolated natural obstacles a strong unity was formed and irregularities of terrain were combined into fortifications extending over several hundred miles.

The bastions were as useful to the soldier with hand arms as to the cannoneer. The arquebusiers needed cover, for their chance of hitting the mark was small and loading was a dangerous, lengthy, and complicated procedure. Rampart and trench, however, made it possible for the man in the front line who had fired his shot to change places with the arquebusier behind him.

The bulwarked front united all weapons effective at a distance: heavy artillery and the culverin, the light arquebus and the heavy musket. Artillery fire was conducted with order and regularity for the first time. Gunpowder had not been really useful for battle until now. Here, in Lower Italy, it determined the character of battles for the first time in military history. The core and the tradition of the Spanish brigades, the army of a future empire whose cohorts were victorious for two centuries, began in the small engagements in which Gonzalo's foot soldiers learned courage.

Countless unexpected factors combined before the astounded world realized that every healthy man could be made into an infantryman. The duel of the Spanish novices with the spoiled darlings of a *Sturm und Drang* epoch was an event of the greatest significance. Once the tactical methods of the Swiss had been established, the Swiss themselves were no longer indispensable.

There were men enough in the world to be organized for the battlefield. Moreover, common men were cheaper than the Swiss whose fame made them arrogant. And for defensive action, the recruits were soon more valuable than the teachers. The Swiss knew nothing of the defensive, used cannon poorly, and were awkward with muskets. Their basic principle, their very existence, was attack. Gonzalo, who crystallized the new forces of war by combining the tactical unity of the Swiss with defensive warfare, not only taught his men to fight, but, in the course of successful battles, to obey. He did not accomplish this by means of commands and regulations. He developed discipline by using the savage impulses of his men in the same way that he used roughness of terrain for defense. He allowed them to keep their spoils, because the soldiers of the period regarded the booty they had seized with their own sweat and blood as their most precious possession.

Gonzalo succeeded in making honor compatible with the prospect of rapine in the minds of his men. He told them that only a victory won in common could provide more than enough for each individual. And he kept his word more punctiliously than other generals thought necessary. He voluntarily sacrificed his own palace in Naples to the pillaging Spaniards. From that day of generosity on, Gonzalo was known among his soldiers only as the *gran capitano*.

After training his soldiers for ten years Gonzalo was finally ready to risk the battle which the French, always eager for attack, were seeking. Not far from Canossa, near Cerignola, he found ideal terrain. Cerignola was situated upon a hill, surrounded by vineyards. Around the vineyards ran a small ditch. In great haste, for the French commander Nemours was approaching by forced marches, Gonzalo had his seven thousand soldiers dig this natural trench deeper and broader. He made them raise ramparts and emplace his thirteen cannon. It was already late in the afternoon. The Spaniards were exhausted from digging and racked with thirst when the French, numerically as strong as they were, began the attack.

"The finest troops in Europe," Gonzalo declared, "now rode in assault upon our center." A gunpowder explosion in the camp of the Spaniards completely hid the Spanish position from the French. The cavalry saw before them not men but turned-up earth fixed with hooks and iron spikes. They halted. The bombardment of the Spaniards confused them completely. After ten minutes, Nemours gave the signal to reconnoiter for another position to attack. By his retreat he offered the flank of his cavalry to the Spanish arquebusiers who discharged their shot in comfort and safety from their ramparts. A musket shot killed Nemours.

Now the assault of the Swiss began. It was bloodier but no more successful. The commander of the Swiss troops fell. In panic, the attackers retreated. Not until then did Gonzalo give the signal to attack. From several sides at once the Spaniards poured down from the tops of their ramparts.

The battle had lasted an hour. Nevertheless it had been the most bloody on Italian soil in centuries. The French left over four thousand men, more than half of their number, dead on the field. The Spaniards had lost scarcely a hundred men.

Cerignola was Gonzalo's golden day and the unforgettable beginning of the tactics which forced the spade and the trench upon all belligerents. "Wars are no longer decided by fierce valour," Gonzalo's contemporary, Giovio wrote, "but by holding one's position prudently and perfecting the art of military method." Rampart and trench could not remain the secret of the Spanish. "Since the great effect of the trench at Cerignola," Gonzalo's general, Fabricius Colonna, wrote, "commanders are devoting the most exacting care to fortification of their encampments." From that day on, all armies entrenched themselves in similar fashion.

Was war to become a constant defensive, restricting all action behind palisades; was it to be nothing but cloaked movement in a labyrinth of trenches? Were the opposing camps to stare at one another for decades, and was the space between their fortifications to become the garden of eternal peace, discovered at last? Was war to make itself impossible, to collapse upon itself because of the tactical and strategical impasse it had arrived at? Had the breath of audacity passed from the god of war at the very moment when France and Spain were becoming World Powers?

No. For battle is eternal. All the practical reason of the

sons of earth is represented by the changing weapons they hold in their hands and the varying manner in which they attack others and defend themselves. When it was recognized that the principle of the bulwarked front was axiomatic, battles did not cease. Instead, an effective unity was created out of the three new elements of war: mass, gunfire, and discipline. After Cerignola, the bulwarked front presented a new tactical problem in all the battles of the century, at Ravenna, Novarra, La Motte, Marignano, Bicocca, and Pavia. How can we weaken the enemy behind his rampart and his trenches? How can we lure him out in the open? How can we force him to give battle? If all other means fail, can we enfilade his defenses so that he will be forced to desert them? The enemy must be made either to attack or retreat!

At Ravenna, the French fired their artillery against the ramparts of the Spanish with a previously unknown ferocity. They tried, with their ordnance, to provoke the enemy to come out of his secure position and attack. At Novarra, the Spanish, covered by a small thicket, went around the French camp, thus avoiding the fire of the artillery. They then threw the whole weight of their infantry against the surprised French mercenaries. At Bicocca, the Spanish did not even wait for the Swiss assault. The moment the Swiss attack began, they marched out from a sunken road to meet them.

Despite all methods of defense, which were advanced to an extraordinary degree of finesse, attack remained the deciding factor. It was necessary for a commander to recognize the necessity of a defensive-offensive from his fortified position. In attack, the climactic point of battle, all curbed energies, all cautious restraint, all moderation, must break out in a desperate rush forward. Crises were still resolved in blood, despite secret paths and bulwarked fronts. The hostile forces of Europe still opposed one another, though now behind ramparts and trenches.

The new way of fighting, however, arose independently of the wills of experts, scholars, and commanders. Men always understand least what affects them most; in this case they changed their traditional ways of making war during the battle, through necessity, without realizing that they were changing warfare fundamentally. The instinct for self-preservation in the conscripts and volunteers of Gonzalo produced the miracle of the surprise attack, just as that instinct in the tirailleurs of the French Revolution produced the same result three centuries later. The legs of the soldiers were frequently more ingenious than the minds of their commanders.

Pure reasoning about battle is always rooted in great, traditional prototypes. It is necessarily always directed backwards and is therefore conservative. Even the wisdom of Machiavelli, the most unprejudiced thinker of his period, was hindered by theories when it came to matters of war. He could not escape the classic example of military greatness, the Roman Republic.

Machiavelli was fascinated by the age-old phenomenon of battle; he wanted to look the god of war straight in the eyes. The battlefield was to him the finest creation of the virtue of rulers. In the course of the centuries, virtù had wandered from battlefield to battlefield, from Assyria to Media, to Persia, to Macedonia, to Rome. Virtù inspired the bravest, cleverest, and subtlest and gave them victory in the midst of dangers, bodily exertions, uncertainties, and accidents.

According to Machiavelli, not military virtues alone, but all virtues, helped determine the outcome of battles. For war is the life of Power. War is no chance occurrence, no derangement of the normal course of life, no official madness, but the indispensable tool of the political intelligence, which is all-determining. Therefore, according to Machiavelli, victories and defeats were inherent in the whole inner make-up of a state and the consequent organization of its army. Out of the character of the country flowed the character of its army. This was true whether that army consisted of mercenaries, militia or professional soldiers, natives or foreigners, volunteers or conscripts, burghers or peasants, patricians or plebeians, knights or slum rabble, unemployed or artisans.

Who organized the troops? How were the soldiers disciplined? How did the monstrous belly of the army function? These were further questions which arose out of the structure of the country. The genius of even the greatest commander is rooted in the spirit and the mechanism of the army. If he desires great successes, he must, when the gears of the army grow rusty, first renew the vitality of the country by an internal, political revolution.

Machiavelli was the first and only thinker of his period who saw in the life of the army during peacetime a microscopic reproduction of the effects of Power on society. Machiavelli was interested in the way individual detachments took up their position; in how the vanguard, the main body, and the rearguard conducted themselves; in the relationship of the musketeers to the arquebusiers, that is, of long-range to short-range weapons; and in the strength and composition of regiments and battalions. This was not merely the anatomy of the army to him; it was also the measure of its effectiveness, of its virtù. Because Niccolo had a new conception of Power, free of self-consciousness and conventionality, and because he looked upon the army as the apex of the political pyramid, he felt that he could deduce the general, empirical theory of war from the component parts of the army and the details of battle. From a complete understanding of military affairs, Machiavelli hoped to lay down rules and methods for achieving victory. "For every science," he wrote, "is based on general principles."

But his insight into the mighty battles of his time was obscured by dogmatism and by his enthusiasm for the Roman legions which had conquered the world. He declared that a country which imitated the mode of fighting and the make-up of the Roman army would hold the key to victory in a mailed fist. Everything the Roman legions did was good. The moderns should do nothing the Roman legions had not done. Roman virtù had conquered the world without gunpowder and therefore Machiavelli recommended that it should not be used. If he admitted the utility of artillery and cannoneers, it was only to avoid seeming old-fashioned, to preserve appearances. Guns were useful to frighten savage peoples or stupid peasants by "the unfamiliar, infernal noise".

In skeptically condemning gunpowder and lead, Machiavelli was in accord with the humanists who, since the time of Petrarch, had uttered a curse every time a cannon spat fire. Many of the foremost soldiers of the period opposed the firearms they themselves used. "It is a shame," declared the noble Bayard, "that the arquebus in the hands of a worthless knave can still a knightly heart by craft and without combat. Are not valor and boldness thus overcome by cowardice?" Marshal Tavanes wrote, "From Germany are coming wicked inventions, gunpowder and Lutheranism." The famous commander of the French in Italy, Tirvulzio, declared that artillery was of almost no importance.

The aversion to gunpowder was especially great among those soldiers who hoped to triumph by the boldness of their assault. Cannon, however, which were effective behind a bulwarked front, were practically useless in the open field. Arquebuses and muskets were sometimes a positive disadvantage in the open field. When the men with firearms had discharged their first salvo, they ran backwards behind the protection of the lancers. In order to kill a single man in a battle it usually took forty bullets.

But these firearms, which were so effective from behind ramparts and trenches, troubled Machiavelli, who conceived of the ideal battle as taking place on open terrain. "The

Romans," he wrote, "almost always sought open battlefields and avoided those with obstacles." Machiavelli wanted to place his troops on smooth plains, as if they were tin soldiers on a piece of cardboard. The heroic tradition allowed only an open field for all possible activities. As a general, Niccolo would not have taken artillery along even if the enemy used it. "I would utilize the sole means of rendering the enemy artillery useless," he wrote. "I would assault it." He would suffer initial losses in order to win the battle. He would win the only success which counted in war; the final victory by hand-to-hand combat. If his ideal army on his ideal battlefield finally came to grips, he wrote, "it is clear as day that neither heavy nor light artillery can do any harm . . . With what valor, sturdiness, and ease the troops will kill the foe. Do you not see that soldiers are so crushed together in close combat that they can scarcely use their swords?"

Nevertheless, Machiavelli was unable to ban reality completely from his conception of war. "If you have few or poorly disciplined troops," he wrote, "then you must seek places which will protect you." Without commentary, as if he wished to keep it secret from himself, he wrote, "Gonzalo always remained behind fortifications and never presented himself in the open field." The bulwarked front, which prevented his ideal battle as much as it contributed to the fury of real battle, was to him the victory of military ineptitude and degeneration. From the elegant heights of classic example he looked down upon the tumult of battle in his epoch like an irate Mars upon deserters.

Machiavelli drew a moral from the battle of Fornovo, where Italian foot soldiers scattered in panic at the sight of the Swiss phalanxes and fled with the Homeric laughter of the German-Swiss roaring behind them like the thunder of cannon; from the campaigns of Charles VIII which crushed the States of Italy; and of Louis XII which plundered them; and of Ferdinand of Spain which ruined them.

The shameful collapse of Florence, Milan, Naples, and Rome in the face of invasion filled him with contempt for the military system of the Peninsula.

Machiavelli did not believe for a minute in the patchwork truce of Lyons, which proclaimed, for the first time, the division of the Peninsula. Naples was made dependent on Spain, Lombardy on France, while all the other territories existed subject to the discretion of the foreign Powers. After ten years of war which had wrecked the Italian State system and interrupted its evolution towards unification, the conquered States were longing desperately for peace. "Everyone is crying for peace," Niccolo wrote, "but this peace will still be no peace." At the end of his description of the first ten years of invasion, Machiavelli wrote, "Florentines, open wide the temple of Mars!"

The truce between Spain and France was but a light, swaying span across the abyss of European conflicts which cut the soil of Italy in two. In Lombardy, the French forces equipped to give battle were very few. From Naples, in the south, the remnants of Louis' army were seeking their way homeward. They vainly entreated the captains of the galleys along the coast for transportation. In desperation, they swam after the ships and were sent to the bottom with blows of oars.

The king had given up Naples and wanted to have nothing more to do with his defeated men. He had not a sou, not a slice of bread nor a word left over for his valiant soldiers. The army of the Lily dissolved into miserable bands of starving vagabonds. Hunted, threatened, jeered at, they looked for food in the garbage dumps of the cities. They perished by the hundreds along the highways. "In Rome they enter houses and cannot be driven out," a chronicler wrote. "Even if they are beaten with clubs, they still refuse to move from the spot. They say, 'Kill us.' "

For the Spanish, however, in good order and encouraged

by their victories, all roads leading to Lombardy stood wide open. Italy was waiting to greet them. The general European situation which included the quarrels over the throne of Spain, the menace of Germany, and Louis' threat to the Pyrenees, prevented Gonzalo from breaking the truce. But he had to fight the temptation daily. He was urged especially to attack Florence. All the neighbors of Tuscany asked why the Republic, Louis' most faithful ally, should remain untouched after the defeat of France.

And Florence set traps for itself. The Republic, included in the truce of Lyons, had purchased the privilege of carrying on the campaign against Pisa. Hence Gonzalo could strike a blow at Tuscany without officially breaking the treaty of peace. A wealth of opportunities offered itself to Gonzalo. He could have engineered a covert, desultory war by playing on the provincial stupidity of offended cities, on the greed of the unemployed or dissatisfied condottieri, and the petty ambitions of sovereign districts. No one could prove who led gangs, who provided them with money and weapons, or who permitted galleys laden with victuals and gunpowder to reach Pisa. Encircled by a dark forest of enmity and intrigue, weaponless Florence fought on against Pisa. The Republic had made the conquest of its hostile neighbor a question of life and death, and it tried to attain its goal with every means at its command only to find them all ineffective.

The old plan of Leonardo da Vinci to divert the flow of the Arno was carried on with desperate persistence. The Signory thought thus to substitute pioneering work for direct assault and so throttle its courageous opponent. Machiavelli was one of the most zealous promoters of this project. The river was to be blocked by a great dam and its waters led away from Pisa in two deep channels to the sea and to the arid lowlands. Engineers calculated that two thousand workers and thirty to forty workdays would be needed to complete the task. Hydraulic experts from Ferrara and contractors from all Italy dredged day and night along the Arno. The river, however, did not flow off into the channels, but the money of the Republic drained into sand and swamp.

This attempt, at once grandiose and impotent, was halted after a number of weeks and another, also the product of desperation, was started. In specified administrative districts the Signory forced the peasants to present themselves to officials. The farmers brought their scythes, spades, pitchforks, shovels, axes, and hammers along and were hastily organized into "despoiling companies". Captains led them to war in Pisan territory against fruit trees, fowl, and crops.

The Pisans, however, not only resisted all spoliation, but even counterattacked. They routed the small detachments of Florentine cavalry in front of their walls. These occurrences made Tuscany tremble with fear. The Florentines thought they could hear the howling of infernal winds bringing danger to the Republic. Temporarily, Florence abandoned the method of slow strangulation to begin direct military assault. The Signory commanded Gian-Paolo Baglioni, its condottiere, to march on Pisa. Baglioni, the ruler of Perugia, was the shining light among the cavalrymen of Italy. At first he did not reply at all to the urgent orders and then answered in ambiguous terms. He finally declared that he could not leave Perugia.

Machiavelli was despatched in all haste to Baglioni. His task was to discover whether Gian-Paolo was merely trying to extort more pay or whether he had already been bought by the enemies of Tuscany. In spite of his suavity, Niccolo spoke roughly and pointedly to Gian-Paolo. He asked him bluntly whether he did not want to keep the treaty or whether the pay was insufficient. "No," Baglioni answered, "I do not need money. The worries and affairs of my territories and fortresses make it impossible for me to leave Perugia at present. I showed the agreement with the

Signory to the most renowned doctors of law at the university. They all explained to me that in view of my own difficulties I am no longer bound by law to make war for you. As a sign of my loyalty, however, I am ready to send you my son as condottiere and as proof of my friendship I promise to deliver fifty cavalrymen to the Signory in the next year without charge. Machiavelli, believe me, I am acting from necessity! I have considered everything carefully, made the sign of the cross more than six times, and implored God to show me the right way."

"Your Excellency is legally cleared of guilt by the professors of the university of Perugia, just as last year when your Excellency was supposed to keep his contract with France," Niccolo replied. "Your Excellency finds himself in the humanly understandable, but nevertheless unpleasant position of having to justify himself each time anew. Whether a prince keeps his sworn word or not is a matter of honor, good faith, and reputation. It therefore is completely beyond the jurisdiction of lawyers." "I struck him right and left," Niccolo concluded his report, "and called him down strongly. His face changed color frequently, but he held to his refusal."

Machiavelli still had to learn the real reasons for the breach of contract. Two men from the entourage of Gian-Paolo who were in the service of the Florentines reported it to him. "For days Baglioni has been very taciturn and no one has seen him laughing. Every morning he sits on a stone bench in the garden of the palace looking very pale, as though he had been up all night troubled by weighty cares. We set out to find the cause for this melancholy and discovered that in the late hours of the night, when all the lights in the windows of Perugia are extinguished, one room of the government palace remains lighted. Each night we observed that masked men were being received. We heard all the details. They are messengers of high rank from Lucca, Siena, Rome, and Naples. They tell Baglioni that his great hour has struck, that if he avoids keeping his contract with the Florentines now, Tuscany will be practically weaponless. And they are carefully discussing all the details of an attack on Tuscany. The arm of this conspiracy is the condottiere in Gonzalo's service, d'Alviano; but the mind that conceived the plan is that of Pandolfo Petrucci, ruler of Siena."

The Signory ordered Machiavelli to ride to the source of the betrayal, Siena. Pandolfo Petrucci received him with open arms and with many curses on his lips against d'Alviano. "Machiavelli," he assured Niccolo, "I have been waiting for you. Florence and Siena have but one enemy, d'Alviano. This violent, ruthless man leads an army, is always under arms, and has no State to lose. His flag promises pillaging and attracts all the brigands and thieves of Italy. Therefore I am ready to sign a contract with you as condottiere for five years. It is, however, still completely pointless for me to enter the lists against d'Alviano openly. Thereby I would only throw myself open to dangers which could also strike you. In addition, I can serve Florence better if I inform the Signory of everything and secretly win away d'Alviano's allies. The precondition of my working for you is silence."

Machiavelli, who would have liked to hint that he saw through the masquerade and the lies, replied, "First it is said that d'Alviano is fighting with Spanish troops and money; then, that Gonzalo will have nothing to do with his condottiere and has commanded him to stop his activities. Then we hear that d'Alviano is a great general or that he is a fool, that he stands in agreement with the Pope, that the Pope is against him. He is supposed to be united with you, and yet his troops are supposed to be plundering the Sienese. I fear that before I return home I shall go mad from all these intrigues. Cannot your Excellency free me from my anxiety?"

"Machiavelli, I will tell you what the King of Naples had his representative say to me when I found myself in a similar position. 'Do not limit yourself. Keep your viewpoint fresh. Alter your resolutions from hour to hour. For these times are too confused and too overwhelming for our brains.' "

Machiavelli could make nothing of these sentiments. He was unable to finish his job. He did not find out whether d'Alviano was going to act on his own account, or in agreement with Gonzalo, or directly in Gonzalo's employ. A precise answer to these questions would have been a certain indication of the direction from which danger threatened. And this information, which Niccolo sought for days to extract from Petrucci and from all his friends and spies, was suddenly given him by Petrucci himself. Siena's ruler called him unbidden and showed him a letter of Gonzalo's which contained a copy of a command to d'Alviano to conduct himself peacefully and not to attack Tuscany.

"What is your Excellency's opinion?" Niccolo asked incredulously and ambiguously. "Will d'Alviano abandon his plans against Florence?"

"Machiavelli," the philosophical Petrucci replied, "reason demands that d'Alviano obey Gonzalo and keep peace. But men do not always act according to reason, and they are often impelled by desperation. Of any four men who act out of desperation, three will be ruined. It is, however, to the good of all that a man driven by desperation should not precipitously fling himself into action. For such acts of madness may set in motion strange chains of events. The possibilities are manifold since disaster may strike even innocent bystanders and those who are far removed. On that account, Florence must be very much on its guard against d'Alviano."

Petrucci thought to conceal his game of duplicity by these oracular comments. He was simultaneously attacking Florence by means of d'Alviano and coming to an agreement with Machiavelli to protect it. However, Niccolo understood him thoroughly now and had sufficient information, although he did not know everything. He returned to Florence, and instead of taking leave of the ruler of Siena in a final audience, he had a message delivered to him, "Many a one whom I saw laughing in the summer I saw bitterly weeping in the winter."

The foreign masters of Italy, who had made much of the condottieri before the invasion, now found these condottieri superfluous. The Spanish, therefore, dismissed d'Alviano from their service. Gonzalo did not share d'Alviano's impatience to act against Florence, for Gonzalo had time and was not forced to live from hand to mouth like a condottiere without a country. The Spanish commander suspected, in addition, that d'Alviano, if he carried on an independent war against Tuscany and saved Pisa, would succumb to the temptation to keep the city for himself.

D'Alviano entered Tuscany at the head of his troops on his own responsibility. In a Florentine border village he awaited his confederates, the troops of Baglioni and Petrucci. These allies, for their part, were waiting for the invader's first victories. Thus d'Alviano, with numerous secret treaties in his pocket, encouraged by everyone only a short while before, found himself isolated and thrown back on his own fifteen hundred cavalrymen. He believed that he had been betrayed, and replied by betrayal. He tried to sell his services to the Florentines in order to take the field against Baglioni and Petrucci. The Florentines did not trust him and refused his offer.

The Signory, however, which feared nothing more than a clear-cut decision by force of arms, thought it would be able to avert direct combat. It knew that d'Alviano had every reason to reach Pisa as swiftly and quietly as possible.

Without making a treaty with him, they smoothed the way for him to relieve the citadel which for a decade had been absorbing the energies of Tuscany! The Signory ordered the commanders of their troops, the Bolognese condottiere, Hercules Bentivoglio, and their political commissioners of war, Antonio Giaccomini, to close their eyes and not see d'Alviano. "For if this bandit goes to the Pisans," the orders read, "there still remain a thousand possibilities of salvation for us; but if we first lose a battle to him, or merely do not win it completely and sacrifice our army, we are lost."

Giaccomini was furious at this imposed impotence, and acted contrary to his orders. He knew all the roads d'Alviano had to pass through and placed himself in the path with far superior forces. Attacking unexpectedly from a small forest, he completely annihilated the enemy. His spoils consisted of a thousand cavalrymen and the entire baggage of the defeated army. Wounded, d'Alviano escaped with only twenty men into the neighboring territory of Siena.

The victory surprised the Republic, which was so accustomed to fears and compromises. For weeks the successful battle altered the feelings of the city, which ordinarily disdained all military effort. Giaccomini intoxicated even sober and moderate men. The citizens, blotting their own past weakness out of their memories, demanded a supreme, decisive undertaking against Pisa. In Antonio Giaccomini they had, for the first time in their lives, a Florentine who knew how to wield the sword. Their popular hero promised triumph at last over the Pisans. The Great Council, prompted by the festive mood of the populace, approved extraordinary taxes and credits for the army.

A few hours' march from Pisa, the Florentine established a huge camp. The go-between for Commander Bentivoglio and the commissioner of war, Giaccomini, on the one side, and the Signory on the other, was Machiavelli. He was sent to the camp several times a week, saw to the regular and timely arrival of munitions and money, supervised the commissariat, reported on the morale, and encouraged the commanders. Florence tried to enlist soldiers in Bologna, the Romagna, and Rome. The Second Chancery attempted to conscript peasants for five weeks. The "despoiling companies" were hurriedly drilled as foot soldiers. Money was to fill the gap wherever military aptitude was lacking. It was a carnival for the unemployed. Everyone was accepted; small troops of mercenaries who had served out their time, untrained peasants from the neighboring villages, and the better class of Florentine citizens who in order to serve as officers had first hastily to learn the art of war.

By August, 1505, there were nearly eight thousand men and twenty cannon in the camp. The assault against Pisa was fixed for the seventh of September. In the glow of dawn the artillery moved up to within a few yards of the walls of the fortress. Within three hours the cannon hammered a breach of one hundred and forty yards. "Behind this breach," Giaccomini wrote, "the Pisans had already erected a rampart and trench during the cannonade, the women working with no less courage than the men."

Three Florentine regiments, lined up in battle array, were waiting for the cannonade to halt before pouring through the breach into the city. The regiment of foot soldiers at the head, one thousand men strong, heard the roll of the drums and the shouts of command to assault. But the Florentine ranks remained numb. Not a man moved. Lightning from some unknown, inexplicable cloud of cowardice had struck them.

The commanders at their head, Giaccomini and Bentivoglio, could not believe their ears and eyes. They screamed till their throats were sore. They writhed like madmen on their horses. They threatened and wept. Giaccomini stood up in the saddle and harangued eloquently of honor, assault bonuses, disgrace, punishment, and victory. The regiment continued to stand motionless as if at the brink of a bottomless deep and stared with frightened curiosity into the distance. It would not; it could not. The men would sooner have let themselves be hacked to bits than attack. The second and third regiments imitated the first. Silently, in formation, they returned to the camp. The whole army marched back to their quarters without the loss of a single man.

In this lack of moral strength to face the bloody battlefield, in which Giaccomini saw "disgrace before all Europe," Machiavelli perceived more. He found decadence not only of soldiers but of all men in the regions which were once guarded by Roman virtù.

Waves of cowardice were laying waste to Italy, Machiavelli thought, since the Romans no longer killed their enemies, hunted them to the four winds, or condemned them to slavery; and since cities were no longer destroyed when conquered. War no longer had vigor, cruelty, and decisiveness. "It is begun without trepidation, carried on without danger, and ended without harm. The soldiers are such poltroons and there reigns such great disorder in the armies," he wrote, "that a horse turning its head or shaking its nosebag marks the difference between victory and defeat." Perhaps a cavalryman did die now and then in a battle—when he drowned in a swamp or was caught in quicksands. The condottieri considered war a game, a well-paid occupation without risk. Enemies existed only in so far as the profession of soldiery called for some sort of opponent. In no case, however, was the conquered opponent killed. He was a colleague with whom one would work to make the next war a prolonged affair. Only those became soldiers who had run away from home or who had time and again been beaten black and blue for not paying their bills in brothels and inns. The rabble of these armies wallowed in every vice. Every single regiment was a colony of criminals. The leaders of these condotta were no better than their men. They were not princes, but blustering adventurers who believed that it was sufficient for a commander "to think of clever retorts in written negotiations, to contrive deceptions, to bedeck himself with gold and gems, to live more splendidly than others, to revel in sensuality, and to take his own words as oracular utterances."

These condottieri who ate like ogres, stole unscrupulously, plundered treasuries, and were incapable of defending the territories entrusted to them, were not the only ones who lacked martial spirit. All Italy had conspired to prevent the peacefulness of the most philistine existence imaginable from being disturbed. The disease of weakness was like death; it made no distinctions. It had infected soldiers and civilians, princes and peoples alike. Rulers were afraid of the ruled, and the ruled afraid of the rulers. Political and personal life resembled military life in its lack of resolution, surprise, dash, and heroism. In war decisiveness had disappeared, as it had in peace. Deceit, robbery, negotiation, and promises replaced decisions. There no longer existed clear-cut affirmations or negations because all swords had become rusted. Power had been put away, and the pacifism which had seized the hearts and minds of men was more devastating than war could ever be. "Heaven is not warlike," Machiavelli complained, "and earth has grown effeminate." In these decades in which the rivalries of Europe had sent incredibly huge masses of men into battle, in which violence, extortion, rapine, brutality, blind courage, and ruthlessness shone bright and unashamed in all phases of life, Machiavelli moaned that the spirit of his age was congealing under the pressure of peacefulness.

An odd mixture of truth, falsehood, and boundless exaggeration, of genius and dilettantism, of dreams of the past, blindness for important aspects of the present, and presentiments concerning centuries to come, were shaped in Machiavelli's mind into a military whole.

It is precisely in this mixture, however, that Machiavelli's significance as a military theoretician is rooted, because the contradictions in him influenced the course of future events. This thin, harassed, peaceable secretary lifted his mind far above the Italian crisis which had arisen out of the great transition from the Middle Ages to modern times.

Machiavelli's passionate, feverish complaint about the condition of the army was in fact criticism of the military medievalism which Italy had never gone beyond. The Peninsula, compared with the rest of Western Europe, was still in a primitive stage of the art of combat. Italian cities had customarily settled their disputes not with infantry but with the polite tournaments of the cavalry—the condottieri. They attempted to fight European armies in the way they had always fought. Hence they could offer no resistance. Such armies could not possibly succeed against the newly-born, ordered brutality of modern military methods. Even though, contrary to Machiavelli's assertion, enough blood flowed in the thousands of minor feuds in Italy, the higher standards of city life had destroyed the martial spirit, the elemental strength for social slaughter on a grand scale. And every society which has lost the inclination to kill wholeheartedly, must go down to destruction. Politics cannot save it. Better methods of production, intensified economic intercourse, art, philosophy, and poetry, not only destroyed the barbarian virtues, but also removed the basis for any sort of territorial unity.

Machiavelli, however, criticized the lack of martial spirit, the methods of combat, and the make-up of the armies which resulted, not from the standpoint of the new military tactics which the rest of Europe was demonstrating, but from that of his unyielding Roman ideal. Therefore he could grasp the realities of new phenomena of war only where he saw in them parallels of classic methods. He emphasized the significance of the infantry and became its inspired prophet! Again and again he proclaimed that it would become the main weapon, that all others would give way before it, and that the victory or defeat of the infantry would be the sole deciding factor in battle.

He wished to fight his battles not only without artillery, but without cavalry. With equal fervor he raised his voice against the mercenaries and advocated a national militia on the Roman pattern. He wanted foot soldiers in a citizens' defense corps! To support this thesis directed against cavalry and mercenaries, Niccolo fictionalized and caricatured battles. He made false reports on the military relationships of Europe, idealized the Swiss phalanxes, and divided the peoples of Europe at his own discretion into armed and unarmed groups according to how closely they approached his ideal. In describing certain types of military actions, he revealed a remarkable untrustworthiness.

Above all, he continually disparaged the condottieri. He had come in contact with them at their lowest ebb and he saw how they could "find neither glory in war nor repose in peace." Because of this, Niccolo forgot their former greatness, their strength which had allowed the Sforzas, Visconti, and Esti to establish ruling houses which lasted for hundreds of years. He forgot that only two generations before Italian cavalry commanders and Italian arquebusiers had been reckoned among the most celebrated warriors of Europe. He blamed the condottieri for the turbulent condition of the Peninsula. As a matter of fact, they themselves were merely victims. They were being driven out of existence by the course of military events and could continue to be active only by continuous and unscrupulous betrayals.

Machiavelli's military caricatures and falsehoods were no more than the common devices of prophets, who since Jeremiah have navigated profitably upon the high seas of exaggeration. Nevertheless, if they were cartoons they were based upon the objective fact that no Italian city was animated by martial spirit and that all Italian cities had useless methods of combat and inadequate military systems.

He felt that his mission against the condottieri was not that of the historian but that of the politician. Not only the example of Roman history, but the violent decay of the condottieri, awakened in his thoughts the desire for national, unhired arms. His general, theoretical demand for a native Tuscan army took shape more concretely the more closely he came to know the Baglionis, the Petruccis and the d'Alvianos. His opposition to the mercenaries hardened to a determination which brought new strength and perseverance into his life. He built up the hatred which, in the decade of official duties soon to begin, he was to use in behalf of the militia and against the condotta. He saw nothing more in the savage struggles of the condottieri than tavern brawls fought out in the golden armor of Saint Michael. All enmities which were not rooted in personal affairs, which were exalted beyond the individual, were incomprehensible to those condottieri, and the bureaucrat, Niccolo, did not understand such disordered emotions. He saw strategy and politics helpless at the hands of a characterless, arbitrary rabble. For him, military and political government could begin only after the condottieri had been overcome.

Those eternal forces which harden men and nerve them to conquer continents, which make ordinary men build pyramids and create believers out of unbelievers, were now being manifested in new shapes. Force had changed; it had acquired new dignity and become *Power!* Niccolo, the mentor of the new Power, despised the disciples of the old school of force who were not rooted in a *State*. His ideas and his conception of Power, not those of the mercenaries, were to become the background of battle and the lifeblood of the evolving military organization. The independent soldiery Niccolo encountered was exuberant with explosive energy and terrifying to the contented. Impressive in its frank enjoyment of danger it killed lightly and illogically and was killed in the same way. But this caste was dying and Florence was condemned to bear the burial costs.

Niccolo revolted against this sacrifice which Tuscany daily made with a portion of its being. He was impelled by practical, official, and personal feeling as well as by national sentiments. Hurt by the defeats of Florence and Italy Machiavelli took refuge in his conception of classic warfare. Through an entire generation, the thought of the Roman battlefield of the past and the disasters of the present shaped his national consciousness. The spiritual process which finally takes place in an entire nation here occurred in one individual, Machiavelli. For every significant event takes place in the individual before it becomes the property of common men. The rich sunshine of platitude which warms the lowlands of society first gleams coldly on the mountain peak of genius. The task of the prophets has always been to link the present with the remote past and to anticipate the future.

Machiavelli believed that the revival of the Roman militia would make Florence the keystone of the Peninsula. He had always been the first to jeer at the obscurity of the ideal and to free politics from the burden of the ought-to-be. But now, without this fiction so dear to his heart, he would not have had the strength to leave the demand for native arms as his bequest for future centuries.

CHAPTER VIII

Machiavelli in the Field

THE IDEA of calling the inhabitants of Tuscany to arms was not born in Machiavelli's mind. It was an ancient request of the extreme populani and a persistent demand of Savonarola's followers. In the revolutionary, anti-Medicean days all the guilds had armed themselves in order to keep the gates to the city closed to the expelled ruler. Along with this city defense, which had been born during an uprising and did not last much longer than the uprising itself, there existed theoretically the right of general levy. In the thirteenth century there had been a militia fixed by parishes in the rural regions. The levying of men from the peasant districts, the despoilers and the foot soldiers who had either been drafted by force or lured by money and led into Pisan territory, had been carried out on the basis of these old laws which for generations had neither been applied nor remembered.

Even the baseness and unreliability of these occasional levies did not invalidate the idea of the militia. With the condottieri and their mercenaries the Republic had not had more fortunate experiencs, merely more protracted and more costly ones. Public opinion favored a standing army, even though each political stratum of the public wanted to see itself exempted from military duties. Despite the sober approval which had greeted a new army as a necessary evil, the conduct of military affairs appeared to remain unchanged.

The Republic lacked the organs for a reform from top to bottom. For a decade since the expulsion of the Medici, the leading authorities had been changed every third, sixth, or eighth month. The law dictated constant instability. The Florentines thought a democracy must change its officials continually. Only thus could they preserve liberty unscathed. The priors, the chiefs of the Guelph party, the magistrates, the Ten of War, the Eight of the Guard, the Six of the Commercial Court, took office and then departed to make room for their successors when they had scarcely become familiar with their duties. The three thousand fully franchised citizens of the city were theoretically eligible and trained to fill any office. This instability was regarded more as a natural state of affairs than as a disadvantage.

As a result, no ruler had enough ambition to begin reforms with a long view. Four years before, stirred by Cesare Borgia's threat to dismember the Republic, the Florentines had sought to establish a fixed point of reference in their Constitution. Piero Soderini was nominated by the Great Council to the office of gonfaloniere for life. The populani, who formed a party into which men were for the most part born, were providing themselves with a party chief. The law confirming Soderini's nomination consisted of nothing but restrictions upon the power of the gonfaloniere, as if it were necessary to make excuses for permanency of office to the three thousand fully franchised citizens.

Piero Soderini was the son of a wealthy family well known for its democratic leanings. For generations the Soderini had learned populani politics from their fathers. Offspring of other propertied houses—especially those of the opposing nobili—continued to be in arrears with their taxes solely in order to be exempt from the privilege and duty of occupying a public office. Thus they avoided subjecting themselves to useless dangers, difficulties, and expense. The Soderini were different. Of five brothers, two served as diplomats, the third was enthroned as a cardinal in Rome, and Piero was dignified with the presidency of the Republic.

The legal restrictions, which were to make it impossible for Soderini to become sole ruler and which made him removable by the joint decree of the various political bodies, were not really necessary. For his own character was the stumbling block between Piero and dictatorship. He was a passionless person who did not feel the allure of ambitious projects.

His jovial, satisfied smile, filled with the dignity of his office, stamped him an optimist. He was always convinced, an opponent wrote, that things would turn out all right. Soderini had proclaimed patience as his first principle of government. He presided over the Great Council and constantly negotiated among the many magistracies of the Republic. These all had expressed different ideas. For twelve years he negotiated more than he governed. He frequently spoke ten or twenty times for the same law in an effort to win over the authorities to his point of view, discussed every detail with dozens of men, lost himself in minutiae, and at the same time always bore in mind his maxim of patience.

Soderini governed exclusively with the Great Council of the three thousand Florentine citizens, the party of the golden mean. True to the wishes of the republican organizations whose representative he was and whose spirit he wholly shared and loved, he fought the pro-Medicean opposition of wealthy nobili, and sought to stem their political and social influence. As the skeptical aristocratic Guicciardini wrote, "he suppressed men of quality and liberally distributed offices and honors, often to people of low birth. The result is that a great many prudent men have been alienated from public cares." Nothing was further from Soderini's mind, however, than hatred for the opposing nobili. It seemed to him a crime against the Republic to sign sentences of death or banishment. He preferred to reconcile all opposition by benevolence.

His normal, healthy intelligence, his assurance, his gravity, which was as great as his dignity, did not permit him to believe in insurmountable obstacles any more than in unique political or human phenomena.

When the gonfaloniere entered the palace of the Signory to inspect the chanceries, he was pleased by the good order prevailing in the office of Machiavelli, with whom he was casually acquainted. Soderini's private and official papers were characterized by a painstaking exactitude. Niccolo's files proudly revealed this same orderliness. Their documents embraced before their hearts had met. Soderini was glad to have a secretary who treated his work with unusual seriousness in these offices where the clerks so carefully cultivated their laziness. Niccolo's bureaucratic and punctilious habits delighted Soderini. Here and there he objected to the somewhat bold conclusions in Niccolo's reports, but this carping was similar in nature to the reply he was said to have given Michelangelo when asked how he liked the *David*, "Good, only the nose is too long."

The gonfaloniere became for Machiavelli the chief obstacle which he had to surmount in order to make his ideas effective in the Republic. The president frequently appeared to Niccolo as the personification of the three thousand contented citizens who sought nothing more than peace and order. But Soderini permitted himself to be persuaded by the genius of this lowly subordinate. When Machiavelli urged extreme measures or bold action, when the logic of his analogies, the gloominess of his fears or the hopefulness of his dreams seemed unsound, the gonfaloniere would listen with quiet interest. At first he regularly said no. He would mention the Constitution, the possible dangers, the costs. But the action which the president occasionally took was solely the result of these conversations with his secretary.

On this account, the president was grateful to him, and for eight years his trust was not broken by either moods or whims. Niccolo could count upon Soderini. He knew that in the long run all hostility and envy would be powerless against him in the upper floors of the Signory where Piero's offices were situated. When Soderini became gonfaloniere, in Machiavelli's sixth year in office, Niccolo was finally able to work effectively, freed of all worry that he might lose his position. Protected by the continual activity of his chief, he could finally draw up the balance of his experience and work for the reform of the army. Before long Niccolo was considered the president's man. His enemies said he was just a rubber stamp for the gonfaloniere.

Man, however, is only outwardly corruptible. In the secret recesses of his soul he cannot be bought. He cannot persuade himself to hold particular convictions, but only to appear to do so. Secretly, Machiavelli was contemptuous of his benefactor, superior, and friend.

Niccolo saw in Piero the man from whom one could learn how not to govern; a leader who had Power and was not inspired by it. Soderini bore a platonic relationship to Power. He was ready to defend it with pen, ink, and the letter of the law, but not with violence, fury, and cunning. Niccolo despised Soderini not because the gonfaloniere vigorously rejected any thought of personal dictatorship, but because he was convinced that a man who was incapable of seizing Power for himself was also incapable of seriously defending the Power of the Florentine Great Council.

When Soderini passed away, Niccolo was said to have written for the president's grave the epitaph:

> "The night that Piero Soderini died
> His soul descended to the depths of Hell:
> Thou fool, no Hell for thee! old Pluto cried,
> Get thee to Limbo where the infants dwell!"

Nothing was more alien to the character of the gonfaloniere than reform of the army. Yet it was his task, as the sole individual with permanence in office, to undertake such reforms. In spite of his love for Florence, he would have liked to see no soldiers at all and to defend the Republic only by skillful alliances. Reform of the army frightened Soderini as it did all the magistrates. This fear also made the nobili of the right and the populani of the left extremely suspicious of the President of the Republic.

Untrustworthy as the condottieri were, they were nevertheless foreigners in the Republic. They could be dismissed at any time. They could do no more than desert, refuse to fight, betray, and cheat. But a national standing army might have ambitions.

Machiavelli argued that the militia, as he envisaged it, would never disturb the peace, would never turn against the Republic. On the contrary, the weapons which the law would put into the hands of the citizens would perform excellent service for the Republic and keep the fatherland free. With an armed citizenry, Rome had lived in freedom for four hundred, Sparta for eight hundred years.

These general ideas were not convincing. However necessary the militia might be in theory, no one was able to predict with certainty its immediate practical consequences.

Machiavelli, who had sweeping military reforms in mind, had to permit his proposals to be limited and determined by the internal politics of Tuscany. Roman and Greek examples did not fit the documental language of the magistrates. The main thing, in spite of all the compromises which altered his plan until it was almost unrecognizable, was to preserve the central idea. The still unarmed republic must have a balanced military organization and the flag, the device of the new soldiers, must be "the insignia of the State". In a private statement he gave legal and administrative assurances that the levy would not interfere in the relationship between master and serf or between the ruling Republic and the subject territories.

These reservations expressed the basic weakness both of

Tuscany and its army reform. Machiavelli explained, almost candidly, the factors which placed limitations upon a general arming of the people. He emphasized the fact that for the present the duty of serving in the militia would apply only to those living in the rural areas of the Republic. Only these districts were peaceable and tractable. Here he hoped in time to be able to organize twenty to thirty thousand men into battalions. The Florentines themselves were not to be armed or regimented because the city was torn by party factions. At any time family feuds might break out into civil war. The regime of the populani would not tolerate the arming of the citizens.

Machiavelli passed lightly over this question. He did not definitely assure the populani that the young sons of the friends of the Medici, the golden youths whom they despised, would not immediately attempt to clean the Soderini out of the Council Hall. But he reassured himself and those with whom he talked by saying that the Florentines were born to command, not to obey. He promised a cavalry militia for the rich, proportionate to their numbers, which would be a guard of honor of dependable populani within the general militia.

The *distretto* had to be weaponless. This was the district where the centers of rebellion lay: Arezzo, Cortona, Volterra, and Pistoia. "The mood of these districts," he wrote, "is like that of a man who would no longer endure any master if he knew that he could stand on his own feet." He did not neglect, however, the theoretical possibility of arming all Tuscany. "The distretto will not be armed," he wrote, "until the militia in your rural regions has taken root and won esteem."

Machiavelli's secret memorandum sought to solve the major problem of Florentine democracy. The Republic needed an army in order to live and at the same time was afraid of one! The Republic had tried many schemes in its eventful past, but had never yet succeeded in reconciling authority with liberty. This same unsolved problem, which continually shook the foundations of the Tuscan Constitution, now arose within the militia also. The contradiction was evident in all positions of leadership both civil and military, from the gonfaloniere down to the last corporal. The power of an individual to issue commands awakened in the Florentine republicans a haunting fear of tyranny. Their Constitution everywhere preferred a council or a committee to individual authority. Niccolo was forced to sacrifice good management within his evolving army to the Florentines' fear for their liberty. The government was suspicious of every army order, no matter how minor.

Niccolo was not permitted to establish any sort of supreme command. Like the civilians, the soldiers also had to be dependent upon a number of authorities. Like the civilians, the soldiers were to obey no single man, but a committee. So he proposed that the army be controlled in peacetime by a committee to be newly created with members who would be changed every eight months: the Council of Nine. In wartime, however, the duties of the Nine were to be taken over by the Council of Ten, the Florentine ministry of internal and foreign affairs.

The only professional officers the military law provided for—the captains—had authority only as instructors. They were to have no more power or esteem than the clerks in the Florentine chanceries. "Care must be taken," Machiavelli wrote in his memorandum, "that no one be permitted to command a company in a district in which he was born, in which he has possessions, or with which he is familiar. Captains from Cassentino are to be taken for Muggello and from Muggello for Cassentino. And because authority, with time, becomes rooted, the captains must be transferred annually." By curtailing the power of the officers, he thought to avoid not only a revolt from above by the generals, but also an insurrection from below. "For a mob without a head," he wrote, "never makes mischief." Finally, after many secret conferences, Soderini agreed to the plan. He gave Machiavelli the means with which to work and won him the necessary support from the various authorities and factions.

Niccolo's personality changed. He became sure and unbending when he was dealing with military affairs. He was firm and knew what he was about. Now it was Machiavelli, not the gonfaloniere or the many shifting city bureaus, who issued orders. The remodeling of the military system, the transformation of mercenaries into militia, was accomplished by the subordinate, Niccolo Machiavelli. Using the works of Titus Livius, his correct and erroneous calculations, his straight and crooked thinking, and his daring dreams as a basis, he drafted an experiment and performed it in the laboratory of Italy.

Machiavelli, who was not accustomed to have more than limited influence, worked for a maximum of unanimity and proceeded as cautiously as if he stood upon an insecure scaffolding. It was necessary to familiarize the common people with the idea of the militia before it was introduced. Consequently, before the new law was passed, several hundred peasants were levied. They were trained quickly and well and then marched through Florence.

Florence watched the parades in astonishment. In the piazza before the Council Hall, along the Arno, in the middle of the main streets, from one end of the city to the other, singing soldiers marched in their newly learned step. At the head of each troop strode the tallest man with the flag in his hand. The soldiers were wearing white doublets, their cuirasses were gleaming, their breeches were the national colors, one leg red, the other white. As one captain wrote, "It was a feast for the eyes". Previously, whenever the Florentines had seen soldiers they had been frightened.

Soldiers had always been either allied French ready to

pillage, or hired condottieri whose true intentions no one knew. The Tuscans had never yet seen a procession of armed forces which they did not need to fear. These trial troops won the populace more swiftly than the magistrates would ever have done with patriotic orations. The apothecary, Landucci, who in his chronicle noted down all the agitation of the streets, was never so delighted as after these parades. "The gonfaloniere," he wrote, "commanded that in all rural districts many thousands of such soldiers be levied, so that it will no longer be necessary to hire foreigners. This was considered the most constructive action ever taken in the city of Florence."

After this, Machiavelli drew up his military law. It was proposed by Soderini and accepted. The law ordered every male inhabitant of Florentine *rural districts* who had reached the age of sixteen years to be entered in the newly formed service lists of the infantry. Militia units were to be raised in even the smallest districts, the *podesteria*. Every ten men were under a corporal. One hundred to three hundred men formed a company which was under the command of a captain. Training took place on every festival day and holiday. Of every hundred men, ninety had naked weapons and ten had guns. The weapons supplied were registered. Twice a year a great army review took place.

All the safety measures and restrictions which Machiavelli, voicing the desires of the ruling populani, had proposed, were carried out. Florence acquired another central authority elected by the guilds and the Great Council jointly, the Council of Nine for military matters! Niccolo was named permanent chancery secretary for these changing Nine, these visitors who were but temporary workers in the war ministry. He also kept his position as Secretary of the Ten. Thus he guided the organization of the army in war as well as in peace. He was able to supervise the execution of his laws himself. He became the recruiting director of Tuscany. "We command," the ordinance empowering him reads, "all who are entered in the scrolls of our Republic to obey Machiavelli, and all magistrates to aid him in his task."

From the very beginning, Niccolo had no intention of levying for active duty all those bound to serve in the militia. He thought of organizing thirty thousand men, but he did not count upon an effective strength in the field of more than ten thousand. The remaining men were to be territorials, staying in their parishes and beating back invasions on their own soil. "To win esteem," he wrote, "large numbers are valuable; for practical purposes, a small number of men is more effective." Machiavelli intended to make the selections and decide on fitness or unfitness himself.

He rode out into the country. Neither cold nor rain nor furious heat made him postpone his trips. He was in a hurry, and if his horse stumbled on the smooth, icy mountain paths, he went on foot for hours. Back and forth through the Republic, up hill and down dale, he sought out one community after the other. The plains and mountains of Tuscany, the valleys, the forests of oaks and cypresses, and the vineyards; these produced the men who were to become soldiers. Niccolo conferred with the government officials of the village and with the priests to find out the mood of the people within each podesteria. He gave them news from Florence and explained the new defense law. The day after his arrival in a village the peasants who had been registered would come. Niccolo examined each man carefully. The country people were suspicious and embarrassed. They did not know exactly what this man from Florence wanted. "What makes them suspicious," Machiavelli reported, "is fear of a new tax or some other spiteful trick."

In one podesteria, only ten out of one hundred conscripts appeared. In another, the peasants declared that it was beneath their dignity to serve with men from their own parish who lived on the other side of the river. In still another community, all the recruits appeared, but as soon as they were given arms they rushed off to settle an old feud. In a fourth podesteria, shortly after inspection, a recruit used abusive language to the captain. The officer raised his cane and struck the insolent soldier's spear. The peasant shouted, "Capricciolai!", the name of his village. Immediately his friends left the ranks. A general brawl ensued which interfered for days with the further organization of the company.

All these countless episodes were attempts by tiny, outlying villages to throw a wrench into the workings of the defense law and to make obstructions in the hope of obtaining special rights and privileges. But Niccolo never for a moment lost patience. He never had the feeling that he was merely recruiting soldiers. He was convinced that he was faced with a great task which must succeed without question. "I believe more than ever in the success of the new army ordinances," he wrote, "provided always that care is taken. We must always be careful when a country is to be reformed." Niccolo did not wish to break the frequently savage resistance of individual peasants and whole communities by using the new Florentine troops as a police force. The recruiting, which despite everything was on the whole proceeding quite well, must not lead to a war against the low country! Niccolo wanted to convince every single community. He talked his heart out with stubborn peasants. This bookworm, politician, and diplomat knew how to popularize his theories and show the farmers the connection between their private affairs and the Republic. "You must consider," he said in one community, "that all the expenditures that you make for fortifications and for the walls of your villages are thrown out the window if you are not organized to defend yourselves and have not learned how to fight."

In the office of the Nine he centralized the entire work

on the militia and made efforts to inspire the other recruiting officers with the same flexibility he himself possessed. The officers had to send daily reports to the Nine wherever possible. Machiavelli insisted that the defense law be obeyed in every detail. "But you must think more of the consequences which arise from severe punishments than of your sense of justice," he wrote to one official. Where punishment was absolutely necessary, it must be done "with humaneness and caution".

If the peasants of a community, in spite of all the urging of Florentine officials and the local priest, were still unwilling to serve, then they should be released, for their refusal demonstrated their rebellious state of mind. "And the arms which we do not give them," Niccolo wrote, "we can consider arms gained."

It was not yet the modern State, where obedience flows like blood through men's veins even before they are put in uniform. Nor was it yet the modern army. Machiavelli was working, however, on the prototype of future armies.

He saw the need for a compound of volition and compulsion: the spiritual energies which work both with and against each other. No army could be established exclusively on a basis of compulsion or exclusively on a basis of volition. A government which is forming a new army must enjoy authority among its subjects. Commands must find an echo in the hearts of the people. "Then, when it finally comes to the point where they must fight in all earnest, those who are left behind will even be annoyed."

The Signory did not have this authority Niccolo dreamed of. He tried to replace the lack by flexibility in administration. Thousands of papers relating to the militia over the course of two or three years bore his signature; thousands more he wrote and had signed by others. Pedantically exact, he concerned himself with all the details of tactical organization, such as the recently introduced marching step and the shovels of the infantrymen.

The Signory was overjoyed to have found a civilian, a powerless clerk who was no threat to democracy, to relieve them of the burdens of military affairs. They gave him a free hand in selecting his assistants and representatives, although they did not permit him to devote himself exclusively to the militia. Soderini's confidence, in fact, which had made possible the reform of the army, repeatedly took Machiavelli away from the army. The man who had been the Florentine envoy to Cesare, seemed to Soderini the right man to represent the Republic in the field camp of Julius II, who was at the moment demanding auxiliary troops from the Signory.

Among the twenty-four cardinals in Julius' entourage, Niccolo felt like the Devil in holy water. The papal army was approaching Perugia, the territory of Baglioni who as condottiere had sold out and betrayed Florence. Baglioni came to meet Julius, declared himself ready to surrender, and arranged for the transfer of gates, fortresses, and other places.

Niccolo did not trust Baglioni's submissiveness. He thought that treachery was at work and reported to Florence, "We will wait and see what time holds in her lap." Julius was impatient, and rode out in advance of his army. Even the youngest cardinals had difficulty in keeping pace with the sixty-four year old man. The Holy Father entered Perugia, which was still in Baglioni's hands, before his own army. In Machiavelli's wishful thinking, Julius had impetuously let himself into a trap from which he could not escape. Niccolo kept his eyes and ears open in order not to lose anything of the color and tone of the events which were about to take place.

For a week, so long as Julius' troops were not in Perugia, expectancy kept Niccolo alert day and night. Julius quite calmly took up residence in Baglioni's palace. Niccolo could not openly inform the Signory of his blasphemous hopes and merely reported: "If Baglioni does nothing evil to him who has come to take away his country, he will be refraining because of generosity and humanity . . . We shall soon see, when the Pope has been here six or eight days." But when Baglioni refused to seize his opportunity, Niccolo noted for himself, as if betrayed in a great hope, "This cowardice of Gian-Paolo struck all sensible men in the Pope's following. They could not understand why he neither destroyed his enemy with a single blow, to his eternal fame, nor loaded himself with spoils . . . One must conclude from this that men are incapable of doing evil for the sake of honor . . . Thus Gian-Paolo did not have the adroitness to perform a deed which would have led everyone to admire his courage and would have made his name immortal. For he would have been the first to show these priests how little one need trouble oneself about them."

After two months, when he had returned from Julius' camp, Niccolo hoped that he would have a chance to devote himself in peace to his reform of the army. But he found the Signory at its wit's end.

The gonfaloniere poured out to him the anxieties that filled his mind. At the assembly of the German Estates, Emperor Maximilian had announced his coronation march to Rome. All Italian States were sending diplomats to Constance to win renewed assurances of the sovereignty of their countries by paying enormous sums to the Emperor. For thirty, fifty, or a hundred thousand ducats, the Emperor was said to be willing, in case he should march to Rome, to consider Florence his ally and guarantee her Pisa.

The forces and tendencies of the continent seemed to the Florentines to be steadily closing in on the Republic like the walls of a pit. Venice wanted to compensate for her losses in the sphere of world trade by acquiring more territories in Italy. The Pope bent every effort to prevent the realization of this plan. The Emperor Maximilian was making the situation constantly more dangerous and complicated by his contradictory attempts to establish sharply defined boundaries against France on the one hand and to revive the medieval world empire on the other.

The more perilous the situation of Tuscany grew, the more confused all the bureaus and boards of the Signory became. Every fresh event in Europe had its echoes within the city, in the parties and in the personnel of the Signory. All old fears, ambitions, and intrigues were revived. Behind the scenes there were furious debates to select the man who was to be the envoy to the emperor. Soderini wished to avoid all surprises and therefore asked Niccolo to go to Germany. He wanted no one else for this mission because the diplomats of the Republic were by and large the sons of well-known nobili and secretly inclined toward the Medici. True, they were in the service of the populani, but their ancient, traditional Ghibelline preference for the aureole of the Roman Empire might well come to life in the presence of His Imperial Majesty.

To Soderini's partisans, however, Niccolo seemed to come from too restricted an environment, and to have too little experience with the world to represent Florence at the court of Maximilian. How could he, of all persons, who during his legations was always begging the Signory for a few ducats, negotiate with Maximilian over hundreds of thousands? They proposed Francesco Vettori, a well-to-do man from an old family of diplomats whose forefathers had always supported the Medici, but who had been in the service of the Republic for years.

Soderini had to give way, and Vettori went to the Emperor. The gonfaloniere, however, declared that he was still unsatisfied. He frightened his followers by suggesting that Vettori, thrown on his own resources, might be too compliant. Under the pretext of delivering new instructions to

Vettori, Machiavelli was sent after him. Crossing Geneva, Constance, Innsbruck, and the Brenner Pass, Niccolo reached Bozen, in Austria, where Vettori and the emperor were.

The two Florentine diplomats were not at all suspicious of each other. Indeed, a friendship arose which was to survive all the changes of the future. They both passed the same judgment on the situation. "If Maximilian should march to Rome," Machiavelli wrote, "then the leaves of all the poplars of Italy, transformed into ducats, would not suffice him. There would then be nothing for which we would not have to pay in cold cash." Vettori and Machiavelli negotiated for over a hundred days and probed the emperor's weaknesses. They found in Germany nothing but hostility and treachery. They saw hostility of the princes against the cities, hostility of the cities against the princes, alliances of the cities with the emperor and betrayal of the emperor by the cities. Whoever, in Germany "does not dare to begin war against his Majesty, dares to refuse him auxiliaries; and whoever has not refused them, still has the courage not to send them. And if he does not dare so much, he still dares to postpone sending them long enough so that they come too late to be of any use."

The Ten in Florence, encouraged by these reports, refused to advance money for the coronation of the emperor. They believed that Maximilian's projected coronation was merely a means for extorting money. They would still be prepared to pay if Maximilian should make his way into the heart of Italy. Soderini was convinced that he had saved the Republic a great deal of money. The oral reports which Machiavelli and Vettori brought back increased the citizens' good humor. Their fears that they would have to pay had been dispelled.

But intervals between worries were brief in Florence. Louis of France, who was now in league with Ferdinand of Spain, made grave accusations against Tuscany. His representative appeared and told Soderini, "The embassy to Maximilian, as well as the long war against Pisa, are a flagrant breach of our alliance with you. We have the right, if we choose, to expel all Florentine merchants from the territories of King Louis and send our galleys to the assistance of the Pisans."

The gonfaloniere, who was always ready to support France, was completely taken aback. In vain he showed the envoy the signatures of Louis and his predecessors to treaties which guaranteed Pisa to the Florentines. In vain he pointed out that no money had been given Maximilian and that the Florentines had merely wanted to protect themselves against him. The French reproaches were the preface to demands for money. Soderini knew this and was prepared to pay. But even before they were through haggling over the sum, the King of Spain sent an ambassador to Pisa and another to Florence. The first renewed old treaties of assistance and encouraged the Pisans to resist the Tuscans under all conditions, while the second quoted to Florence the price for the annulment of the old and new treaties with Pisa.

Soderini was unwilling to pay Ferdinand and Louis in secret so that the two monarchs could then cheat the Signory separately. He wanted them to face one another and he proposed that all three, France, Spain, and Florence, negotiate together. For months the envoys sat around a table and resolved all oaths and treaties into ducats. The French demanded 125,000; the Spanish would have been satisfied with 50,000 ducats. Honor, however, forbade Ferdinand to demand less than Louis. Soderini, therefore, negotiated with Louis' envoys behind the backs of the Spaniards. Publicly France declared itself to be satisfied with 50,000 ducats. In a secret treaty, however, it received an additional 50,000, and the king's ministers received 25,000 ducats for their personal use. Florence also promised to enter the League of Cambrai, consisting of Spain, France, the Pope, Ferrara, and Mantua, against Venice.

For Florence, all political trails led to the walls of Pisa. At the same time that Venice was carrying on an astounding struggle against all of Europe, the Signory had eyes for only a few square miles within the borders of the neighboring city on the Arno. The turmoil of world events scarcely concerned the Florentines. The internal situation of the State dulled their adroitness, their clarity and their intelligence. They could do nothing but bow to immediate necessity. Compulsion dictated. Florence needed Pisa as Lyons needs Marseilles, Berlin Hamburg, and Manchester Liverpool.

As Machiavelli put it, after all the open maws had been stuffed with gold, the diplomatic road to Pisa was clear. Now all Florence had to do was conquer her old enemy by force of arms. The Signory ordered the spoliation of all neighboring territories befriending Pisa. Lucca, especially, had to bear the brunt. With an artistry such as is ordinarily applied only to the laying out of a garden, the bands of militia destroyed woods and fields. In a broad arc about the besieged city, the landscape was soon withered and scorched.

Three camps were set up about Pisa—the first to guard the Arno, the second to close the highways to Lucca, and the third to attend to all other roads. These camps, communicating with one another by a number of large detachments and patrols, surrounded Pisa on land. From the sea, the mouth of the Arno was blockaded by rows of piles and stakes. Along the coast cruised recently hired cutters, galleons, and brigantines. Hundreds of smugglers attempted to circumvent these obstacles and help the besieged city. They could easily hide in the broken, frequently marshy terrain and in the mountainous ravines, or among chalk and sandstone cliffs. The soldiers of the Tuscan militia learned combat at close quarters in their struggles with these courageous smugglers. And soon the Florentines had to try their strength in greater conflicts. Eight hundred Genoese tried to fight their way through to Pisa with their goods and were driven off.

The spirit behind this desultory warfare, this methodical annihilation, was Machiavelli. The year-long siege, which extended over an unusually broad territory, was to be the test of his army. For three years he had been shaping it from his office and in the villages. Now it was in the field. Never before had militia been mobilized for such a long time. He prevented desertion by appealing to the honor of his men. A third of the army still consisted of mercenaries. Niccolo stirred up the atrophied hatreds of his conscripted peasants, stung to life their ambition to be superior to the professional soldiers.

Whole companies voluntarily gave up their leave and learned to love their arms and the dangers that faced them. When new recruits came, Niccolo distributed them among the various camps and accompanied them to their quarters himself. Often he left the front line for several days in order to conduct inspections. Besides this, he guided the affairs of the army administration and took care of pay and munitions. He negotiated on his own responsibility with foreign cities for the delivery of grain, functioned as "Commissioner of Spoliation" pointing out new territories for the axe and the flaming torch, inspected those already despoiled, and supervised the work of damming the Arno. All day long he rode and at night dictated long reports to the Signory.

Although Niccolo was the organizer of all the work within the army, he did not hold the highest office. The Commissioner General of the Republic for the army was Niccolo Capponi. For more than ten years Machiavelli had been accustomed to do the lion's share of the work and nevertheless remain nominally the assistant. This time, however, he took no consideration of his chief. He worked as if he alone had the power to command, and because of this a dispute developed. Capponi could not even meet his assistant to reprove him—for Machiavelli was everywhere and nowhere. Above all, he avoided being where Capponi was staying. The Commissioner General protested to the board to which he was subordinate, the Ten. He offered to resign his office.

As long as Machiavelli was doing the major part of the work and no one objected to it, the Ten were glad to avoid being involved in disputes over jurisdiction within the army, which were just as complicated as those within the Signory. They preferred their well-established habit of using their Secretary of the Chancery for all military affairs. They spurred him on, prodded his native industriousness. "Command and perform whatever is possible," they wrote him. "For we have placed all the care for affairs of the camp on your shoulders."

This order reflected their true attitude and the actual situation. Niccolo Capponi, however, not only had tradition on his side, but also many followers. These trumpeted to the four winds the word: scandal, scandal! Machiavelli's work in the campaign was considered arrogant and impudent by many colleagues in the Signory. Spiteful sayings and suspicions flew from the bureaus into the city. "The Secretary of the Chancery is playing the commander! Why should he be permitted to? Because the Ten understand nothing about war and because the gonfaloniere's rubber stamp is working for his master."

The Ten in office at the time were extreme, bigoted republicans who wanted to fight Soderini's influence in the army. They were afraid that they had perhaps allowed his friend, Machiavelli, too much independence after all. They half capitulated. The Ten wrote an urgent order to Machiavelli to place himself at the disposal of Niccolo Capponi and report to him promptly. Machiavelli replied with the request that he be removed at once from his post.

The Ten, however, wanted neither to give his place to

another nor to grant him leave. It sufficed them to have reminded him of his subordinate position. Moreover, they could show the copy of their commands to all of Capponi's friends. The gonfaloniere was the most upset of all about the affair. In the prevailing atmosphere of distrust, however, he did not wish to correspond directly with his protegé, and sent for Blasius. "Yesterday I had a long talk with the Superius,"[1] Blasius wrote to Niccolo. "He commissioned me to write you and advise you to have patience on his account. Capponi is remonstrating and abusing . . . The bigwigs are always right, you know . . . But you are accustomed to exercise patience . . . If one looks at the matter closely, it is fundamentally a triviality . . . If a few reports can satisfy Capponi, they are easy enough to write. There must be no more talk of leaving . . . They are afraid here that they will not be able to get along without you."

From then on Machiavelli reported all inessential matters to Capponi. He wrote to him, especially, that there was nothing to report and that all the difficulties of the war rested on the shoulders of the Commissioner General and all successes were Capponi's work. Everything remained as it had been before the dispute. Niccolo saw to it that the work of the military did not suffer from the intrigues over jurisdiction.

Pisa was facing death. For the first time in fifteen years the Pisans saw no hope. In all the world, no one was helping her any longer. Her friends had been bought by Florence, and her ally, Venice, had been beaten in battle by the might and superior numbers of the League of Cambrai. Pisa felt its great isolation and was forced to look for miracles. Hunger discouraged the Pisan peasants, broke their defiance, and stifled their eagerness for war. For months they had been starving in the city as refugees while their fields were lying fallow and their villages were ravaged.

[1] The gonfaloniere's nickname.

The rulers of Pisa conferred continually in the Town Hall. They looked back upon fifteen years of struggle and pleaded with fate for one last battle to the death. The peasants, however, wanted to see their fields and were feverishly eager to go home. They rebelled, surrounded the Town Hall of the battle-hardened Pisans, and declared that they would not move until a peace delegation to Florence had been named. The councilors could not fight simultaneously against their own people and against Tuscany. In spite of their defiant declarations, they gave in. Five city men and four representatives of the rural communities traveled to the neighboring city of Piombino, whose Duke was willing to act as mediator.

In a hall of the castle at Piombino, Machiavelli waited for them. He had so often, here and there, in Italy and Europe, pleaded the helplessness of Florence. Now he could at last enjoy victory! The Pisans, however, humbled though they were, destroyed Niccolo's dream with their first sentence. They had assumed, their spokesman declared, that Florence would send an important man, an ambassador, to negotiate. Instead they, the Pisans, were insulted at the outset at being forced to discuss the fate of their city with a Secretary of the Chancery.

Exasperated, Niccolo reminded them of their position and demanded to see their diplomatic papers giving them the power to negotiate the capitulation. The Pisans had none, but they tried to talk of conditions. Machiavelli interrupted them. "Do you want peace or do you want war? If it is war you want, you will have enough and more than enough." Niccolo broke off the negotiations.

However, the treaty of peace which Soderini and Machiavelli drew up did not reflect this tone. It granted amnesty to the Pisans and restored to them all old rights which they had had before their secession in 1494. No confiscations were made and commercial privileges were not revoked.

Hunger and the treaty, which was announced everywhere even before it was accepted, extinguished the last sparks of military defiance in Pisa. The besieged inhabitants did not even wait for their authorities to finish with all the formalities of capitulation. By the thousands they went out to the camps of the victors and pleaded for food. They were greeted joyfully. The hatred of fifteen years was forgotten like a single night. "We want to wipe out the cruelty caused by years of Pisan courage," a Florentine Commissioner reported.

On June 8, 1509, a rider with the olive branch came to Florence and reported to the Signory that the treaty had been ratified by Pisa. Tuscan troops would be able to march into the conquered city early in the morning. It was the day of Corpus Christi and in the packed churches of Florence everyone passed word to his neighbor about the rider and his message. The crowds from all the churches marched, deeply moved, to the Signory. The greatest of all miracles seemed to have taken place. Because this fifteen-year-long war, during which youths had grown to men and men had become greybeards, was over, it seemed to them that the eternal peace of the entire world had this day begun its merciful rule. By evening the city had been transformed into a garden of pleasure. "Everyone is crazy for joy," an assistant in the Second Chancery wrote to Niccolo. "There is nothing lacking but that Heaven should for its part also reveal some new blessing. Rejoicing is so great . . . I do not know what I am saying."

When Machiavelli arrived in Florence, Soderini embraced him as the modest and successful negotiator of a difficult task. The great Florentine commander, Giaccomini, kept away from the army by intrigues, shook hands with him silently. Francesco Vettori congratulated him with smiling countenance. The Ten pronounced a "laudation" upon him in the name of the Republic—always stingy with honors.

The ever-faithful Blasius and a number of assistants from the bureaus celebrated him in their favorite tavern on the Arno. With thick tongues they toasted him over their wine as the greatest military commander of all times and proclaimed him their private general.

Niccolo knew no other triumph. No laurels grew in Florence for a Secretary of the Chancery!

CHAPTER IX

The Return of the Medici

SEVEN years previously, Machiavelli had informed the Signory of a rumor he had picked up in Cesare's camp. Niccolo had said, "A man showed me a letter which read to the effect that in Portugal ships full of spices have arrived direct from Calcutta. That will seriously depress the price of these wares." Niccolo had not given too much thought to this report. The Republic of Venice herself did not yet know that she was to be the chief sufferer from the reshuffling of the world markets.

After the Republic of the Doges had, in her own commercial manner, impressed her heritage of Roman law upon the far-flung shores of the Mediterranean, and after she had brought the Mediterranean itself under the thrall of her commercial monopoly, she was ruined by the circumnavigation of Africa. This meant that direct traffic was established between Lisbon and India. The historical transition was not brought about by a mighty individual, but by the prosaic means of a trade and price revolution.

Venice could no longer at her pleasure close the Eastern Mediterranean in Cyprus, Candia, Cairo, and all the intersections of the Levant because her key position had ceased to exist. The scepter of Neptune fell from the hand of the Republic, and she lost her dictatorship over prices. In the market place at Lisbon, ginger, cloves, pepper, pearls, lac, and dye-wood were cheaper by two thirds than in the halls of the Rialto where Venetian commodities were stored and then transshipped to north and west Europe at a high jobber's profit. Germany, France, Holland, England, and even Italy bought less and less in the City of the Lagoons. The Venetian agents in Tunis, Catalonia, Oran, and deep into Africa as far as Timbuktu were working at a loss. Famous established houses along the well-tended canals helped spread panic, uncertainty, and bankruptcy. From the loss of the major source of profit—jobbing—the native branches of the manufacturing industry—textiles, glass, and metals—also suffered. Credit, formerly so liquid, was lacking. Other countries no longer saw in Venice a profitable refuge for their money and foreign merchants no longer came to have their noble metal stamped into the coin of the Republic.

The Venetians had two lions in mosaic in the church of San Marco as the symbol of their past. One lion had his face turned toward the sea; he was large and strong. The other was looking inland; he was scrawny and weak. As long as the Republic had been Queen of the Sea, she had neglected her native hinterland. She had had no territorial ambitions in Italy. Now, however, that she had to look fearfully on while Lisbon took away more and more of her commercial profits, she began seeking continental markets on the Peninsula itself and grew eager for commercial rights in the best ports. Rapidly and energetically, Venice tried to build new settlements up and down the length of Italy. She sought to complete in Italy in the space of a decade the work she had done along the coasts of the Adriatic, Greece, and Asia Minor during a glorious thousand years.

For this reason, Venice had hoped for the invasions and welcomed the destruction of the balance of power in Italy. She had been one of the prime sinners in bringing it about. The mobs of foreign armies which since 1494 had been pouring through all the roads and passes of Italy and spreading out over the whole Peninsula, offered the best of prospects to the City of the Doges.

"The lords of Venice are very clever," the French ambassador, Commines, declared. "They sit in conference daily. Their neighbors will soon feel it." The Venetians planted their flag in the shadow of disasters. They annexed cities in a thousand devious ways. During the struggle of the Spanish in South Italy, the Republic had occupied the five best ports of Apulia. They were menacing the Pope in Mantua and Ferrara, the French in Lombardy, Emperor Maximilian in Dalmatia and Istria, the Hungarians in Albania, and the Florentines in Pisa.

A powerful coalition, molded in the fires of hatred and envy, rose up against Venice. The splendor of the Republic of the Doges was a moral provocation to rapine. How many wars could be waged with the wealth of Venice! In Paris, Constance, Madrid, Rome, and Florence, imprecations were poured down in prose and rhyme upon the "cowardly shopkeepers" of Venice. Claude de Seyssel describes the mood of the continent when he cries out, "Who can observe without revulsion the manner in which this nation seeks to attain sovereignty over land and sea by deceit, thievery, and foul cunning, and threatens all kings and princes."

France, the Holy Roman Empire, and Spain, had needed fifteen years to reach the point where they would unite against Venice. Under the leadership of Julius II, they defeated her decisively in the Battle of Vaila. Venice had not believed in the danger of a European coalition, which was the first since the Crusades. Her diplomats, whose reports in their precision and clarity are typical of this remarkable age, were trained in tradition and thought that the nature of political life was always the same. They did not clearly understand the character of Julius II, who succeeded in uniting the Powers of the world despite their antagonisms, and who was able to speed up all political processes.

This unexpected side of Julius' character, the product not of swift changes of mind but of the scope of his vision,

ENGRAVING BY MORACE
FROM PAINTING BY RAPHAEL

POPE JULIUS II

"Succeeded in uniting the Powers of the world despite their antagonisms and was able to speed up all political processes."

PAINTING BY CLOUET

KING FRANCIS I

In a last attempt to take Milan for France he had embroidered on the sleeves of his bodyguard, "Once more and never again."

made him save Venice from total destruction after it had been defeated. Julius had forced Venice to abandon territorial ambitions in Italy and he had beaten her into moderation. Now there was a greater goal; the freeing of the Peninsula from foreigners. He suddenly began to hate Louis, as he had formerly hated Cesare after having made use of him. If he had never served in Paris for long years he could not have hated France more. His hatred was to open anew the way of Spain and the emperor into the Peninsula.

But now he was aware only of the immediate fact that there were French lances in Ferrara, Brescia, Genoa, and Milan. He felt as if they were directed against his own breast. They robbed him of sleep and appetite and he paced his room for many nights moaning in a choked voice, "Punish Louis! Punish the French!" Toward morning he would send for the Venetian ambassador and say to him, "Never, never, will I be Louis' chaplain. I am Pope in spite of him." Julius attacked the French positions in Italy without declaring war. He secretly sent troops to his native city, Genoa, to incite the port to rebellion against Louis. In midwinter, with a speed that made him the terror of his own generals, he marched over the icy paths of the Apennines in cuirass and helmet and took the field against Ferrara.

The soldiers, in marching to Genoa, crossed through Tuscany without asking permission of the Signory. The Council of Ten and Soderini trembled. Their dream of security had been brief. It had been pleasant to be in league with Louis and with Julius. Suddenly this alliance had become a pincers and Florence was about to be cracked like a nut. To oppose Julius was impossible. This powerful and violent greybeard, once he was in motion, would strike before Louis could even answer a question about his stand, let alone send troops. The king, however, was their ally, and it meant a flagrant breach of the treaty to permit papal soldiers to march through Tuscany.

Machiavelli had to betake himself immediately to France to explain the dependent position and the dilemma of the Republic.

He found the French court in Blois unoriented and indecisive. All had the feeling that they were on the brink of a profound crisis which would open the door to all sorts of perilous situations. Neither Louis nor his chancellor, Robertet, nor the nuncio who was assailed on all sides, nor the ambassadors of France, Spain or Maximilian, knew whether there was to be peace or war in Italy.

The initiative lay in Julius' hands alone. Niccolo heard nothing but curses against the Vatican. The boldness of the Holy Father took these men aback at the same time that it enraged them. What did the Pope want? Was it not enough for him to have been the head of a world coalition? He had extended his territory and made his State secure? Why had he concluded a separate peace with Venice? On whom was he counting to aid his weak forces in their attack on the French positions in Italy? Was he trying only to extort new concessions, or did he intend to start a war which would spread far beyond the boundaries of Italy? "Machiavelli," one diplomat asked, "is this Pope sent to us by God to destroy the world?" Chancellor Robertet, red with anger, swore that France would give Julius notice that their obedience to the Church was at an end; that they would indict him before a consilium and make any connections between French clerics and Rome punishable by death.

The revolt against the Curia made Machiavelli's mission easier. He had expected a storm of indignation against Florence, but instead, he was received amicably. Louis was gracious and spoke in a tone which indicated that he was willing to make advances. "Mr. Secretary, I am in a state of war with neither Rome nor any other country. In these times, when friendships change so swiftly, I must know who are my allies and who my opponents. I want to know on whom I can depend."

Niccolo assured him that the Signory's own interests made it imperative for Florence to preserve the alliance faithfully. Were not the richest branches of Florentine business located on French soil? The troops of the Ecclesiastical State had been permitted passage because the Florentines thought Julius still the ally of France. None could have suspected the change in the Pope's attitude. Now, however, that there was serious possibility of war, he felt it his duty to describe in detail the topographical limitations of Tuscany. Three quarters of the country bordered on Julius' States. The Pope could invade the country along a frontier many miles long. The king must not ask the Signory to take the offensive. He must allow the Florentines to defend themselves solely on their own territory. The strength of his fatherland was insufficient for anything more.

Louis was satisfied with this defensive confirmation of the alliance, which, of course, gave the Florentines opportunity for underground negotiations with everyone. Niccolo's actual mission had been successfully completed. He did not leave the court, however, because he saw that Louis was inclined toward peace and because the perils threatening Florence made it imperative for him to work for this peace.

The situation forced a task upon him which went far beyond the narrow outlines of his mission. He became the intermediary between Julius and Louis! None needed peace between Rome and France more urgently than Florence. Encouraged by Chancellor Robertet, he described to the Signory the measures which might appease Julius. He urged Soderini to send negotiators to the Pope; he wanted diplomats on all the roads leading from Rome to Florence. By exaggerating the inclination of the French to leniency, he tried to win time for a truce.

At the same time, he placed his experience in Italian

matters at the service of Louis and Chancellor Robertet. Since the death of the king's intimate, Cardinal d'Amboise, Roman affairs had been left to chance. "The king is not accustomed to going into the details of affairs," Machiavelli wrote. "He lets things drift, and those who govern are not industrious enough. They not only do things wrong, but they have no clear conception of how matters stand."

Louis and his chancellor were glad to be advised by Niccolo. In order not to offend the two noble lords, he gave his advice with masterful modesty. His skill at flattery, acquired over many years, won him the chancellor's sympathy. To be sure, Niccolo lectured, the Pope had not only insulted France provocatively, but also attacked her. It was imperative to combat Julius. Nevertheless, it would be preposterous to forge coalitions against Rome and set all Europe in motion. The broader a coalition against Rome was, the more unstable it would become within a short time. For the Pope enjoyed the adoration of the faithful everywhere. As a friend, the Pope was of slight advantage, but as an enemy he was one of the most dangerous. He could always say that religion was being threatened. He could set emotional forces in motion against which his Majesty would be powerless. But there were other methods of destroying Julius; excellent and tested means! In the Romagna, in Rome, and in the Campagna, lived the sons of the condottieri whom France had always used against the Curia. With only a part of the forces and sums which a large-scale war would cost, these rebels, at present intimidated, could be encouraged to start a thousand minor fights against Julius. This would avoid great battles, great coalitions, and the formation of new, as yet unknown countercoalitions.

The chancellor was of one mind with Niccolo. The king said, "If the Holy Father will offer me but one fingernail, I will extend him my whole arm." For two weeks Niccolo could hope that he had prevented war and protected

Florence from fearful decisions, battles on her borders, and the possibility of invasion by friends or foes.

The Pope, however, was as obstinate in his hatred as he had been at the beginning. At the head of his army he saw only the fortresses of his enemies and did not hear their words of peace. To provoke the king even more, Julius arrested a French cardinal. The king, treated contemptuously by Rome, and perilously menaced in the positions he had conquered, now fell into a fury against Julius. "I will make a new heaven and a new earth in Italy," he swore. In the face of the Pope's persistence, Niccolo's peaceful phrases sounded like very unworldly advice. He parted from Chancellor Robertet overcome with dread and anxiety.

But the chancellor had not lost sympathy with his adviser. He consoled him, slapped him amicably on the shoulder, and declared that Louis, shielded by the benevolent neutrality of Spain and England and supported by Maximilian, would march into Italy at the head of new armies. Niccolo gave warning. He declared that Julius had his secret, trustworthy friends in England and in Germany and that in all probability he was acting in secret agreement with Spain. Robertet replied that they were certain of the friendship of the Powers, but that he could not reveal all the details of the treaties. Faced with such firm confidence, Niccolo wavered in his disbelief. Perhaps the chancellor, who had carried on the negotiations with Europe and must have a precise knowledge of all the documents, was right after all. Perhaps, as in the previous year against Venice, a superpowerful coalition was being formed against Rome? The Pope, since he was beginning the war, was the one to bear the blame. Niccolo hated him not only as pontifex, but as the man who menaced Tuscany. Nothing, he wrote to the Signory, is more emphatically to be wished, than that Robertet is right and that "our shameless priests will also get a taste of the bitterness of this world."

Machiavelli's diplomatic success won Tuscany the privilege of remaining on the defensive in spite of all treaties with Louis and gave the Republic a chance to maneuver somewhat. Florence could let herself drift in the waves of world politics for a while yet. But suddenly, with a rapidity unsuspected by Machiavelli, by the Signory or by Tuscany, the French were victorious in the greatest battle since the beginning of the century, Ravenna. All roads leading to Rome stood open to them.

The Pope, near the end of his life, and faced with invasion of his own territories, was nevertheless successful in turning the great French victory into a decisive French defeat. Europe, seduced within a few weeks by the magic potions of Julian politics, rose against Louis. The League of Cambrai became the "Holy League" for the defense of threatened Christendom. From Switzerland, twenty thousand Helvetians were moving into Milanese territory against the French army. In Navarre, Louis was menaced by Spain in the south; in Calais by the English in the north. Threatened by revolt in the cities of Lombardy and hampered by constant engagements during their retreat, the French left Italy. A more unsuccessful victory than that of Ravenna Europe had never seen!

Before the Republic could estimate the tremendous effect of the French disaster, she was encircled on the north and east by foreign armies. Soderini and his men, fine artists at prolonged negotiations, were caught unprepared by the swiftness of events. The quick victory of the French, their sudden defeat, and the triumph of the Pope, paralyzed them. Could not he lose the victory which he had won overnight with equal speed? Could not some secure ground, no matter how narrow, be found between the battlefields? It was unbelievable that the situation could have changed fundamentally so often in the past two years. The Pope had been defeated twice and so had Louis. Emperor Maximilian had been in league with Louis against the Pope twice and twice with the Pope against Louis. England had been allied with France against Spain once and once with Spain against France. In the first excitement, each new situation had seemed congealed, as if poured into a mold for all time.

Soderini, the Great Council, the Council of Eighty and the Ten of Liberty did not even think of using their own military strength. They fled into negotiations. Commissions and subcommissions were in permanent session. The Signory was hoping that dissension within the Holy League would save the independence of the Republic. Neither Emperor Maximilian nor Ferdinand of Spain would permit Florence to fall to the Pope. The two rulers promised Tuscany freedom if she paid for it. The Signory, however, had been cheated so often that at this time, of all times, the gentlemen of the Council demanded repeated assurances from these potentates, who were now quite willing to consider terms.

The indecision of the Holy League was its destruction. The victory went neither to the King of Spain, who lived far from Italy, nor to Emperor Maximilian, who could not make up his mind, but to Julius, whom Florence had offended. Julius wanted to destroy the pro-French regime of the populani and drive out Soderini. He turned the question of the Republic over to the house of Medici.

Eighteen years before, at the time of Savonarola's revolution, the Medici had been expelled from Florence. Since then they had been living in Rome. Cardinal Giovanni Medici, later Pope Leo X, was the head of the family. He had woven a network of secret agents about the Republic and countless times he had come to the borders of his native land. There he had given audiences to burghers and peasants, consoled rich and poor, and promised the arrival of the golden age. No important gate into the Republic, no road that led to the heart of the country, was free of his men. From the month of June to the month of August the Cardinal had won more adherents daily than formerly during a year.

His friends within the narrow circle of well-known nobili were usually concerned more with poetry and Roman history than with politics, but now they became noisy, intriguing party leaders. How they laughed at Soderini during this summer of the year 1512! The good, upright philistine at the head of the State could find nothing more decisive to do in his fight for the Republic than to prove his honesty in long orations and to make public a model budget. Meanwhile, it seemed as if all the springs of continental and Italian dissension were pouring floods of misfortune into the Arno. Even nature joined with politics and made life difficult for Tuscany by the withering fever of a month-long drought. Trembling hearts, filled with heaviness and desperation, could already hear the tread of the Spanish and the victory songs of the imperial, the Venetian, and the papal armies. Fleeing men, women, and children streamed from towns and villages into the capital.

At the gates of Florence hundreds of carts piled up, filled with children, old men, cats, oil, linen, and locked chests. Amid all this misery, which prevailed throughout the country, the followers of the Medici offered consolation. Everyone felt that they were the rulers of the morrow. The country would belong to them. They worked their way into the hearts of the people because they offered the only hope. Many a friend of the populani caught himself in sinful, Medicean thoughts. Had not the times of Lorenzo the Magnificent been glorious? Were they not the most splendid days the fatherland had known? A chattering monk had driven forth the old regime. Was an eternally moralizing gonfaloniere to be allowed to run the State for the benefit of his friends?

The people thronged into the piazza before the Signory. Would there be war? Misery and curiosity, but no determination, showed in most of the faces of the crowd. Some shouted,

"Long live the gonfaloniere!" but not very enthusiastically. Others at once interrupted, asking, "Shall the whole city perish for one man, for Soderini?" The discussions gave way to angry debates. A few courageous men, for the most part members of the Lesser Guilds, went to the Council of Ten and demanded that the Florentines be armed. "We resisted Charles VIII when he set his heart on the restoration of the Medici, resisted him even when he was right in the city," they declared. "Shall we capitulate to the foe now, when he is only on the borders of the country?"

The Ten told both the timid and the resolute that the fate of the city would be decided within a few hours. All the boards, presided over by the gonfaloniere, were to hold session together. The Signory received an ultimatum from the Spanish viceroy and another from the Pope. The war of the Holy League, the notes stated, was not aimed at the independence of the Republic. Rather, the League was eager to free the Republic from Soderini and its alliance with France. The notes demanded the immediate deposition of the gonfaloniere. For the Medici they demanded neither throne nor office, but solely the right to dwell within their homeland.

The sixty-four year old Piero Soderini arose and stood before his followers, who were as bitterly earnest as he himself. There was no one here whom he had to convince; these men knew what it was all about. Like him, they would sacrifice all the gold in their coffers in order to avoid war. But they loved themselves, liberty, and Florence, and they were ready to endure this unfortunate struggle patiently as though it were a bad dream. Reason showed them no other alternative. Soderini spoke to them reasonably, without lofty words, as if he were discussing a sewerage project. If he did not have to bear the sole responsibility, if he could share it with others, he could find inner peace.

Everyone in this Great Council—he scarcely needed to assure them—knew that he would give up his office if the war were directed at him and not at the Republic. "And if it were really a question solely of permitting the Medici to live among us as citizens, then we would not place obstacles in the way of their return . . . But the Medici would not be content to live in our midst as private persons. Deprived of their property by the Republic, brought up in exile, supported by foreign armies, they will think only of ruling and avenging. If today, armed as you are, you surrender, if you do not fight, then you will learn the value of freedom only after you have lost it . . . The misfortunes which would then descend upon us make me tremble."

The council heard its own sentiments in Soderini's speech and decided not to sacrifice the gonfaloniere. In order, however, even at the last minute, to leave the way open for further negotiations, the demand for the return of the Medici was not rejected but passed over in silence. This half-decision, which indicated the dilemma the citizens were in, this public "yes" and secret "no" in their minds, was typical of the entire war.

In the effective strength of their troops, in reserves, in arms, and opportunities for follow-up attacks and for provisioning, the Florentines were superior to the Spanish. The military plans of the Republic called for strictly defensive tactics. Ten thousand militiamen were to be concentrated at Prato, a day's march from the capital. Along the border, the local bodies of troops would have to guard the country from isolated enemy expeditions.

A council of war, however, changed this original plan. The area to be defended was narrowed. It shrank alarmingly and no longer extended over the full territory of Tuscany. The compact, larger half of the militia formations, the axis of resistance, was no longer to be at Prato but under the walls of the capital itself. Florence, the council of war thought, with its thousands of republicans and its easily barricaded streets, was an ideal support for the resistance.

While the council of war was still in session, the Spanish had already crossed the borders of the Republic, reached the sources of the Arno, and put the local, poorly armed militia to flight. The ties of the border villages with the Signory were for the most part broken and information was a matter of chance. The more inaccurate the knowledge of the numbers and strength of the Spaniards, the more distinctly were they seen everywhere. Faintheartedness obscured clear vision and caused a general turmoil which proved an obstacle to all military operations.

Not until three days after the Spanish had entered Tuscan territory, and after Machiavelli had urged it vigorously, was the appointment of a commander in chief finally agreed upon. Jacopo Savelli was selected. And Savelli, after the Signory had given him the position, disappeared without leaving a trace. Messengers searched for him in vain throughout the city. In his stead, Niccolo was now the most important man in the military organization. He was given enormous powers. He had to guard the authority of the Signory, using the condottieri of the Republic as well as the militia. His word and his commands were respected and obeyed.

Everyone knew that resistance had been decided upon as a result of his work with the militia. It was he who had overcome the timidity of the Signory and driven it to defend the regime of the populani. But his great powers were of no advantage to him now, just as his small powers had been no handicap at Pisa. He multiplied himself like Krishna, being seen everywhere and nowhere. He rode to Firenzola where two thousand picked soldiers of the militia were encamped nearly three thousand feet up on the slope of the Apennines. They were to threaten the Spanish flank. But there was not a trace of the enemy in Firenzola. From there he rode along the border encouraging local troops, having trenches dug, and ramparts erected in the passes of the Apennines. He tried in vain to get artillery and munitions from Florence to support weak spots in the defense, and to organize detachments on a small scale in all places where the enemy was not. Niccolo was oppressed by the number of turns the situation might take, and found himself living from hand to mouth, as it were. He did not have the army commander's ability to survey a situation easily.

The weakness of Florence, which at the very moment of decision undermined its determination, also affected Machiavelli's energy and weighed upon his military imagination. The weak morale of the Republic sapped her physical power and decreased the number of her troops, the efficiency of her armament, and the courage of her reserve forces. Niccolo was swamped in the flood of national helplessness. His vision was more dependent on the writing desk than even he knew. He had the eyes of the critic, not of the man of action. He could not proceed in the manner of the ideal man of his imagination, could not act as his man of virtù would act. He was not able to take the government under his wing, terrorize the Medicean opposition, inspire all with his own determination, and become a pillar of resistance. The Florentines could not have waged their war more thoughtlessly and more weakly had Machiavelli not been there. He had been present at the council of war and had not raised his voice against the crippling of the defense.

Machiavelli, who impressed the necessity of battle and of firm decision upon the world, did not even think of the significance of the war, of his purpose, or of swift marches and forays. It is true, however, that greater soldiers than he, men who had led fearful massacres and gathered much experience, had also tried to destroy the foe by maneuvering, without giving battle. Even the Spanish General, Pescara, declared, "May God grant me a hundred years of war and not a single day of battle!" The Spaniard, Mendoza, wrote, "One should steal into battle slowly and cautiously, with leaden foot." Many generals thought that if a commander merely moved his own troops well, the enemy, if not destroyed, could be so worn down and exhausted by the problem of providing pay, by lack of provisions, by searing heat and terrible cold, and by the hostility of the population, that he would gladly compromise in order to avoid disaster.

The entire situation, not merely the spiritual weakness of the Tuscans, spoke in favor of using Fabian tactics against the enemy of the Republic. The Holy League was no longer as flourishing as it had once been. Venice and the Pope were not supplying the Spanish with subsidies and Spain sent its own troops no money. The Spanish command was bankrupt; the troops, victorious and impoverished, had neither reserves, munitions, nor artillery. Before the Spaniards entered Tuscany, a loaf of bread and a few figs each day were all that was distributed to each soldier. Had it not been for Cardinal Giovanni Medici and the papal legates among them, they would, in their distress, have signed any sort of compromise.

The Cardinal kept the army from falling apart. He pictured to them the wealth of Florence; stimulated the appetite of their eyes and bellies. He persuaded Viceroy Cardona to move forward faster telling him the resistance of the Florentines had been broken by the Medicean party. He showed him the lists of his agents and spies; told of friends who were throwing water on the Florentines' gunpowder and of others who were in command of Republican troops at the fortifications of Tuscan cities. He spoke of the conspiracy which would break out against the Signory any moment. His words lent wings to the feet of the viceroy, the officers, and the soldiers, and encouraged the cowardly, the brave, the bandits, the invalids, and the wounded. The flood of his oratory drove them on.

On Saturday, August 28, 1512, ten thousand Spaniards stood before the tall, narrow walls of Prato. They surrounded the city and began to fire on the battlements of the fort. Prato remained silent, as if it were an invulnerable fairy castle cast under a spell. It did not return the enemy fire. None of the three thousand men in the garrison dared to climb the walls to shoot. Seeing this lack of courage, Viceroy Cardona sounded the signal for assault. But the Spanish were beaten back from the tops of the palisades. The viceroy, nonplussed at this unexpected opposition, remembered the perilous situation of his army and halted.

The next morning he reviewed his men. "We have no choice," he told them. "Either we starve to death or we take Prato." After this speech the signal for assault was again sounded. The Spaniards, an eyewitness wrote, ran like raging dogs toward the breach in the wall. This hole, like an open window, was little more than four yards high and two wide. The moment the Tuscans saw the first Spaniards passing through the breach, they ran like frightened rats. Along the whole inner wall, from the palisades and bastions, the Tuscans threw away their weapons instead of hurrying to the threatened spot. They fled madly, but found no open gate. They themselves had walled up all the exits. The victors began their terrible, cold-blooded butchery. Not only the soldiers, but everything that bore a human countenance, paid for the hour of its birth. The Spaniards boiled men in oil, quartered them alive, strangled them with cords, ripped out hair with their bare hands, blew bodies full of air with bellows, roasted the soles of men's feet. They tortured until they had found the hiding place of every last gold ducat.

Cardinal Giovanni Medici rode through the city while the massacre was going on. The horror of it put him in a melancholy mood. "The pillaging is not proceeding without some cruelty in killing," he wrote to the Pope. "I feel somewhat displeased at this. But Prato has a good side also. It will serve as a frightful example to others." Even had the Cardinal wished to order a halt to the massacre, none would have obeyed him. "It is difficult," General Pescara declared, "to serve Christ and Mars at the same time." It was on their predilection for such cruelty that the might of the Spanish, the foremost infantry in the world, rested! This cruelty was with them everywhere, gave them unity in combat and impetus in assault. It supplemented experience and replaced drilling which was unknown to them.

Machiavelli's militia, ten thousand strong, which at that time stood idle before the walls of the capital, knew nothing of these furies of battle. The men of the militia had scented neither blood nor booty and they knew neither the privation of long weeks of marching nor the desperation which drives men forward. They had no experience in battle. The hard work and theories of Niccolo were no substitute for the practise which the Spaniards had had in the plains of Calabria, in Lombardy, Africa, Aragon, and Castile.

When he thought of the Roman militia, Machiavelli had erred in a backward direction by fifteen hundred years and in a forward direction by two centuries. He saw correctly that the structure of society conditioned the character of the army, but he identified Florence with ancient Rome to too great an extent. It was to take two hundred years of political and military change for the *misera plebs* to be educated for battle, trained by drill, discipline, and the barracks. The right to march to war for the fatherland had first to be won on the frontiers of Europe by the common men of all countries. At this time the first ingenious and tragic attempt to summon up an entire people collapsed.

The tempest which swept out of Prato scattered the regiments like dry leaves. In the face of such horrors and such frightfulness, the soldiers fled. In Florence, everyone who did not have Medicean sentiments sought to depart or to find some corner into which he could creep and where he could remain unnoticed.

The Signory was ready to dismiss the army in order not to provoke Cardona further. In the terms of surrender, the viceroy demanded the removal of the gonfaloniere, the return of the Medici as private persons, and presented a bill as penalty for the week-long attempt at resistance. He demanded enormous sums for the emperor, for Ferdinand, for himself, and for his army. Only under these conditions was Cardona willing to remain in Prato and not enter Florence. The signori were ready to pay. They declared, however, although with a tremor in their voices, that they could not abandon Soderini. They were willing to pay additional sums if he were permitted to remain in office.

The nobili of the city, in league with the viceroy, settled the question of the gonfaloniere themselves. Within half an hour they drove off the militia guards of the populani and occupied the entrances and exits to the Council Hall, the piazza in front of it, and all the bridges of the city. Triumphantly they fetched a dozen followers of the Medici out of the prison. Thirty young men from bankrupt, noble Florentine families made their way into Soderini's office and dragged the frightened man to the home of one of the nobili. The gonfaloniere was a prisoner, although legally still the head of the Republic.

Francesco Vettori, who was everybody's friend, Soderini's, Machiavelli's, the nobili's, and a supporter of the populani regime, visited the imprisoned president. He consoled him as only a son can console his unfortunate, grey-haired father. Then he hurried to the great hall of the Signory where the magistrates were in session. With folded arms, in a voice choked by tears, Vettori told the populani, who were ready for anything, that in order to save the life of their beloved and worthy president they must remove him from office. The Council was no less touched than Vettori and declared that Soderini's term of office had expired. That same night the president left Florence. The body whose duty it was, and no other, had removed the gonfaloniere. The Constitution was besprinkled with tears, but no one could be said to have done violence to it.

With the help of Spain, Venice, the Pope, and the emperor, the Medici had climbed once more to their old ruling position. By the conspiracy with the nobili they succeeded in a far more delicate task. Despite their invasion, despite their wars, despite Prato, they had not offended against a single letter of the Constitution.

The Medici had learned from their forebears to attain their goals indirectly, through the activities of friends, as though they were not concerned. They had learned to keep up appearances. Even now, after eighteen years of exile, after eighteen years of struggle and intrigue in all the capitals of the world, when they could face, with overwhelmingly superior forces the conquered regime of the populani which they hated so bitterly, they did not want to appear openly contemptuous of the Constitution and the laws. The Medici were afraid to let their fate depend upon the passing victory of foreign armies. They knew that in this city of burghers they could not live in continual enmity with the burghers. They wished to erect their Temple of Power in the cool shadow of legality.

Pursuing this diplomatic course, they left their military garments and their victorious Spanish retinue at the gates of the city. Giuliano Medici entered Florence in all modesty, surrounded by a few friends and wearing the republican red tunic and wide velvet girdle.

III

AFTER DEFEAT

CHAPTER X

Small Joys and Great Sorrows

ON THE morning of September 2nd, 1512, when Machiavelli entered his chancery, the only man missing in the palace of the Signory was Piero Soderini. If one of the officials had not come, he would with good reason have been considered a rebel. He and not the Mediceans would have been manifesting an attitude dangerous to the Constitution. If masters changed, it was the duty of servants to show the loyalty required of them and to keep silence.

The fears and hopes stirring in the clerks gave rise to wild speculations which they discussed with one another without restraint. Their familiar offices seemed as uncomfortable to them as if they had no doors or windows, for they did not know precisely to whom they were to be loyal. On the one hand, the institutions of the populani were still intact; on the other hand, the insignia of the Medici had sprung up overnight and was glittering everywhere in Florence. The clerks felt as if they were at a funeral repast. But they devoted only a few stray thoughts to the vanished Piero Soderini because all their hopes flew toward the House of Medici.

The families of nobili and of populani were not divided along rigid caste lines in the little city of Florence. Friendships, business connections, acquaintances, and marriages, often crossed political lines. Not only the Cardinal but nearly fifty other fortunate persons bore the name Medici or formed part of the family through marriage. There were the Cardinal's brother, his three sisters, his cousins, brothers-in-law, uncles, his numerous nephews, the younger Medici line descended from old Cosimo's brother, and the natural children of the dynasty who had all been legitimatized. To find some link with a member of this numerous family became the major occupation of the day. The memories of the timid, vain, and ambitious became wonderfully clear.

People ransacked the distant past to find friendships, a word or two exchanged in passing, or a greeting, which would give them a claim to being old adherents of the Medici. Machiavelli, too, was among this horde. Like his colleagues in office, he was determined not to lose his position. Until the first of September he had avoided no toil and hesitated before no danger in order to defend Soderini. On September 2nd he no longer was willing to become a martyr for a lost cause. No man is willing to die for a government which tries to maintain itself by surrendering its power piecemeal and for a leader who has fled for a thousand cogent reasons. Niccolo could not approach the Medici through his friends, Francesco Guicciardini and Francesco Vettori. They themselves were too new in the party of the victors and more than busy trying to cover up the trails of their own political journeys. Niccolo was forced to rely on his own pen.

He composed, for a high-ranking woman of the Medici, Alfonsina Orsini, the widow of the expelled Pietro, a detailed description of the Florentine revolution. In it he portrayed clearly the hopes of the populani and the reasons for their defeat. Showing a just impartiality toward Soderini, he awkwardly mentioned the ravaging of Prato and with timid optimism proclaimed the Medici to be his lords and patrons. To Cardinal Giovanni Medici, Niccolo wrote that he should be on his guard against the yapping enemies of Soderini, since they would be only a burden to the new rulers and were capable of building their own party within the party of the restoration. Even this advice was not enough for Machiavelli, so he wrote the Cardinal that the persons who had acquired portions of the property of Lorenzo Medici as a result of Savonarola's revolution should not be seized, "for men complain more when an estate is taken from them than when their father or their brother is killed. The brother or the father will not again awaken. But the next upheaval might return the estate."

Among all the flatterers of Florence, Niccolo, who always boasted to his friends of his skill at dissimulation, revealed himself as the poorest liar. He found nothing wiser to do than offer the victors, who were already hostile toward him, advice which was as unasked for and unpleasant as it was correct. The concept of "Machiavellism" which has been fictionized and made a byword through the centuries, fits no one less than this poor, petty secretary oppressed by the weight of his cares. In spite of his fluent pen, he could not even compose a plain little eulogy. After every sentence which was supposed to bring forth the magical fragrance of pious incense, he slipped back into cold reason.

The misfortune of the man who sees truth and reality is not that he "may" not lie or will not, but that he cannot; he suffers from a literalness bordering on folly. In comparison, how skillfully Niccolo's friends, the masters of Florentine skepticism, could eulogize! On the first of September, Francesco Guicciardini, the sage of thirty years, had composed a memorandum on the consolidation of the republican regime. On the sixth of September, in a new paper, he advocated exactly the opposite. And Jacopo Nardi, the theoretician and historian of the Great Council, knew how to sing hymns to the name of Medici.

The Cardinal and his sister-in-law, who were friendly with Francesco Guicciardini and Jacopo Nardi, and who had sent messages of forgiveness even to Piero Soderini in his exile, both warned the Medici against Machiavelli. If the two Medici had read his memorial, it had only awakened new animosity toward the founder of the militia.

Niccolo, daily more humble and taciturn, was permitted to enter his chancery and take care of records for two months longer—he left the office quickly when his work was done—only because the Medici did not yet enjoy sole rule and still allowed the magistrates of the populani to go on debating in peace over constitutional changes. Like Machiavelli and his colleagues, the gentlemen of the Council and the magistracies were glad to assume officially that nothing had changed. Unofficially, however, their days and nights were full of anxiety as they waited to hear what the Medici would demand. But the Medici would not speak. Their silence was a consuming, withering flame to the magistrates. The Signory thought that by proceeding carefully it would be able to save the basis of the populani regime. It wanted to surprise the Medici by friendly measures, make their position legal. The magistrates, in joint session, therefore decided to dissolve the militia and to change the term of office of the gonfaloniere from life to a year. After a swift election, Florentines who stood close to the Medici were placed in office in all government departments. The Great Council, however, the body of three thousand citizens who made the final decisions, was to continue in existence, although with more limited rights.

From the House of Medici there still came no reply to these reforms. The secret battle of nerves, the exchange of unspoken words and thoughts between Cardinal Giovanni and the populani, was not ended. Giovanni's traits of character, which he forged into political weapons, made the restoration a thing of elegance. He built up his power by his skill in avoiding everything unpleasant, by his disinclination for severity and exertion, by his deliberate slowness, by his habit of never openly saying no, and by his art in trapping his enemies with lies. His sparkling compound of cool dignity, wit, laxness, and generosity was irresistibly attractive. Apparently deeply moved, without a shadow of reproach, he listened to the tales of the many converts and condoned their sins. Weeping bitterly, or impudently denying their pasts, the most prominent members of the recent regime made their peace with the Cardinal. And although not all left Giovanni's room with a new post, none left without great hopes. Piero wrote to his brother, Francesco Guicciardini, "Here things are turning out for the best. The public has been calmed by the affable benevolence of the Medici."

The new friends were, as a matter of fact, dearer to Giovanni than the old. The new were ready to give up everything but the old made demands. The new were silent, but the old declared, "Coming events must take place as we desire them." Both old and new friends, however, were united against the magistrates of the Signory who were still chattering about the Constitution. The heads of populani organizations were, in the Cardinal's eyes, only an isolated few who could not find the smooth, clear path to submissiveness. He made a road for them by sending his brother, Giuliano, into the palace of the moribund populani regime with a few soldiers. At the sight of the victor, the signori grew silent. One signore rose and asked Giuliano what his family wanted. "We want nothing," Giuliano answered, "except guarantees of our freedom and assurances that we shall have equal rights. We want nothing but revision of the Constitution by the loyal people of Florence."

That same evening the bells of the city called the Florentines to a plebiscite which was to take place by a raising of hands in front of the Council Hall. "My people," Savonarola had said twenty years before, "when you hear the bells calling you to the Parliament, arise, draw your swords and cry, 'What do you want? Cannot the Great Council do all that is necessary? What kind of law do you want? Cannot the Great Council make it?' "

This particular evening, however, the tumultuous, but carefully guided Parliament did away with the Great Council, the fundamental force of the previous two decades in Florence. From now on the regime of the Medici was to keep watch in the halls of the three thousand. In front of the Signory, the people, with soldiers scattered among them and occupying all side streets, shouted their enthusiasm for the new Constitution, which was really the old Constitution of Lorenzo Medici. Any one of those present had the right to shout "nay", but it would have been the last word he ever said.

A commission of forty-five men, the *Balia,* whose names were read aloud and who were the staunchest adherents of the Medici, were authorized to appoint a Council of Seventy for a life term, and a Council of One Hundred who were to be chosen every six months. The various boards and magistracies of the Republic continued to meet. But the men in them were guided by invisible strings which were held in the hands of the Balia. The head of the Balia, who never appeared before it, but issued orders from his palaces, was the head of the House of Medici.

After a gonfaloniere had been appointed for a period of two months and most of his personal affairs had been settled, the Cardinal went to Rome. He left Florence, by the law of primogeniture, to his twenty-one year old nephew, Lorenzo. There was time now to examine the clerks of the chanceries more closely. The new masters were not excessively vengeful. They wanted, however, to have their own men, their own spies, and eavesdroppers in the Signory. The officials were inspected one by one as if they were pieces of furniture to see whether they fitted in with the new establishment. Every official strove to seem small and insignificant, no more important than the rug or the cuspidor. Marcello Virgilio, Niccolo's direct superior, was considered the living rubber stamp of his chancery and was permitted to continue in office. He had always been cautious and had always guarded against doing more than his duty.

The considerations, however, which were in his favor spoke for Niccolo's dismissal. Machiavelli would never stop being overzealous, never stop wanting to play politics. It did not matter how humbly he protested his loyalty. The men now in charge of distributing posts were shrewd enough to know that a character such as his could never change. He seemed like an evil spirit from the past, Soderini's most capable aide, the man who had always urged extreme measures against the Medici. Niccolo received a gruff announcement of dismissal, "We remove Niccolo, the son of Bernardo Machiavelli, from his office as Secretary of the Second Chancery and we release him from all his other duties."

The discharged forty-three year old Machiavelli drew up the balance sheet of his life. It was the moment in life when the past, as it had been, and the present, as it was, arose before him. Because he did not believe in God, he stripped the veil of illusion from all his experience, and past and present flowed together into a single ominous picture. Difficult as life had been for him up to this time, his practical tasks had always enabled him to keep up his courage. He had been able to forget himself in the stream of events. He had been able to read the destiny of peoples in the eyes of the mighty. Where was he to go now and what was he to do with his hours, days, and years? What was to be the work of his hands? Dismissed, forbidden to take up any duties, he continued to busy himself with his chancery and tried to give advice to his successor; he bothered his former colleagues so much that they could not get him out of the offices. Then a new command of the Signory delivered the final blow. He was forbidden on pain of imprisonment to enter the Council Hall. This humiliation brought new despair to him. He wept bitterly. When he saw a man without cares he stared after him. Other men could do many things. "But I know nothing of silk or the weaving of wool," he wrote, "nothing of profit and loss. All that I have any knowledge of is the State."

In the service of the State he had remained poverty-stricken. Great as his distress had been up to now, at the end of every month he at least had had a few days' comfort and security. Now he was faced by real poverty. He felt it at his throat, ready any moment to leap upon him. He was ashamed of his own misfortune. "Poverty is making me ridiculous," he wrote. He had never been able to count his pennies. With the freeman's lofty defiance of poverty, he had unconcernedly given away the small sums which so quickly mount to large sums. Now he could no longer do this. He was reduced to his tiny inheritance and he would have to see in the eyes of his wife and four children the silent demand for an accounting.

"I should like to find out," he wrote, "whether Fortune will not finally grow ashamed of kicking me." Destiny, however, seemed to want revenge for his temerity in praising Power in the face of the dark malignity of Fortuna.

Machiavelli was arrested without warning.

Two young Florentines of noble family, Agostino Capponi and Paolo Boscoli, had conceived a ridiculous plot against Giuliano Medici. They intended to kill him. On a scrap of paper they had written the names of a number of men whom they believed ready for rebellion. Machiavelli's name was on this list. Chance helped to betray the conspirators and the childish but compromising paper fell into the hands of the Signory.

Machiavelli was chained in a gloomy, filthy dungeon of the Florentine prison. "On the walls are lice as large as butterflies." The stench choked him. Nearby he could hear the screams of an unfortunate who was chained too high above the floor. One morning he heard the steps of Capponi and Boscoli as they were being led to their deaths. In the minds of these two youths, the pious republic of Savonarola was in conflict with that of the Roman Brutus. They looked on death as a welcome salvation. On their last walk, they tried to prove to the confessor that Thomas Aquinas did not count the violent destruction of a tyrant as a sin. The two of them did not fear death, but they did fear dying as heathens. "Father," Boscoli moaned when they were before the executioner, "drive Brutus out of my mind so that I may leave the world as a Christian."

Although Niccolo had the same enthusiasm for Brutus as Boscoli, he considered the attempt of the conspirators a ridiculous act which now was threatening to draw him down to a ruin he did not deserve. Would his turn come, now that these two had died? His nerves were as little able to endure imprisonment as Savonarola's had been, though the latter had brought his Heaven to prison with him. Niccolo was tortured, drawn up by the rope six times. In the fever of his pain he wrote sonnets to Giuliano proclaiming his loyalty and mentioning their common friends. He praised the Medici while his whole body was still sore from the blows of their servants.

Not the humble tones of his lyre, however, but the confessions of the two conspirators released him after four weeks in the darkness of the cell. He was a free man. But Niccolo did not go home immediately. He wandered about for days in festive Florence, which was celebrating the election of the thirty-seven year old Cardinal, Giovanni Medici, as Pope Leo X.

Such a bacchanal of joy neither Machiavelli nor any of his contemporaries had ever seen. The city was rejoicing uproariously, participating in a gigantic banquet. Wine poured out of the fountains; oxcarts distributed roasts, cake, and barrels of chianti. For three nights in succession, the brother, nephews, and brothers-in-law of the new Pope threw gold ducats from loaded sacks into the crowd. "And when a sack was almost empty," an eyewitness wrote, "the lords and ladies threw it down. Wherever they saw the most people they cast the most sacks." Silver beakers, hats, coats, bonnets, velvets, and silks became a cloud of good fortune that rained down upon the Florentines. The wealthiest families imitated this extravagance in honor of the new Prince of the Church. From the palaces of the Houses of Salviati, Rucellai, and Strozzi, flowed streams of gifts.

From the first day of the restoration on, Niccolo had been placing his hopes on this all-forgiving generosity of the Medici. His mind was still confused from his weeks of imprisonment as he watched the fabulous shower. He knew that the riches being tossed away in Florence were but a fraction of the brilliant papal bounty in Rome itself.

"A stone could sooner fly into the air," Niccolo's acquaintances said, "than the Holy Father save a thousand ducats." Machiavelli writhed when he thought of the literati around the Pope's throne. Their song rang, "Leo gives gold for the silver tones of the lyre." In his first breve, the Pope had proudly proclaimed that he had been brought up by his father Lorenzo among books and codices, surrounded by all the loveliest creations of art. He considered it the duty of the Church to guard and increase libraries, to collect the treasures of antiquity, and to encourage the dreams of architects, painters, sculptors, poets, composers, and historians. He made the best Latinists of Italy his secretaries, representatives, and familiars. The administration of the theologians was forced out of the Chancery of the Curia and replaced by that of the disorderly, madcap humanists.

The literati of all countries made pilgrimages to Rome. The swarm of poets and poetasters persecuted the Holy Father more mercilessly than grumbling Luther at the head of his iconoclasts might have done. Neither in his bedroom nor his bath did Leo find protection against importunates.

He never lost patience, however, and was fond of being called "Patron of Literature". Niccolo looked with sorrowful eyes on the splendor of the libraries of Rome, on the exclusive villas of the courtezans and the open brothels, on the fame, if not the art of Raphael, Bramante, and Michelangelo. He heard of Giovio, the historian, of the theatre, of political free speech and satire, of the papal hunts in the company of European celebrities, and of the table of the banker, Chighi, who served his numerous literary guests with ducats along with the roast. But for him the liberality of Rome was a soap bubble. No path led into these Elysian fields. "Only I," he wrote, "amid so much Florentine good fortune, must remain among the ruins of Pergamon."

However, things which do not kill a man strengthen him. Prison had not only given Niccolo liberty but life. His lethargy was broken. The well of misfortune was infinitely deep, but Niccolo had suffered so much that he now seemed superior to all sorrow and eager only for merriment. Despite his innocence, he felt that only a miracle had rescued him from the abyss of Justice, from indifferent judges and torture. "I am enjoying my regained life," he wrote, "and I think I am dreaming." He had the consolation of the skeptic who tries to live by being ironical with himself.

Niccolo found his way to his own kind, to his comrades in misery, and rejoiced in their foolishness. He sat for hours on a bench in front of his house with a certain Girolamo del Garbo whose wife had died a few days previously. Together they studied every passing woman to see whether she might do for remarriage. He laughed till the tears came at Count Orlando who was infatuated with a boy from Ragusa and whose inane actions knew no bounds. He quarreled for a week with the feeble-minded Tomaso because he had paid four soldi for a pound of veal for a lunch the two were to have together. Toward evening, he and all his friends would go to the home of Donna Sandra di Pero who enjoyed an income from a salon of easy ladies. From the windows of the Donna's house, the friends watched the procession in honor of Pope Leo X. Niccolo's companions danced a religious dance for the newly crowned Prince of the Church and got the girls to play the parts of abbesses and novitiates.

At dawn the friends went home. But Niccolo remained at Sandra's for a week. Here was a refuge from his family, from the festive city, and from the good luck of others. He told the girls a thousand stories of the Pope, of the emperor and of the King of France. He invented gallant fables and unlikely encounters and told them of their many sisters whom he had met in France and Italy. Glad not to have to guard his tongue, Niccolo became as talkative as he had been during the days of his success. The prostitutes sat about him listening with their large, handsome eyes shut, gratefully caressing this warrior of life. These women were more to him than a bottle of wine, more than the consolations of a friend, more than Dante's Beatrice; they were the gifts of circumstance whom wise men enjoy wisely and stupid men stupidly. They had always made life easier for Niccolo. In his darkest days they had been helpful, good-natured and generous. It was their chatter, their laughter, and their crude voices, and not platonic dialogues with bluestockings or duchesses, that gave him courage and consoled him. "Politics have always brought me misfortune," he wrote; "women nothing but joy and pleasure."

He celebrated his escape also with another woman, his mistress Riccia who was plump and almost faithful to him alone. She embraced him joyfully. But he bothered her when she was cooking and he broke her crockery. "These wise men," she complained, "never know what they are doing. They hold everything the wrong way. These wise men are nothing but fools after all."

Finally, however, he had to return home to reality! His good Marietta crossed herself for joy at the sight of him.

Niccolo told her that he had come as quickly as his feet would bring him directly from the cell, and he showed her and the children the marks of the chains on his ankles.

Meanwhile, the authorities had not forgotten him. They did not even grant him the repose of his mournful home. The tormentors in the chanceries could now avenge themselves for all his witticisms and for his days of glory. He was summoned by his successor and had to give an account of his bookkeeping, justify every penny spent. The daily running back and forth to the Council Hall, expecting any day to be thrown back into prison, ended with relief when a decree of banishment to his hereditary estate was proclaimed against him. For at this low point of his existence he still felt the spark that was in him.

"If in the future someone should read our letters," he wrote to Francesco Vettori, "he would at first believe that we are thoroughly earnest men filled with noble and great thoughts. But on turning the page he would reverse his opinion and think that we are merely frivolous, fickle, and shameless, and that we fritter away our energies with inanities. We are, however, but imitating nature, which is so many-sided. And whoever does that is above all reproach."

CHAPTER XI

Misfortune and Immortality

FRANCESCO VETTORI, through whose intercession Machiavelli still hoped to win his way into the graces of the Medici, became the ambassador of Florence to the Holy See. Since the Medici were reigning both in the Vatican and in Tuscany, however, there remained to this high diplomatic office only the name of its former radiance. The post of ambassador became a form of elegant banishment for this man who was well known and well spoken of by all parties and whom a group of the victorious faction, from pure envy, preferred to have away from Florence. To Niccolo, who was pleading for help, Francesco pointed out his own precarious position. But Vettori's exile was upward into the vestibule of Power and Machiavelli's downward into the land of the humble. Vettori's bad luck was that of the fortunate man whose days, even in misfortune, are rich in rewards; Niccolo's was the evil destiny of the poor man who is an eternal victim of events.

Vettori was a clever egoist who would not waste a tear and who did not even allow his friend the pleasure of a complaint. His mind was busy only with himself. The troubles he described to Niccolo were merely pleasant, amorous dilemmas. He received many beautiful Roman women who easily and gladly shed their virtue, so that he suffered only the pain of making the most agreeable of choices. His luxurious dwelling was in the neighborhood of the Vatican gardens. The carefully tended rooms with their rich carpets and fine tableware, the bindings of the books, and the pictures, all bore the stamp of a highly selective taste. This aristocrat was without wealth but also without financial worries, and he could wait patiently and sensibly for the favor of the Holy Father. Reason, which for him consisted in proper moderation, he loved in all things. Even of his mistress he wrote that she possessed "reasonable beauty". He disliked a neighbor because her radiant grace pleased him too much. Such pleasure might become a passion and a vice. For a married man, father of a grown daughter for whom he must provide a dowry, such a neighbor was dangerous tinder and thoroughly unreasonable.

The same reason assured him that he would soon take a seat at the freshly covered board of the Medici. He made his reason hide his burning ambition under a show of indifference. Vettori was in the Vatican daily, but he spoke to the Pope as little as possible. He let the others from all the countries of Europe crowd ahead of him. He would not demand anything for himself or his friends. He often lunched with Cardinal Giulio Medici, the personal representative of the Holy Father, and complained about the horde of Florentine pleaders.

Pope Leo, Vettori declared, had no cause to be grateful to his native city, for it had shown itself more fickle toward the Medici than the loosest woman. In general he thought that those gentlemen who were accustomed, when the mood was on them, to ring the bells of the Signory and call for rebellion should not be treated so leniently. Vettori could easily list the names of those who had been burning with enthusiasm first for Lorenzo the Magnificent, then for Savonarola, then for Soderini, and finally for Leo himself. He did not even keep silent about populani color of his own past. He smiled at it as a venial, understandable, youthful sin. Now, however, years and events had taught him the futility and ugliness of all feverish enthusiasms. The celebrated "liberty" of the Florentines was nothing more than a fantasy, a word that they could play with as children play with snowballs.

"Aside from the utopian Republic of Plato and the one described by the Englishman, Thomas More," Vettori wrote, "there is no form of rule which does not reek of tyranny. All forms of Power have their roots in usurpation."

All sovereignty was to him the rule of one part of the population over the other. The signori, who talked so much about liberty, would do better to think of the logical consequences of this word. With minds obscured by the word liberty, the populace might demand the redistribution of property. Vettori recommended to the Medici that they avoid forming a party based on only one level of the population, whether it be the middle class, the plebs, or the nobili. The Medici should not burden themselves with a party, for a party ordinarily became a caste which raised its voice against its master. If the Medici won the support of the ambitious from all classes Vettori thought that would constitute the firmest basis for rule. Ambitious men not only were inclined to rebellion, but they were also ready to risk their lives. They could be won if they were given the illusion that they were part of the government and that the Power they enjoyed was their own.

Vettori, however, rarely lectured in so stern a tone. As a temperate lover of human infirmity, he was far removed from any rash desire to improve or reform. The advice he gave was discreet and unobtrusive and of a kind which, he said, "should not be written down".

The beautiful and pleasant aspects of life existed, in his opinion, because of the frailty of the world. Deceit was both the basis of earthly existence and the good in that existence. Deceit kept everything alive, shaped thoughts, and released energies. Deceit alone made for progress in human society. Men wracked their brains to find new tricks to deceive other men and the others sharpened their wits to defend themselves against these tricks. Priests were the most skilled masters of deceit and they were the determining force in society; next came the lawyers, then the physicians and astrologists, and finally all secular rulers and their satellites.

Machiavelli was in thorough agreement with his friend on the usefulness of subtlety and artifice. But Niccolo's perception did not stop there. Deceit was to him a second degree necessity. He recognized elemental motives and laws in the life of nations which could not be deflected by any artifice. The politician was no cobbler sewing facts together with the thread of deceit, but a man who quailed before no necessity and who sought to penetrate the obscure future with the eye of his spirit and the force of his character.

Francesco did not quarrel with Niccolo over this difference of opinion in their outline of the eternal problems which beset mankind. Vettori asked his friend, whom he considered the most intelligent of his circle, for reports on various political situations. He promised to hand them to the Pope, hoping thus to aid Niccolo. The Holy Father read the reports but overlooked the name of their author. The timid attempt to help Machiavelli was unsuccessful. Niccolo became inwardly more proud and outwardly more humble.

"The Medici," he wrote to Vettori, "must take me into their service even though, for a beginning, I merely overturn a cliff for them." Francesco apologized for not yet having done anything for him and dropped a hint about his awkwardness at making requests. Since a political career was closed to his fallen friend, he repeatedly tried to amuse Niccolo by describing his amorous adventures. Here Niccolo could not let himself be outdone by Vettori! He wrote numerous little tales in which he appeared as the youthful and always fortunate hero. "I am nearing the fifties, but I permit neither my years to weigh upon me nor rough roads to tire me when it is a question of an amour," he wrote to Vettori.

In reality, however, he was troubled by quite different cares. He whined his complaint in exile like a wounded animal. He tilled the soil on his estate, Sant' Andrea, in the district of Perugia, a day's journey from Florence. His sole link with the world was his correspondence with Vettori. Every morning he arose with the sun, put on peasant's clothes and supervised the work in the fields. He decided to have his tiny forest of oaks cut down, hoping to be able to pay his taxes and more pressing debts with the proceeds. He urged the woodcutters to hurry and inspected the work constantly. Then came the question of selling the wood. Every member of his Florentine society of fools wanted a cord at a special rate. One paid ten lire less than he promised because, he claimed, Niccolo owed him money from a game of cards four years ago. Another, who had bought a wagonload, had his wife, his maids, and his sons help in loading, so that Niccolo had nearly half of the wood stolen from him. He acted quickly and resolutely, declaring that he no longer had any wood for acquaintances.

Each morning, after two or three busy hours, Machiavelli began to feel the threatening silence of the day which was just beginning. The silent soil, the wind rustling through the treetops, and the yellow leaves of autumn covering the earth, angered him and stripped him of his patience. He had to talk, he had to escape from this humdrum nature. Any man was more welcome than none, and he went searching for people and installed himself in the inn on the highway. At the window of the tavern, which was on a level with the street, he spoke to the passers-by, asked them questions and skillfully entangled them in long conversations. He tried to keep them talking to him, and he believed that he was profiting by it. "I hear all sorts of tales, and pay attention to the various tastes and whims and worries of people."

For lunch he went to his home where he met his wife and children. They could eat only what the estate produced. Nothing was bought in the city. Cheese, bread, beans, figs, pears, and smoked meats made up their unchanging fare. After eating he went back to the inn. There he sat for long hours in the company of a butcher, a miller, and two tile-makers. These people were already tired of his stories. He knew their troubles and they knew his. They no longer listened except when he was telling them a particularly spicy tale. Otherwise he had to bow to their wishes. They were in the majority and dictated. Machiavelli played cards and dice, dice and cards with them until he was nearly mad. Often the group quarreled, and their shouting could be heard all over the village.

"So I grow moldy among this rabble," he wrote, "and give free rein to all sorts of scurvy habits."

He never entered his study until it began to grow dark. Here the solitude which he regularly sought at this hour enveloped him; the solitude of his thoughts, not the deep silence of nature. "At the threshold I take off my peasant clothes, dirty and spotted with mud, and don royal and festive garments. Thus worthily dressed, I step among the men of antiquity and, feeling no weariness, forgetting all my troubles, and neither fearing poverty nor dreading death, I live wholly among them. And since Dante says that knowledge is unfruitful unless well retained, I have noted down what I have gained from my intercourse with them."

The golden age of the Roman Republic, as Titus Livius described it, was the epoch he was looking for. He listened to the divine speech of the Will and moved among the troops of Scipio's peasant legions. Fresh and new, without wounds or shadows, he saw the Roman world as it never was. Everything that pleased him he took over uncritically into his book, the *Discourses*. Expert testimony can offer documents to contradict almost every one of his historical instances. But from the whole of the book there arises the impression of an eternal reality. Besides Livy, Polybius and Aristotle were his guiding stars. It was an arbitrary compounding of the elements of antiquity wherein Aristotle with his politics of the city-state and his description of tyranny had more to say for Italy of the fifteenth and sixteenth centuries than Titus Livius. In his political criticism and in his maxims, Niccolo leaned more heavily upon Aristotle than upon the others, even though Livy is mentioned by name more frequently. His own aspirations and that of the century were measured against the ideal standard of two dozen political axioms.

Cesare Borgia, the militia, French, Spanish, and imperial politics, his many legations, the party disputes of the Florentines and their struggles for existence—everything he had learned in the "school of misfortune" as he called his experience—were passed before the infallible judges of antiquity. And in spite of the fact that he fitted his own period into the mold of the past, in spite of the fact that he placed the second century before Christ above the fifteenth and sixteenth centuries, in spite of his intense subjectivity, he repeatedly forced himself to realize that Rome was merely the symbol he was using and that his true subject was Italy and the present. He struggled for objectivity and fled from his own axioms.

He wanted to escape from single examples and generalities in order to set foot upon the firmer soil of experience. Experience was to him more determinative than ideal reason. For Machiavelli, man had been the same since primitive times and would be the same for all times. Human thoughts were always the same in newer guises. The finest and best men, the men who made the best subjects of the State, were as Niccolo contended the men of classic, republican Rome. He had been thinking about these men for a quarter of a century. Now he was describing, classifying them in his *Discourses.*

Why, however, if man always remained the same, did he not have the superiority of pre-Christian times? "Because he had lost the Roman experience!" Niccolo answered. In order to show the man of the present the heights man had attained in the Livian epoch, Niccolo described the experiences of Rome. Classic experience was in his eyes summed up in the institutions of the Republic. These institutions had arisen in the course of a long process of internal class struggles fought in a free city. Rome, the conqueror of the world, had been born during this struggle between the haves and the have-nots for the division of property. The freedom of action resulting from this internal class conflict had kept alive in Rome all the virtues of discipline and of war.

"If we condemn the struggles between the Roman common people and the nobility," Machiavelli wrote, "then we are carping at the primary cause of the retention of Roman liberty. We are then observing the noise and the tumult of these struggles rather than the good effects which resulted from them. We are then not considering that in every republic the aims of the nobles and of the people are at variance and that from their discord come all laws which confer liberty."

Nothing, however, is more difficult than obtaining liberty, preserving her, and guarding her against assaults from without. Nothing is rarer than that liberty should become an event of universal, historic significance. Liberty, which Niccolo defined as "the golden age in which everyone has his own opinion and the right to defend it", can be menaced by the republican privilege of censure, for this often becomes unrestrained slander. The have-nots are eager to avenge themselves by robbing the others; they are eager to acquire wealth of their own and to fill the offices their enemies abuse. Liberty is threatened by the people themselves. Because they have been so often deceived, they no longer place their trust in any man and rush inevitably to their destruction with the motto which Dante had already voiced, "Long live my death; die, my life!"

As a consequence of the mistakes, infirmities and omissions of rulers, bold men are capable of killing freedom in unforeseen, hidden ways. Machiavelli traced all the paths which a would-be dictator must tread. He wanted to write down as an eternal warning the alluring ideas which the sight of a tyrant created in the mass of men and the hopes of the propertied minorities which drove them into the arms of an autocrat. His pen eavesdropped on all the moods, all the general situations and particular factors which destroy liberty.

As a check to the victorious, autocratic individual, he outlined all the possibilities for conspiracy. He wrote the most telling pages that have ever been written about tyrannicide. Here his dramatic, theatrical turn of mind united with his sense of political reality to create for posterity the most fascinating chapters in historical literature. Machiavelli followed the political assassin step by step. He looked into his soul, discovered his fears. He was with him at the first conception of the murder, with him when he was assailed by doubts, when he took counsel with others, when he betrayed himself by want of caution, when his hand trembled, when he drove the dagger deep into the breast of his foe, when his deed failed, when he was seized, and when he was led to the scaffold. Niccolo warned against playing with assassination. "Without having made the test, let no one depend upon his courage in such great matters . . . The majesty of the prince and the respect which his presence inspires is so great that the murderer easily becomes confused and timid."

Niccolo did not lose track of his subject, however, for he analyzed all the methods and motives of conspirators. He pointed out that the attempts at tyrannicide which were likely to be most successful were made by persons who were either old or new friends of the prince, persons in other words who were close to the prince and who had turned against him. Many such assassinations occurred as much because the prince's benevolence was too great as because his misdeeds and offences were monstrous. "Princes must not raise their favorites to such an eminence that there remains no space between them and the throne and nothing still to be desired in between. Otherwise they will rarely die a natural death."

He then described the "grand tyrannicide", which has its origin in some man's consuming desire to free his native land from enslavement by a single individual. "From such attacks no tyrant can guard himself unless he curbs his appetite for unlimited power. Since, however, none do this, most tyrants come to a bad end."

He told all tyrants to their faces, "The prince must be on his guard, for he can never so rob a man that there remains to him no knife by which he can avenge himself."

Although the threat of tyrannicide was to Machiavelli liberty's act of desperation, her final, uncertain attempt to escape extinction, he felt that dictatorship by law was her constant protection against internal and external dangers. "The ordinary course of affairs in republics is dilatory," he wrote. "No council or magistrate can decide everything alone . . . Much time passes before all the various opinions and desires have been brought under one head. But danger does not wait."

The virtues of liberty must not cause her to become a hunted animal! It is her duty to maintain a front of warlike energy. The transient necessity of putting Power into a single hand should not be left to the last moment. Power should not become the plaything of uncontrollable forces. In a republic, even in the face of monstrous perils, none should be permitted to proclaim himself dictator at his own pleasure. No man should be allowed fortuitously to become the man of the hour. The lawgiver in a free State must be empowered to provide for dictatorship.

The idea or the name dictatorship cannot be harmful to liberty if the checks and balances among the governing forces are just and proper. "Neither the word nor the office of dictator reduced Rome to bondage . . . Had the title of dictator not existed in Rome, some other title would have been found. Power easily creates names for itself, but names do not create Power."

Suddenly Machiavelli's work came to a halt. The chapters he had begun, his notes and his books, seemed alike of no importance to him. Time was no longer meaningless and the hours struck loudly impressing him with the fact of their passing. Niccolo was no longer looking on Rome, liberty and virtù. He could now see nothing but his room, the little room with the barred window which served as his office during the day and which smelled of dung. Only yesterday he had been thinking that he could capture in clauses and sentences the new thoughts which no one yet dreamed of, but now he suddenly saw that the consolation which writing gave him was an evil drug. It cast a magic spell over his miserable condition. It caressed him during the long evenings as only thoughts can caress. The most petty post in the Signory or the most obscure place at a desk in the Vatican Chancery would have been a tremendous step upward in comparison with this meditation in poverty and exile.

Machiavelli had received a letter from Vettori. There, stated with the nonchalance of the man without cares, stood the news that the Pope was thinking of giving his brother Giovanni and his cousin Lorenzo official positions. To Niccolo, who had never had ambitions to be a scholar, who had studied Livy to find fundamental principles for the present, not the truths of the past, this news from his friend seemed to be a supreme command to act immediately. What did the *Discourses* mean to him? Of what use were they to him? Except for a dozen or so friends, no one would read them. They would bring him nothing, not even a bottle of wine or a day's journey to Florence. Why write in general about Power? Why not think for the Powerful themselves, for the few who were in a position to reward the writers of books?

He extracted material for the *Prince* from the *Discourses,* which he laid aside with relief and completed eventually only after years of spasmodic work at them. He wrote the *Prince* swiftly, within the space of a few months, and dedicated the work to Lorenzo Medici. "I have written a small book, *De principatibus* . . . It will undoubtedly be welcome to a prince and especially to one who has newly acquired sovereignty . . . The strait necessity which oppresses me impelled the dedication."

He had made up his mind to flatter, to use his pen to prove to the Medici, "that I have neither squandered nor idled away the fifteen years I have devoted to the study of statecraft". Man, however, is master neither of his good nor his bad intentions. He is governed in his actions not by one, but by countless motives. Machiavelli vacillated. The wish to increase the might of the Medici appealed to him, yet at the same time a free Rome appeared before his inner vision. He wanted to have faith in Italy, but could not refrain from laughing at the disunion of the princes and at the totally worthless soldiery. Suddenly in the midst of his work a knowledge of the real condition of Italy broke upon him in his solitude and revealed to him the shape of worlds in the making. His own wretched plight seemed but a reflection of Italy's condition. He wept over himself and over Italy simultaneously. He was no longer his own man, but the begging prophet of the most beautiful and the most unhappy land in Europe.

Italy's inhabitants, he wrote, "have fallen to the lowest depths of misery. They are more enslaved than the Israelites, more oppressed than the Persians, more scattered than the Athenians. They are without a leader, without order, beaten, plundered, torn, and overrun by foreigners."

With vivid, stunning clarity, the wonderful opportunities of the Medici presented themselves to him. For the first time, Tuscany and Rome, all the territory washed by the waters of the Adriatic and the Mediterannean from Naples to the plain of the Po, made up *one* country in the hands of one family, the Medici. Niccolo's hopes were the same as those of the three soldiers, Scharnhorst, Gneisenau, and Clausewitz, who three centuries later transformed Prussia into Germany; and as those of Cavour in the nineteenth century, who created a united Italy out of Piedmont.

In order to make Rome and Tuscany together the pivot of national independence, a man of virtù, a man of mighty ambitions, a deliverer must appear. "At this time Italy can place her hopes in nothing but your illustrious House," Machiavelli wrote Lorenzo Medici, the ruler of Florence. Niccolo dreamt for Lorenzo the dream of Power and with his pen he sought to furrow the fields of Italy more deeply than all the plows in the country. He tried to lure Lorenzo not only by the magnificence, but also by the difficulties of the task. "For a new ruler," the *Prince* reads, "it is a gift of fortune when enemies rise up against him and he has the opportunity to overcome them and thus to climb upward upon the ladder his enemies hold for him."

In order to prove his point, Niccolo adduced as emphatic examples for Lorenzo the establishers of new States of his own time. He cited Cesare Borgia above all others because he had created the ecclesiastical state out of nothingness and had had far fewer resources with which to build up his Power. Niccolo would have liked to pour the spirit of Cesare, his far reaching vision, his shrewd cunning, and his sanguinary boldness into Lorenzo's soul. Why should not the methods successful in the Ecclesiastical State be successful in all Italy? Niccolo sang Lorenzo the siren song of another founder of a State, Ferdinand of Spain.

In his fifteen years of service Machiavelli had always felt the danger of Spain. He shuddered at Ferdinand and was fascinated by his baseness which "it was not well to name". He could not restrain his admiration for the manner in which Ferdinand, king of a torn land, mounted a powerless throne and then "with the money of the Church and of the people . . . always under the cloak of religion . . . with a shamelessness which was unparalleled, first drove the Maranos, the baptized Jews, from his kingdom, created an army with their money during the war itself, and then devoted himself with a pious cruelty to making war on Africa, invading Italy, and finally attacking France . . . thereby keeping the minds of his subjects in suspense and admiration." Machiavelli recommended these methods to the Medici. Ferdinand was to him, and must also be to the Medici, the great master who permitted his will and his intellect to submit only to the law of prudence. Ferdinand allowed his subjects free rein to exercise their murderous impulses and evil instincts, so long as these did not interfere with his goal. "And he always preached peace and good faith."

Ferdinand and Cesare Borgia were to become the spirit of the Medicean dictatorship over Italy.

Had Machiavelli forgotten his song of liberty in the *Discourses?* Were the melodies he had sung there merely the fantasy of a dreamer, and were the principles of the *Prince* the truths of a panderer? No! The world as it was, and not the author of the *Prince,* had caused the abandonment of the ideals of liberty in the *Discourses* because those ideals were unrealistic. Niccolo had not buried his image of liberty. Even in the *Discourses* he had never been a soft-minded, prettifying author who obscured the outlines of things by bowing over his papers and causing the true pictures of life and death to be distorted. "He who gives a republic a constitution and laws must take it for granted that all men are evil," the *Discourses* declare. And in the *Discourses* as well as in the *Prince* he speaks of the duty of setting up a dictatorship for self-preservation. "Republics which in a time of urgent danger do not take refuge in dictatorship or some similar power will always be ruined when difficulties mount." Indeed, dictatorship of this kind had meant liberty to Rome.

Italy of the year 1514, however, the Italy of the *Prince*, which was constantly being threatened with dismemberment by Emperor Maximilian, Ferdinand of Spain, and the King of France, had no Roman Republics. The Peninsula was a mosaic of powerless States with a structure which had already been discarded by the rest of Europe.

In face of this weakness, no politically trained man, no man who was acquainted with the whole and with the details of the whole, could hope for a revolt from below. In Niccolo's opinion, only a mighty sword, wielded from above, at the head of an armed people's militia, could both eliminate the last traces of medievalism and fight the foreign enemy. Theoretically Machiavelli stopped in Italy the gap filled in Spain by Ferdinand and in France by Louis. But he was ensnaring his mind in a romantic view of liberty.

Only a united Italy could become the realm of liberty. Dictatorship, however, could serve during the transition and could combat both external enemies and internal flabbiness and decay. It could work as a means of compulsion and reform. The soldier who reorganized the scrapped Florentine militia and used it dictatorially to wage war against the barbarians would be preparing the way for future liberty. Moreover, the dictator would at least be teaching the Italians to observe the laws. For liberty can never maintain itself without respect for law. The dictator, who was called for by every factor of the political situation, would bring liberty in his train. The Power of the ideal dictator would so order and arrange the House of State that the builder would become superfluous. Even if the way was muddy, the goal was clean. To be sure, Niccolo wrote, "in everything there is hidden an evil proper to it." If, however, Lorenzo Medici were really the deliverer, then he would also have the strength to make himself superfluous by regenerating the entire body politic.

Once he had declared himself a partisan of Lorenzo Medici's dictatorship, Niccolo was no longer satisfied with giving examples and summoning to action in general terms. He wanted to give detailed instructions and tell the dictator how he was to conduct himself every hour of the day. He wished Lorenzo to be no tyrant of the old school, no hysteric about Power who trembled at his own shadow and touched himself in the morning to find out whether he were still living. Such men were eventually destroyed by the intrigues of friends or murdered by their own families. Just like the dictator in the Roman Republic, he was to be free to make his own decisions and possess independent command over the army. His rule was to have a broad basis of popular support. The people's dictator of the *Discourses* appears again in the *Prince!*

The image of Cesare Borgia, the memory of the way the Pope's son caressed his murderers with one hand and the common people with the other, became a permanent part of Machiavelli's thinking. He believed that only those dictators understood their trade "who have the mass of the people on their side and the lords against them. For then their power has a stronger basis than when they have the people against them and the nobility with them." This ancient observation and teaching which Aristotle, Thucydides, and Xenophon had already made before him, the theory of plebeian tyranny, had been forgotten during the Middle Ages because the territories of the feudal lords were small and narrow. The Church alone had remained faithful to this Greek axiom. Niccolo rescued the theory from oblivion. He felt that the common people were more loyal and dependable, more easily ruled, than conspiring nobili or an obstinate aristocracy. The internal struggle of dictatorship must be directed against the upper class.

Lorenzo Medici was to reign through the love of the populace, not through fortifications. Like his grandfather of the same name, he was to "show attention to the guilds and societies, and sometimes come to their meetings, offering an example of courtesy and generosity, but always maintaining the dignity of his station, for this he must not in any circumstance allow to be diminished." Lorenzo was to be an enlightened, unprejudiced despot, sensitive to all the eddies and currents of Power.

Machiavelli's crowning of Lorenzo, however, did not accord with the actual conditions in Rome and Florence. Lorenzo, who owes his immortality in the memory of men solely to the fact that Niccolo dedicated the *Prince* to him, was an arrogant young man. He had neither ideas nor political ambitions. Vanity, selfishness, and family intrigues filled his life. His highest goal was to sit in state as the master of a princely court. He surrounded himself in Florence with a circle of aristocratic young men. Tabards of heavy silk, servants' liveries, embroidered or emblazoned arms, the colors of the tapestries in his rooms, knicknacks and beautifully carved furniture—these were his passions. He often sought solitude, and his associates considered him a dreamer. By night he roamed through the streets in disguise to pick his women from among the people. He thought that he would never be a real prince in Florence, still a Republic according to its Constitution, until he had established his legitimacy by marrying a duchess of the reigning family of France.

All his political activity was directed toward becoming

a kinsman of the King of France. Francesco Vettori, who had risen swiftly in the favor of the Medici, became his trusted emissary and negotiated for the hand of the bride in France. Lorenzo revealed his fears and cares to Vettori. "We must make my royal marriage our major concern," he wrote to him. "I think of nothing else, desire nothing else. Only thus can I share in the good fortune of the papacy . . . The kin and nephews of the Popes have always in the past been so pursued by misfortune that I continually think of nothing but how I can guard myself against an ill fate. I see no other way than that of a royal marriage." In order to eliminate all the barriers that stood in the way of this marriage, Lorenzo and Vettori, as far as it lay in their power, followed a course at odds with the policies of Leo X, who did not want to bind himself exclusively to France. When the king finally married Lorenzo to his kinswoman, Madelaine de la Tour d'Auvergne,[1] Lorenzo became nothing more than a tool of Paris.

One forenoon, before the hunt with his greyhounds in the garden of his palace, a lackey brought him a copy of the *Prince,* handsomely handwritten on parchment. He did not take a second look at it. In the evening, after the hunt, he saw the carefully bound manuscript on the desk of his seldom used workroom. Lorenzo recognized the binding. He read the name of the author, rang for a servant, and ordered him to take two bottles of wine to Machiavelli as a sign of his gratitude.

Aside from a few friends, for whom the faithful Buonaccorsi industriously copied out the manuscript of the *Prince,* no one was the least concerned about the book. In vain Niccolo waited for even the faintest echo. He felt that he had written in water. He never lived even to see the book in print.

[1] Out of this marriage was born Catherine di Medici, Queen of France.

The consequences which the *Prince* was to have through the centuries seemed to be punishing the despairing Niccolo with the torment of failure that the words of the Evangelist might be fulfilled, "It must needs be that offences come; but woe to that man by whom the offence cometh."

CHAPTER XII

In the Service of the Medici

MACHIAVELLI remained in the country longer than his banishment required. For over five years more, necessity forced on him the selfsame, narrow peasant existence. During this period, in the course of which age was beginning to creep upon him, the stream of his experiences, thoughts, and melancholias found the firm channel of regular, patient work. Cast away on a lonely island of misfortune, he accused, cursed, and lamented—and wrote the best prose in Italy. He completed the *Discourses,* began his book on the art of war, wrote novellas, comedies, carnival songs, bad occasional poems and a dialogue on language.

He was an alien among the literati. No one mentioned him. Every common rhymester, comedian, historian or storyteller was regarded more highly than this fifty year old man who for long years sat at his lamp in the evening and with the energy of a youth described the men of his world. In his *Orlando Furioso,* Ariosto had mentioned every writer in Italy, omitting Niccolo alone. "If you meet Ariosto in Rome," he asked a friend, "send him my regards. Tell him, too, that he forgot me alone like a dog among so many poets."

Niccolo's patience was unassailable. He wrote the best comedy in Italy up to his time, *Mandragola.* In it he slashed at the class of men who he believed had persecuted him most bitterly, the hypocrites! Machiavelli was on the trail of Tartuffe, and he showed him in the garb of a priest. Timoteo, the father confessor in *Mandragola,* condones everything in return for money. He proves that nothing is more honorable than that a nun in a convent should practice abortion, for thus the honor of the convent and of her family are saved. He proves to a virtuous woman of the middle class, Lucretia, whose husband is sterile, that it is by no means a sin for her to bear a child. For it is a worthy deed to make the gift of a new-born human being to Heaven. The good, he says to Lucretia, must never be avoided for fear of evil.

All the characters in this play—the husband, the mother, and the acquaintances of Lucretia—unite to bring about the downfall of virtue. The characters are placed in every imaginable situation, so that not even a saint can decide who is good and who is evil. The fools make sage remarks, and the sages talk like fools. And Lucretia, still virtuous in the third act, believes in the fourth that her lewd and inquisitive mother, her stupid husband, and her basely treacherous father-confessor are expressing the will of God, though in fact they are merely trying to sweeten lust by adding the syrup of good conscience.

Among Niccolo's friends and acquaintances, *Mandragola* inspired enthusiastic merriment. Day after day messengers brought congratulations, requests, invitations, and promises to him. *Mandragola* was played in villas, at banquets, and by itinerant troupes. A wealthy Florentine merchant had it produced in his garden in the presence of members of the Medici family who also had it performed. In Faenza, Bologna, Venice, and Rome as well, *Mandragola* was greeted jubilantly. Fifteen years in the service of the State and seven years of literary free-lancing in the service of Power had not made his name as well known as this comedy. Niccolo had had to leave public life as a clerk; he greeted it again as a poet.

Mandragola did not entirely free Niccolo of cares. But he no longer had the feeling that his bad luck was an incurable disease. He could listen to the soft music of suppressed hopes. His literary success made it easier for his friends in high places to work in his behalf. Vettori, Guicciardini, and the wealthy Filippo Strozzi no longer had to talk in favor of a bird of ill omen, for Niccolo was now a hero of the hour and his name was its own recommendation. Leo X thought he already had plenty of political advisers. But a man who could write good dialogue for the stage was no ordinary pleader and he might perhaps have something new to say in politics. For the first time the Pope was inclined to listen when Machiavelli's name was called to his attention. He asked to see the play and made general promises to help Niccolo, although he did not rush to fulfil them. Machiavelli waited for political favor and took his fill of enjoyment from the success of *Mandragola.* The unpredictable, mysterious combination of events which brings a man recognition was now helping Niccolo at last, in the autumn of his life. In spite of all his new joys, however, his deep sigh for his lost political life could be heard. He pays his respects and offers his excuses in the prologue to *Mandragola:*

> "It is denied to me in other realms
> To test the talents given unto me,
> For my endeavors are unrecognized."

After long years of loneliness, the lights, sounds, masks, and faces of the stage were a fairyland become reality. Barbara, the actress who took the leading role in *Mandragola,* became his mistress. She was a married woman who, whether she liked it or not, was soon to celebrate her fortieth year. With thorough unconcern she would sing all the ballads of Tuscany and all the street songs of Florence. She could imitate the voices of priests and self-important magistrates perfectly. Barbara's circle was a joyous company which greeted the morning reveling, slept through the day, and celebrated every evening anew. Here Niccolo's witticisms found appreciation in an audience eager to laugh. He and Barbara tossed sallies back and forth. They outshouted all other voices, put their own good spirits at the disposal of their friends, and were always the last to go home. "Tell Machiavelli," Francesco Vettori wrote to a friend, "that it is much more pleasant to eat with Barbara of evenings than to be here in Rome at mealtimes waiting behind a door to pay respects."

Niccolo, who could get nothing definite for himself in Rome, tried to help his mistress. He wanted Filippo Strozzi to procure her an engagement as a singer in the Vatican. Niccolo was her impresario; he wrote songs for her and studied the texts and the music with her. He wanted his friend, Guicciardini, the papal governor, to make a tour of the Romagna possible for her. Niccolo wrote to him, "Prepare lodgings for Barbara among monks, and if they do not lose their heads, then I am not worth a centesimo." Guicciardini, ordinarily sober-minded and austere, was all excited about this tour. He declared that all other affairs of his office ended with uncertain success, "but if we make efforts to further the production of a comedy, we at least do not risk wasting our time."

As Niccolo worked for Barbara in Rome, so Barbara worked for Niccolo in Florence. After his dismissal he had become a citizen of the second class which meant that according to the letter of the law he could never again hold office. The good Barbara, however, had other means of persuading the gentlemen of the Signory than those of Filippo Strozzi and other high protectors of her friend. Machiavelli was again made eligible to hold political office; he was officially rehabilitated. The historian Nerli wrote to his friend, Niccolo, that this was due to Barbara.

Even the literary circles in Florence were interested in Machiavelli. The Rucellai family, relatives of the Medici, opened the gates of their gardens to him. In the palace of the

Rucellai, which housed the wealth of generations, art and literature were happily united in the best Tuscan tradition.

Cosimo Rucellai, the youngest son of the family, lying paralyzed on a sedan chair, held a literary court. In the shade of great trees and in the peaceful stillness of the garden, professors, poets, Latinists, and novelists spoke of ancient Rome, Hellas, and the future of Italy. Niccolo frequently irritated the professional scholars by asserting that the savants of the pulpit, to be sure, knew everything, but, alas! no more than everything. His *Discourses,* which he dedicated to the head of the house, Cosimo Rucellai, and his dialogue, the *Art of War,* which was a post-mortem theory based on his experience as founder of the militia, soon brought him high esteem.

From time to time, literary conversations drifted off into political discussions which troubled the pleasant harmony of the garden. Although Cosimo Rucellai was not happy when their discussions sounded like the meetings of a political club, and although he preferred to hear nothing of factional struggles, he nevertheless avoided patronizing his friends and directing their conversations. But more and more frequently notes of dissatisfaction from the city echoed in the free-flowing talk and the somewhat formalized debates, which usually lasted from early afternoon until the garden grew dark.

The death of Lorenzo Medici, who died in his twenty-seventh year already an old man, gave the populani an unhoped for opportunity to show their discontent without danger of punishment. A number of *priori* from the guilds walked in Lorenzo's funeral procession wearing red republican tunics. Florence gave the dead man a hopeful, joyous escort. In the light of candles, behind mourning veils and black pennants, the citizens congratulated one another as if they were entering into the inheritance of some great fortune. Many actually thought they would be able to inherit the government of the city. But the Florentines were united more by their common ridicule of the elegant, dissipated, tyrannical arrogance of the deceased than by their love of liberty.

The nephew of the Holy Father, Cardinal Giulio, who was staying in Florence as the successor to Lorenzo, recognized this hostile temper. Giulio had always had nothing but contempt for Lorenzo's indolent living and he was inclined to conciliate all classes of the population, the extreme nobili as well as the populani. He thought that he might most easily hear the desires of the city by listening to the conversation in Rucellai's garden. But instead he was received with orations on liberty.

Youths of the upper class declared, with eyes alight, that the Republic alone could become the source of a clean government. The Cardinal was an unprejudiced, patient, and experienced man. He had hoped to hear practical suggestions here, and he heard nothing but unrealistic fancies. Everyone, he answered, should have learned from experience by now that the Florentines, fond of innovations as they were, could not live without an overlord. Had not the Signory of its own free will once elected Piero Soderini as gonfaloniere for life? Why should not the Florentines voluntarily put their faith in a Medici who would bring wealth to Tuscany and support the country in the face of the world with the high authority of his family and of the Holy See?

The Cardinal had his guards in the city, his men sat in all important offices, and the power of the Pope protected him. He had nothing to fear. Least of all could these literati hold any danger for him. Giulio, however, all his life had liked to listen to advice. His inborn wavering sought direction from the thoughts of others. His liking for advice and negotiation gave Giulio's continual vacillation the appearance of profound reflection. The Cardinal asked Rucellai's guests, among whom Machiavelli was included, for opinions on the present and the future of Florence.

In his memorial, Niccolo proceeded on the assumption that the dissatisfaction with the Medici was recognized. "There are two ways," he declared, "to resolve the crisis. It can be done either by intimidating the citizens in such a manner that they will no longer dare to speak when they are not spoken to, as Lorenzo of blessed memory did, or by so managing the Constitution of the city that they can govern by themselves and the Cardinal need merely supervise them from a distance. The second way guards against dangers and vexations, the first only against vexations." Machiavelli recommended, as the sole device against discontent, that the Great Council be reestablished and the elections influenced by a secret system. The rule of the Medici would thus be in no danger because the Cardinal would continue to hold the most important offices of the Republic. He would be in command of the army, of the financial system, and the administration of justice. For the future, however, when the House of Medici had passed out of existence, Niccolo demanded complete liberty for Florence.

Machiavelli wrote as if he did not know that the great ambition of the Medici was the achievement of a frictionless sovereignty for their dynasty. In the Florentine palace of the Cardinal, two boys were being educated for Power. One of them, Ippolito, nephew of Leo X, was the son of Giuliano by his Ferrarese mistress; the other, Alessandro, was the son of the late Lorenzo by the wife of a drayman. The Cardinal himself was an illegitimate son whose birth records had been falsified in order to clear the way for his entrance into the Church. He made the two Medici bastards his successors and attempted to keep the younger line, descended from Cosimo, *pater patriae*, from Power.

Giulio did not take Niccolo's memorial amiss. The Cardinal saw that Machiavelli was trying to square the circle and to satisfy at once the Medicean demands for supremacy and the ideals of the republicans. The candor of Machiavelli's opinions pleased him. What was left unsaid pleased him equally well. The Cardinal found concrete proposals in the memorandum and he expressed his satisfaction. Such words of recognition always raced through the city, and everyone who heard them added his bit. Niccolo's friends declared that his hour had come. Filippo Strozzi called him a "man with a great future". Rumor had it that Machiavelli was to accompany the Cardinal to France; other rumors declared that there no longer stood anything in the way of his recovering his old post in the Signory. Niccolo waited in a fever of expectancy. But the whims and favor of the mighty are unpredictable. The suspicious Cardinal was not to be won as easily or as quickly as the applauding spectators in the theatre. Contrary to the practise of all the other Medici, Giulio liked to test the patience of converts. Not until a year had passed was Machiavelli sent for.

How glad he would be to abandon his literary successes for the turbulent sea of political life! From Machiavelli's house to the Signory was but twenty minutes' walk. Every step was bringing him closer to Power, every step cast his imagination further under a spell. Was the world of action really opening up to him? And once he had won the confidence of the Cardinal, would it not be easy to enter upon the paths that led to his goals? When he arrived at the second floor of the Council Hall his dreams were suddenly dashed. The secretary informed him that it pleased the Cardinal to send him, Niccolo, to neighboring Lucca. It was an unimportant, unpolitical mission for which any ordinary jurist would have done. In Lucca, Machiavelli was to fight for the private demands of some Tuscan citizens. He consoled himself quickly, however. After all, the Cardinal was not responsible for his hopes. And this task, minor as it was, still meant the first outward expression of Medicean favor.

Burdened with legal drudgery, Niccolo had to remain in Lucca for several months. He had a great deal of time on his hands. In his days of despair, literature had shown him the way to success. Since his good luck with *Mandragola* he recognized writing as a bridge which led to reconciliation with himself and the world. And he used the bridge. He wrote for his friends in the garden of Rucellai the romantic life story of Castruccio Castracani, a prince of Lucca at the beginning of the fourteenth century. In this so-called biography, Niccolo developed the characteristics which he had demanded of a ruler in the *Prince*. "Grateful to his friends, but terrible to his enemies; just to his subjects, faithless to strangers; he never sought to overcome by force those whom he could overcome by deceit, for he was wont to say that it was victory that brought glory and not the manner of securing it . . . He used to say that God is a lover of strong men, for one always sees that the weak are punished by the strong."

This little book aroused great enthusiasm among the guests when it was read aloud in the gardens of the Rucellai. Even though a few professors pointed out that the portrayal of Castruccio was a product more of the imagination than of reality, the majority believed that Niccolo was the man destined to write the history of Florence. He should be given charge of the chronicles of Tuscany. He alone, they declared, would be able to make dry facts live. The Cardinal and the Pope put in a word for Niccolo. A yearly pension of one hundred ducats was granted him.

Some of the young men of the Rucellai garden had quite a different conception of politics from Niccolo. Brutus, liberty, and the Republic still lurked in their minds. At the news of the death of Pope Leo X, they thought the moment had come to rid themselves and Florence of his nephew, the Cardinal. Supported by the brother of Gonfaloniere Soderini, they plotted the murder of the lenient ruler, Giulio. The heads of the conspiracy were close friends of Niccolo, intellectual followers to whom he had dedicated the *Discourses* and the *Life of Castruccio,* disciples who quoted his phrases enthusiastically and everywhere proclaimed his fame. Nerli declared that the attempt at assassination came fresh from the chapter on conspiracies in the *Discourses.* "Had these youths understood Machiavelli better, however, they either would never have done the deed or they would have gone about their work far more circumspectly." A friend wrote to him that Nerli's words, kindly as they were, nevertheless established a direct connection between him and the assassins. What would his enemies, what would the Cardinal say?

Once more the past rose up to threaten Niccolo. Circumstances spoke against him a thousand times more strongly than they had ten years before when he had had to pay for the confused fervor of two republican youths. The Cardinal, however, did not believe for a moment in Niccolo's complicity. Official historians are not wont to brandish daggers. Giulio, as head of the family, had buried all rancor against Niccolo.

Machiavelli did not attempt to return this lukewarm Medicean favor by kowtowing to the Medici in his history of Florence. He was no imprisoned writer or domestic servant industriously weaving laurel-wreaths for his employer. His panoramic view of the transition in Europe, of the make-up of the army, and of the party conflicts in Florence, was so clear that he forgot that his real commission was to fabricate a court history for the Medici. He wrote to Guicciardini that the work was a joy to him because it enabled him to indict the princes who had done everything possible to destroy Italy.

Niccolo was contributing to the communal spirit of liberty which for more than a century had animated all systems and doctrines, agitated studios and academies, and stirred aristocratic and Platonic circles. This liberty, with its blemishes, its pamphlets, its hollow audacities, and its wanton arrogance, stamped its brand on the Florentine-Roman Renaissance and particularly on the Medicean period. Intellectual independence and freedom of research are not consequences of the Reformation or of the French Revolution. They were first realized in the pre-Lutheran Curia. The Church in its wisdom had fed even its own antithesis. Before the Reformation forced the Holy See to frown upon its former tolerance, Catholicism had been so many-sided that it could accommodate the various phenomena of genius. It had been the grand home of mankind where were gathered the splendor and the poetry of all things new and old, of all great thoughts and intense sensations. The Popes had felt no contradiction between truth and the interests of the ecclesiastical organization. They felt as little imperiled by science as by the fact that two times two were four.

The Church gave intellectuals their daily bread. And the giver is always the master. These masters were not parvenus. They were imbued with the idea of the dignity of man, man who was the image of God. Since the dependence of writers upon patrons was a fact of nature like disease or death, it was more bearable to be dependent upon princes than upon the mass of the people. Between intellectual men and an aristocracy there could exist a certain concord within the framework of dependency which could not possibly exist between intellectuals and the masses.

Machiavelli and the circle of political and historical thinkers of his epoch sought to reconcile by skepticism the contradiction which must always exist between art and bread. This skepticism was useful to their work. It stood guard over their writing like a scarecrow and frightened away the shadows of their bondage. The intellectuals of post-Lutheran times made a show of virtue; those of the Renaissance boasted of affected vices. "In hypocrisy," Machiavelli wrote, "I have long since received baptism, confirmation, and communion. In lying I even possess a doctor's degree. Life has taught me to temper falsehood with truth and truth with falsehood."

The great historian, Giovio, who enjoyed his leisure at the papal court for thirty-seven years, was accustomed to boast, "I have a golden pen and an iron pen; the golden one for those who pay, the iron one for those who do not pay." In his work, however, he did not spare his patron, the Church, and he suppressed no facts. Leo X followed his work with eager interest. Frequently Giovio had to read the book aloud to him until the dawn. The Pope listened in suspense as his historian berated the papal-Medicean policies as "shameless injustice and countless infamies".

Guicciardini, skilled in deceit and grown grey in the service of three popes, revealed in his history of Italy a savagery without parallel. The actors step onto the stage, exchange friendly courtesies, and strangle each other. He did not see faces, but masks. In hundreds of pages he analyzed the present. He showed all passions and all emotions. But contrary to Machiavelli, in his thinking no single action had its source in religion, conscience, or virtue. From the beginning of the world to the end of all time, he saw only selfishness, ambition, and vice as the determining causes of events.

Francesco Guicciardini had held the highest offices and dignities the Ecclesiastical State could give. In the course of his career he had been lieutenant general of the papal army, governor of the Romagna and of Bologna, Parma, and Reggio. In addition, he was considered the oracle of Europe. Charles V was wont to say, "In a moment I can create a hundred Spanish grandees, but in a hundred years not a single Guicciardini."

Francesco became close friends with the aging Niccolo, and there arose a constant exchange of ideas between them. Guicciardini criticized the *Discourses,* and his criticism was the fruit of the political experience which came from having held offices of power. He saw events differently, not with the broad view of the eagle, but from close up. He looked more into the pores of things than at the flow of events. Therefore he frequently saw details more crudely and more correctly.

At present he was governor of Modena. He kept his distance from most men, but he wanted to have Niccolo near him. He had often invited him to visit. Now Niccolo was finally in his territory, a few miles from his residence, on a minor official mission. The wool guild had sent him to the Franciscan monastery at Carpi to find a preacher for the Florentines. The governor general of the Pope was merry all day long at the thought. "What an idea," he wrote to Niccolo, "to send you, of all people, to find a preacher."

"I have always served the Republic to the best of my knowledge and ability," Niccolo answered him. "In this particular case, however, I am not in agreement with my fellow citizens. They want a preacher who will show them the way to Paradise. I want to find one who will show them the way to the Devil. I want to find a base liar and hypocrite. For to find the true path to Paradise one must know the way to Hell and then avoid it.

Every day Guicciardini sent him a courier with letters. Soon the Franciscans believed that Niccolo was an extremely important papal official with a vital mission, so they opened the treasures of their wine cellars and their kitchen to him. Niccolo was living in a utopia. He stretched his limbs on white beddings, let himself be wooed and waited on all day long, and continually pricked the curiosity of the naïve monks. He would murmur aloud, as if to himself, sentences from Guicciardini's letters. He wanted the brethren to believe that he was staying in their monastery to wait for a messenger from the emperor and that the governor general was daily sending him the instructions of the Holy Father. "While I write this," one letter from Niccolo to Guicciardini reads, "the clerics are standing in a circle around me with their mouths wide open. Because I have been sitting over the paper for some time, they are looking at me spellbound, as if there were a holy aura about me. In order to astound them still further, I gravely stop writing from time to time, move about restlessly, and play with the pen with an air of great importance. If they knew what I am writing they would be even more astounded than they already are." Guicciardini answered him that he should use his stay in the monastery to incite the brethren against one another and create an infernal mix-up. But he should guard against becoming as hardened a rascal as those devout souls were. Niccolo vouched for himself that he could not possibly become more corrupt than he already was.

The joke ended because Machiavelli was afraid that the Prior of Carpi—"who is cleverer than thirty thousand devils"—was beginning to see through the correspondence. He rode off to Modena to his friend. There they could laugh over the farce of Carpi at their leisure.

Papal officials like Francesco Guicciardini and Francesco Vettori, and papal historians like Giovio and Machiavelli could never have existed after the storms of the Reformation. In the new world, in which terrible schoolmasters taught mankind the duty of being earnest, there was no longer any room for splendid minds which lived by cleverness and irony and which played with all things great and lowly.

CHAPTER XIII

World Crisis and the Death of Machiavelli

TO THE Dutchman Hadrian, the successor of Leo X, the seat of papal Power seemed the tomb of God. The paintings of Raphael and the works of Bramante and Michelangelo were to him like visions of the Evil One. His eyes were horrified at the marble Apollo, the torso of Hercules, the Venus, and the statues of the gods of the Tiber and the Nile. At the sight of these things the tall, wasted old man grew dizzy and thought he was viewing the fall of mankind. Divorced from Christ, man was plunging into the bottomless abyss of heathenism. Hadrian grew more and more horrified. Everywhere he looked he saw only sin and still more sin. Before the Laocoön he covered his face with both hands and said weeping, "Nothing but idols, nothing but idols!"

Hadrian would have preferred to flee from the Vatican and take up his residence in a plain summer house. It took the pleas of his Netherland friends and the remonstrances of the ambassador of the emperor to persuade him to remain in the palace of the popes. However, he turned the Vatican into a monastery and lived like a monk. He had the gates locked which led into the gardens of Belvedere where the ancient statues stood, and he took the keys into his own keeping. The pupils of Raphael could not finish the paintings they had begun. Every hammer and brush was put away. Hadrian spent his time in a small study filled with theological books. His day was so strictly regulated that every hour had its place. He received few visitors, daily made the holy sacrifice, and sought everywhere for a place to anchor the heavily pitching ship of Christ which was being buffeted from all sides.

Leo had had nearly a hundred servants and pages; his successor was satisfied with two servants and an old Dutchwoman to cook for him. The Cardinals had given banquets at which seventy-five courses were served, and on fast days they had eaten sturgeon at eighteen ducats apiece. Hadrian gave his servant one ducat every evening for the meals of the next day. With holy zeal he tried to curb the Cardinals. He forbade their carrying weapons and supervised their incomes. He followed up every charge that was brought against them and announced that no prelate could have more than one prebend. He took radical steps to abolish nepotism, simony, and trade in favors and papal bulls. He dismissed humanists from the chanceries and replaced them with theologians.

As a learned searcher after God, Hadrian yearned to restore the science of theology to the high place it had once held. All the benefices and pensions which had been conferred upon men of letters were rescinded. The historian, Giovio, was the only man to receive continued support, and that only because it was explained that Giovio was not a poet. Hadrian took steps against the poets immediately after he came to power and overnight hundreds of intellectuals lost their means of support. He declared that they were responsible for all the lewdness in the Church, that they toyed with heathen gods and wantoned with vice. The plaint of the literati rose to a murderous cry against the Vatican. They shouted in furious satires and rhymes that Rome had been taken by barbarians. Everything about the Pope was jeered at, his miserliness, his harsh Latin speech, his outlandish German and Dutch associates. "Rome is no longer Rome," one letter reads. "This Pope recognizes no great names; no one ever sees a gift or a reward. Everyone is full of despair."

Hadrian wished to destroy the glory of the Medici, but he was no misguided ascetic. The efforts he made during his short pontificate were of universal historical significance. The unity of the Church had to be preserved against the attacks of Martin Luther. The Holy Father tried to do this by thinking the problem through and pointing out the same evils Luther attacked, without the latter's blasphemies. "We know," the instructions of the Pope to his nuncio read, "that for a considerable time much that is abhorrent has taken place in the Holy See. From the head the corruption has spread to the limbs, from the Pope to the prelates. We have all become lax. There is none who has done good, not even one."

The new driving forces loose in Europe, however, were not to be restrained by piety, sermons, and repentance. In broad regions, religion had become autonomous. Martin Luther was about to change the world more fundamentally than the discovery of America, the circumnavigation of Africa, and the invention of gunpowder and printing. Martin Luther declared every Christian to be his own Pope. He kindled the "inner light" in everyone. Conscience rose in the souls of millions of men and arrogated to itself the right to settle all questions of mortality and eternity. In miserable hovels, in the houses of rich and poor, and in the palaces of princes, there arose the longing of mankind for innovation. Impelled by new hopes, wild forces stormed through city and country, raging against the old Church, slandering and deriding her. The world grew pregnant with expectation. Cities trembled and men felt themselves spiritually no longer alone. The hands of devout men sought their swords as their eyes sought their Savior. Countless men sat in study, absorbing the spirit and the letter of the Bible. For the first time the Bible became the book of the people. Bottomless springs of warlike energies welled beneath the surface of Europe which the least political earthquake would release to inundate the continent. To the new converts, battles became as tame as diseases of childhood. They enjoyed danger and lamented the day in which they did not increase the host of the pious by one more convert.

Hadrian, whether he willed or no, had to desert his whispered prayers and look about for the strongest arm with which to defend the Church.

The strongest arm was that of Maximilian's successor, Emperor Charles V. To the youthful Charles, the grandson of Maximilian, Martin Luther was proof that the limbs of the "*corpus christianum*" were rotting because of the weakness of the central, imperial Power. From that weakness arose infectious, miasmic vapors. Charles was in a position to oppose the forces which were rising out of the depths of an exploding world. For he had strengthened the crumbled imperial power of his forefathers with the might of his Spanish House. He felt he had the dual mission of commanding both the secular and the ecclesiastical empire!

To become ruler of the West, however, it was necessary to rule Italy. Not only for traditional reasons, not only because the idea of empire was united with the idea of Rome, but also because Lombardy formed the bridge from Austria along the Rhine to the Netherlands. Lombardy, however, was also the focal point of French interests. Lombardy in the possession of the emperor would mean the recognition of the supremacy of Spain-Austria in Europe. At the same time, Lombardy in the hands of the emperor was a threat to Rome. The Spanish were already entrenched in the south of Italy in Naples. If they now established themselves in the north, then Rome would be surrounded by the forces of the emperor and the Pope would lose not only his spiritual but his territorial independence. He would be the domestic chaplain of the Spaniards and no longer the Prince of Christendom. Such were the confusing problems which rose before the pious mind of Hadrian. He, who had believed only in the purity of the Faith, saw himself as the captive of the various political tendencies and contradictions. He was forced to remember bitterly the words of Cardinal Soderini who had told him from the very beginning that in order to combat the new heresy successfully, wars without number would have to be waged. Hadrian, this lonely man upon the throne of Peter, was frightened by reality. After a pontificate of eight months, his heart ceased to beat.

His successor, Cardinal Giulio Medici, the ruler of Florence, who took the name of Clement VII, aroused great hopes. His sobriety, his industry, his gravity, and his long years of experience with worldly matters stamped him in the eyes of initiates as a statesman of destiny. Prosaic by nature, Clement possessed neither the asceticism of Hadrian, the extravagance of Leo, nor the tremendous energy of Julius II. He strove for a peaceful, orderly pontificate. He was a realist, but he was not always in close touch with reality. For he did not perceive the whole significance of the rivalry of Spain and France, whose Italian struggles were struggles for all of Europe. He thought that the art of politics was merely a crafty maneuvering back and forth.

Clement negotiated publicly with the emperor and secretly with Francis I. He followed every gesture towards one of the two monarchs by intimate confidences to the other. Often he was in league with each of them against the other. The Vatican diplomats were either pro-French or pro-empire and consequently they defeated each other's efforts. Both factions, the party of the French and the party of the emperor, had their armed followers in the Ecclesiastical State. These followers hesitated at nothing and were ready to open the gates of Rome to the enemy. The Pope frequently brooded in silence over the labyrinth of his diplomatic correspondence. Ambassadors, secret emissaries, French and Spanish generals had audiences with him one after the other. They had no inkling of his thoughts. Each of them heard from the mouth of the Holy Father only generalities and assurances. "The Pope is the most secretive man in the world," the imperial ambassador reported to his emperor, "and more full of puzzles than anyone I have ever talked to."

These policies, which might serve as an example of supreme deceit, were nothing more than a proof of supreme weakness. By chance, at the beginning of the year 1525, Clement happened to be on France's side instead of the emperor's. In the twenty-first year of the French struggle for Lombardy, Francis I was about to begin a new attempt to take Milan. On the sleeves of his bodyguard he had the words embroidered, "Once more and never again."

At Pavia Francis I was beaten and taken prisoner by the Spanish general, Pescara. The battle of Pavia opened the way for the emperor to France, to Lyons, and Avignon. Pavia fettered Central Europe to Spain. It gave the emperor, who now reigned in Milan, Vienna, Constance, Geneva, and Amsterdam, reason to celebrate his new, supranational Power as portent of the World Empire.

The widespread feeling in frightened Europe that Charles was destined to become ruler of the continent removed all chances that the Pope might find a force to oppose him. Clement was stunned with dread. An eyewitness reported that he seemed lifeless. Seeking to escape by submission, he sent courier after courier to the imperial generals, made unlimited promises, and declared himself ready to give up everything. Clement signed a humiliating treaty by which the emperor agreed, in return for huge sums of money, to take under his protection the Medici in Rome and in Tuscany, and to withdraw all his troops from the Ecclesiastical State.

But Clement sealed his own doom because, instead of keeping quiet, he toyed for days and weeks with plans which were far beyond the scope of his will and character. Like a losing gambler, he superstitiously allowed himself to be guided by all sorts of omens. His indecision and cowardice were greater than his impotence. Little men are not made great by the mighty thoughts which are pressed upon them. And the ideas of the Italian patriots, especially those of Bishop Ghilberti, Clement's Secretary of State, were stamped with an audacity which put them beyond the scope of Clement's craftiness. The Holy Father was held captive by the visionary plans of others. To be sure, Clement was in league with the emperor, according to the recent peace treaty. But this very alliance, the Italians thought, might serve as a shield behind which they could prepare their opposition to the superior might of Charles. The Italian patriots did not, however, have the military energy and the readiness of the nation behind them. On this account, they placed even greater reliance on political machinations.

At this time high treason was becoming more and more an essential part of European politics, and every potentate thought that his neighbor might exercise his customary privilege of having a revolution. The Grand Dignitary of France, Connetable de Bourbon, was leading the armies of Charles V against France. The German princes were in alliance with Francis I against the emperor. And the Italians too were looking for some grand traitor. They felt they had found him in General Pescara, the commander who had captured Francis I at Pavia. Pescara had been offended by Charles V. He was an Italian and, radiant with the halo of a great, victorious battle, was the very man, according to the calculations of the Italian patriots, to be their commander in chief.

The victory of Pavia, terrifying as it had been, could not quell the ferment, the pressure of healthy, revolutionary forces, the impulse to action, within the peoples of Europe. Not peace, but the confused alarms of a world crisis spread over the continent. It was a crisis of greater moment than any Europe was to experience until the Napoleonic wars because it challenged everything traditional; all agrarian property relationships; all boundaries, every faith, and every throne. In Germany, the revolting peasants burnt to the ground everything they hated. Luther was no longer master of these new converts, but the lightning of the revolt he started set fire even to the palaces of his protectors. In Spain, the cities rose in bloody, desperate fury against Charles. On the Danube, the enigmatic, warlike power of the Mussulman was beginning to appear. England was arming suspiciously against Madrid. In France, the capture of Francis I had aroused among the French not despair but a determination to exist as a nation.

The papacy, with its great possibilities, seemed to the Italians the ideal point about which to rally the anti-imperial forces. They saw the Vatican Chancery as the center of resistance. The fervent hope and ambition of the nationalists around Clement was to merge themselves with the new lust for life which was everywhere stirring; to guide into their own stream of resistance every will which was determinedly opposed to the domination of the empire. They were conscious that the hour was ripe. "Now it is not a question of injured honor," Bishop Ghilberti wrote, "nor of vengeance, nor of the claims of this or that city, but a question for Italy of the freedom or eternal servitude. Never has there been a more favorable opportunity."

Even Francesco Guicciardini's usual doubts left him. He looked upon the undertaking against Emperor Charles as a holy imperative. When he wrote to Machiavelli, Guicciardini was not overenthusiastic, but he revealed the maximum confidence of which he was capable. "I hope that each one will do his duty, so that everything will proceed, if not with the necessary precision and speed, still, not so slowly that the favorable moment will slip away from us."

At this apex of the crisis, while Italy waited tensely, Machiavelli and Guicciardini—the two cleverest spokesmen of the political life of their times, as Leopold von Ranke calls them—both shared the same hope. For months, Niccolo had no personal life; he disappeared in the stream of events. The faith to which Italian soil suddenly gave birth, rejuvenated the fifty-seven-year-old Machiavelli. Sick, gnawed by a disease of the intestines, he nevertheless felt cheerful. He had even greater faith in the success of the enterprise because Guicciardini stood at the head of the national resistance.

Encouraged by his friend, Niccolo went to Rome in all haste to hand his history of Florence over to the Pope. This, however, was only a pretext to get close to the center of the opposition around the Holy Father at a time when any moment might bring war.

Clement received him with tender good will. Their conversation touched upon the book only in passing. More as a sign of his favor than from interest, Clement, who was usually stingy, increased Machiavelli's pension for the completion of the book. The feeling that this was the eve of coming struggles lent Niccolo a hasty, but nevertheless worldly blandishment. The Pope was intoxicated by the picture of the vigorous populani energies which his historian drew for him. After but a few hours, the Holy Father was in accord with the idea of founding a militia. Clement sent Niccolo to Guicciardini, the Governor of the Romagna, to discuss recruiting on a new, broad basis. He gave the two of them full powers in this matter so important to Italian resistance. "With Niccolo Machiavelli," the breve to Guicciardini read, "we have examined the entire matter and studied it intensively. He will inform you of all our plans and aims. The matter is important for the well-being of the Church, of the State, of all Italy, indeed, of all Christendom."

Machiavelli was convinced that he would be able to win Francesco's approval for the militia. Overjoyed, Guicciardini embraced him when he arrived. He was happy to find that Niccolo was on an important official mission and high in the confidence of the Pope. He could not have wished a better man to work with. These two foremost Italian patriots, however, were divided on the military question by a fundamental difference in their temperaments, characters, and conception of human affairs. Guicciardini could not warm to the idea of conscription. He shuddered when he thought of arming the people, "that dark monster with countless feet and no head". His penetrating knowledge of practise, if not of theory, and his understanding of Clement based on long personal association, told him that the Pope's acceptance of the idea sprang from low, not lofty motives.

Machiavelli had told Clement that the militia needed no advances of money from the State. The communities would have to arm themselves. The Holy Father, who daily was more distressed by the expenditures for the army, had received ready made from Niccolo, the longed-for excuse to foster his miserliness. And if Machiavelli had forgotten the defeat at Prato, Guicciardini had not. Were they to fight with frightened Romagnolese peasants against the soldiers of Pavia, the soldiers of the celebrated Frundsberg, against the Spanish brigades which had so recently won universal fame? These peasants hated the rule of Clement, whom they knew, far more than that of the most ferocious enemy, whom they did not know. To Guicciardini, the whole idea of establishing a militia when war was about to break out was merely one of his friend's pet academic theories.

But the disagreement left no shadow of discord behind it. Machiavelli did not let his ideas become a besetting mania which might interfere with his further activities.

As a result of the recently manifested papal confidence and the vigorous recommendations of Francesco Guicciardini, Niccolo was now one of the most influential men in signorial circles. He applied pressure to obtain some military office and was appointed Chancellor of the Commission on Fortifications. Enthusiastically he took hold of the new work, made plans, and altered those already in force. He was at the outer edge of the city half the day, and in spite of all financial and bureaucratic obstacles, attempted to make Florence the foremost fortress in Europe. He became so involved in his work that he even forgot his correspondence with Guicciardini. "Pardon me for not having written so long. My mind is full of bastions," he wrote him.

With each new report that reached Florence, the fortification of the city seemed more urgent. It was as if events had already passed out of the hands of the men concerned. They burst like flares in such rapid succession that the eyes of the Italians were blinded.

Although the secret negotiations of Rome had resulted in an alliance with France and Venice—the League of Cognac—this alliance was a tragic disappointment. Within a few weeks, one hope after the other vanished. Pescara would not desert the emperor; the English king sent no money; and the French and Venetians did not send troops. The world coalition which had been welcomed with such great expectations left Rome isolated, and thus paralyzed all forces of attack and defense. The elements of the continental crisis, upon which the patriots of the Vatican had placed their hopes, were those seething energies and permanent tendencies which had now become physical forces at once stronger and weaker than an army.

Vettori wrote that he hoped in vain for the news "that the Turks have taken Hungary and are marching to Vienna, that the Lutherans have conquered in Germany, and the Moors have driven the emperor out of Aragon and Valencia." War, however, was more concrete than hopes; battles were fought on a narrower canvas. The world crisis did not raise any battalions to help the Italians. The imperial armies, on the other hand, crossed the Alps unopposed and arrived at San Giovanni, not far from Bologna and close to the inactive Italian army. Overnight the roads to the two richest cities of the Peninsula, Rome and Florence, were opened to Charles' army.

The two centers of national opposition, Florence and Rome, became centers of panic. In Rome, Clement was being threatened by the baronial family of the Colonnesi. Suddenly terrified, he was prepared to make peace with Charles V. The weak and fearful Pope infected the army of the League with his own timidity.

In Florence, the prevalent atmosphere was one of rebellion against papal leadership. The frosty air of danger made the city shiver. The Medicean ruler of Tuscany, Cardinal de' Passerini, was a caricature of all the weaknesses of his papal master. In the Signory, no one knew anything about the situation of Bologna, of Rome, of the Alpine valleys, of Genoa, or of Livorno where the allied fleet of the French was being awaited in vain. In order to get information, the signori sent Machiavelli to Guicciardini, the Pope's commissioner-general with the army of the League.

That wintry spring of the year 1527, both friends experienced all the despair of helplessness. The anger in their hearts burned ever deeper because they so often saw a chance for victory almost within their grasp. But all the advantages of the Italians became calamities and all these calamities were advantageous to the imperial forces. Furious complaints thundered out of Niccolo's reports. Written hastily by the light of a campfire, their effect died out in a labyrinth of ineptitude and laziness. In the councils of war of the commandants he heard only the "impotent barking of dogs" and felt that the officers were cowardly and conceited. The Duke of Urbino, who was generalissimo of the League, was in his eyes a man whose mind was even weaker than his body. If some miracle did not produce a common plan with courage and manly discipline, an Italian disaster would be inevitable. At the walls of the Vatican, Clement was menaced by the Colonnesi, and from Naples in the south to Siena in the north he was threatened by the troops of the empire. He attempted to purchase peace.

Niccolo realized that the disintegration of the enemy army was imminent, but that it was being postponed by the continual negotiations of the Pope. The emperor's mercenaries, however, lured by the weakness of the enemy, shouted down their own commanders. This time, once and for all, they determined to free themselves of poverty. The only thing which held Charles' army together was the practise instigated two decades earlier by the Spanish command, of giving over to the soldiers for spoliation the country in which there was fighting. The emperor's general, Connetable de Bourbon, was the spokesman for the spoils-hungry soldiers. To prevent him from involving himself in negotiations for peace, a soldiers' council supervised his activities. Bourbon lusted for gold as much as the soldiers. He not only wanted to ravage Rome or Florence, but to be paid for promising to refrain from plundering. The connetable negotiated for the price of a truce, pocketed the money for his starving men, and marched on. His army was already on Tuscan soil in Arezzo, and Machiavelli was still unable to report whether his hordes would pour down upon Florence or Rome. Bourbon himself did not know, for he was not leading, he was being driven.

Now that Italy was lost, at least Florence might be saved. Guicciardini and Machiavelli succeeded in concentrating troops of the League on the roads which led north from Arezzo to Florence. Niccolo sent report after report to the Signory ordering that Florence itself and all the surrounding country be fortified. He tried to keep Tuscany from falling into a state of panic. He wrote that it was not necessary to attack and that merely a determined defense would unquestionably cause the dissolution of the imperial armies.

Bourbon avoided meeting the Tuscan opposition and took the easier, more tempting road to Rome. The imperial army, in torn clothes, without shoes, pay or food, and accompanied by hundreds of beggars, sped across swollen rivers and high mountain paths toward the Tiber.

Clement, who usually never placed his trust in any single man and always oscillated like a pendulum between yes and no, this time believed implicitly in da Ceri, his commandant of the city. Da Ceri laughed at Guicciardini's message that the Holy Father should flee Rome, refused the offer of six thousand auxiliaries, and declared that the eternal city was impregnable. On the morning of the fifth of May, 1527, the seat of Christendom awoke for the last time as the richest city in the world. At dusk of the same day, twenty-five thousand savage beggars with swords and torches in their hands poured over Rome shouting the battle cry, "Empire, Spain, Victory!"

"Then everyone had to die who was found in the streets, whether young or old, layman, priest, or monk." The plunderers of all countries had come over seas and valleys to ravage the halls of wealth with their claws and then squander it all in one evening of incomparable revelry. The churches became stables, the cardinals and barons water carriers. Prothonotaries, heads of religious orders, and bankers were used as servants in their own palaces and villas. The finest ladies, marchionesses, countesses, and baronesses were embraced so roughly that from that day on they were known by no other name than "the relics of the sack of Rome". The soldiers dressed themselves in priestly garments, rode to St. Peter's accompanied by half-naked women, and had themselves crowned pope. Drunkards bedecked asses with sacred vestments and forced bishops to give the animals the sacrament. On all sides, were heard "shouting, the rumble of guns, the screams and howls of women and children, the crackling of flames and the crash of collapsing roofs," wrote one man who saw the carnage from the battlements of the Castel Sant' Angelo to which the Pope had fled. Soon this last fortress was also taken. Dryly the captain of the German mercenaries, Schärtlin, reported to his dear ones in Wurttemberg, "In that place we found Pope Clement with twelve Cardinals in a small hall; we took him prisoner. There was great mourning among them; they wept deeply. We all became very rich."

All that was mortal of the grandeur that was Rome perished. Strange is the incongruity of this world. Here but a short time before, the emperor and the Pope had issued a joint manifesto against the world revolution, defending the ideal of traditional European order and proclaiming the salvation of Church and hearth from the attacks of unbelievers and criminals. But the city of Christendom was burning, set afire by the soldiers of that emperor whose soul nevertheless experienced all the mysteries of the Eucharist in the strictest Catholic sense, who was ready to send a brigade to defend every individual dogma and to take the field against every heretical doctrine.

History gives life to the old through the new, and to the new through the old. All forces are in a constant conspiracy to confuse the perceptions, though not the will, of man. The will has but one impulse, to win Power. Rejuvenated by the new elements at large, Power rose out of the universal crisis and crowned a Caesar, Charles V. The effects produced by people and events were more far-reaching than ever before. Martin Luther, the discovery of the New World, the revolution of prices, the devaluation of gold, the Turkish offensive against Europe, and the independence of the peoples around the Baltic Sea, all played a part. Without regard for doctrine, the material and spiritual links of this political chain were added, subtracted, multiplied, and divided by the policies of the emperor.

If fate in these months had once more raised Machiavelli into the field of action and had taken him into the presence of the men in command after years of bitterly felt political exile, it was only in order that he might see more clearly the waves of defeat. It seemed as though the man who had loved Italy's freedom waited to close the eyes of the dead Italia and then could not long survive her death.

In Civitavecchia, where Niccolo stayed for a few days under orders from Guicciardini, he was able to see how virtù, the virtue of rulers of which he had spoken, was punishing the eternal city with ruin. He heard the thunder of events he knew would come to pass and was overwhelmed by sorrow and pain. His orders to ask Andrea Doria, the French admiral, to help the Pope, now seemed unimportant to him. He knew that the high priest, whose weaknesses had not been proof against the storm of events, could no longer be helped. The admiral indulged in the most friendly evasions and made no move to help Rome.

Niccolo staggered feebly through the streets. The port was filled to overflowing with refugees from Rome, among them Florentine merchants who had been able to pay ransom for their freedom. Niccolo hid away. For the first time in his life his eye was clouded and his lips were shut. He sat alone in a tavern and waited for his servant. Shortly before he left, he heard the great news. There was a revolution in Florence! Against the will of the Medici, the Florentines had taken up arms against Spain. Florence believed that by freeing its military leadership and its diplomatic affairs from the captive Pope it would be able to escape the fate of Rome.

So long as some men stirred to oppose the flood of defeat, Niccolo could banish the misery of his mind and the weariness of his body and continue to cry as he had on the first day of the resistance, "Kill the Spaniards; they are animals. They are only voices, not whole men!"

He rode home as swiftly as his feverish brow and trembling knees would permit him. Valleys and meadows, villages and castles revealed one after another scenes of wretchedness. The land had been withered by war, fear, and pestilence. Peasants had taken to the woods. Fields were lying uncultivated and cities and market places were dead. Only the highways were crowded. Silently, with empty minds, refugees from Rome moved slowly along them into the distance as into an unknown, black ocean.

But Florence was merry. The people were rejoicing because after fifteen years they were able to throw the insignia and standards of the Medici into the Arno. The Florentines celebrated the change from the Medicean to the republican extreme in orations and songs. The old groupings of the days of Savonarola and Soderini rose again in the first hour of freedom as if the dictatorship had been but a passing wind. The Great Council met for the first time in fifteen years and waited in defiance and anger for the struggle with Spain.

The new Signory rapidly examined the officials on their pasts and their republican attitudes. The man who under the Medici had held Niccolo's post as Secretary of the Second Chancery was dismissed. Immediately Machiavelli applied.

Since the day of his arrival in Florence, however, he had sensed about him a cold ring of hostility which he did not understand and had not wanted to recognize. Acquaintances passed him by without speaking. Followers, disciples, and men of letters were avoiding him. The new government looked at citizens through the eyes of the small and the bigoted; the men of moral earnestness were at their philistine work. Although Niccolo was not considered an outright traitor, he nevertheless seemed suspect to all parties including the old and the new republicans. Other men who had grown rich and grey in the favor of the ruling family played the part of new republicans uncontested. The greater part of the nobili, frightened by the weakness and the endless evasions of the Pope, deserted Clement and his illegitimate dynasty.

For all these men, however, the peculiar personal qualities which were always present in Niccolo were not troublesome. Even Vettori and Guicciardini, his friends and comrades in doubt and skepticism if not in belief, would rather have appeared among an average group of their fellow citizens without their breeches than without a dignified mien. Because he always scorned disgruntled men, and because he had had the merrymakers, the revellers, and the few really intelligent men on his side, Machiavelli had believed that he was well liked. But all who feared his tongue, all who felt that his incessant financial worries were a breach of decency, all who were astounded at his impudence, discovered his great sin: the *Prince*. Copies of the still unprinted book went from hand to hand. Its author was looked upon as the apologist for absolutism, as the man who had shown the Medici the way to every imaginable intrigue against Florence. Of a sudden Niccolo's every trait was displeasing. In the eyes of his fellow citizens, his face became a horrid, grinning mask. Had he not even spoken evil of himself? Machiavelli was to learn that there is nothing more dangerous than to make fun of oneself in the presence of stupid men. For the underlying meaning of remarks remains concealed from them, but the echo is always given distorted expression at some important future moment. The little man, who always demands seriousness, takes his revenge.

On June 10, 1527, the candidacy of Niccolo Machiavelli stood on the agenda of the Great Council. Of the nine who took the floor, eight spoke bitterly against him. The first declared, "Niccolo has slandered the Florentines, caricatured them, and made them the mockery of foreigners." The second, "Machiavelli's work is to write obscene comedies, but not to serve the State." The third, "Machiavelli does not know Florence at all. He has been away for years and has thus become alienated from his fellow citizens." The fourth, "Machiavelli is not a good Italian; he likes to glorify the customs of foreigners across the Alps." The fifth, "Where was Citizen Machiavelli when the people fought in the streets against the Medici?" The sixth, "Perhaps Machiavelli is a good writer, but he is no official, no man who can be depended upon to fulfil his duties punctually." The seventh, "Machiavelli learned the art of robbing the poor and knifing freedom while he was with Cesare Borgia. His association with that tyrant ruined him for life." The eighth, "Machiavelli laughed at Savonarola and even jeered at his patron, Soderini. He leads an extremely wanton and impious life. He is worse than a Lutheran."

Luigi Alamani alone, a friend and writer from the Rucellai garden, rose and defended the slandered Niccolo. "Machiavelli," he said, "is known as a serious man among serious men and as a fool among fools. It is true that he is well liked by princes, but not because he has sold out liberty. He is admired for his intelligence. The very confidence they have in him should predestine him to serve the Republic in diplomatic work. For fourteen years he was in the service of the Signory, and every page of the records and documents he kept during his service to the Republic proves his extraordinary merits. After countless missions, after decades filled with hard toil, he is among the most poverty-stricken of men. He is an honorable man from top to toe. To this very day, in the fifty-eighth year of his life, he has betrayed no one and has always served faithfully. You can count upon him under any conditions. For what do you really reproach him? For working in the service of Clement? For helping to defend Florence? How many among you were the friends of the Medici only the day before yesterday?"

Here the speech was interrupted by the offended majesty of the populani. Furious shouts and clenched fists transformed the Great Council into a bedlam. "Traitor! Death to the Medici! Stop!" they screamed at Alamani. Niccolo Capponi, the gonfaloniere, put an end to the uproar by calling for a vote on Machiavelli's fitness for office. The count gave Niccolo twelve votes out of six hundred!

Niccolo himself was lying deathly sick in his Florentine home listening to reports on the speeches that were being made about him. He no longer understood completely what was going on. He was reliving the scenes and events of his life. All thought and hope seemed vain and hollow to him. Through his life he had reflected on Power and placed his hopes in virtù, in Cesare, Leo, Lorenzo, Florence, and Italy. But he had known only the tragic side of events and the ridiculous side of men. Now he was again despised as he had been fifteen years before! Was he to lose himself once more on the paths of humility and in the web of poverty? Was he to sit once more in the tavern at his Sant' Andrea estate playing incessant tric-trac with the peasants and looking out of the window, a pathetic old man, to plead with passers-by for news of the city and the country? The dying man felt that he must steal away, escape from all the misery that faced him. His thoughts returned from the distance. He saw his wife and his five children standing about his bed. Tenderly he caressed Marietta's hand, thanking her for life. He looked at his sons in silence. He could no longer speak; they vanished in the darkness in which the light of his soul was extinguished forever. . . .

* * *

June 22, 1527, the same day he died, he was buried. Only his family and a few friends accompanied the body to the grave. His death remained unnoted in the conflict which was flaring up in Florence.

The peaceful city crowned and ended its existence as an independent state in a three-year struggle against Clement, who was now in league with Charles V. The flame of warfare burst out in Tuscany itself, which for centuries had been the refuge of the noblest thoughts and manners of life.

It lit up the sword of Michelangelo—the Florentine "governor and procurator-general in charge of the construction and the fortification of the city walls". The conflict was not only over the words of a constitution or the independence of Italy, but over the integral spirit of Florence. Tuscany was defending her eternal love of liberty. This ideal of liberty outlived all the mighty forces which it had released. A day of liberty shatters the seemingly eternal pyramids which slavery has built. Liberty comes again and again, caresses men, shows them their dignity, the god within their breasts. And it tests their swords.

Tuscany was defeated. It lost its liberty and its genius, but it retained the gratitude and admiration which the human race will always have for the heights which Florence attained in its glorious past.

Not until after the defeat, five years after Machiavelli's death, was his *Prince* published. It swiftly became the primer of kings. Because the *Prince* was the sparkling expression of the period of evolving absolutism, all rulers kept it close at hand. They wrote commentaries on it, uncovered its hidden meanings, heard the hearts of their enemies beating in it, tried to surpass it. Through it they learned the significance of statecraft. Charles V of Spain was said to have known whole chapters by heart. The Queen of France, Catherine de' Medici, felt a kinship with the book because it had been dedicated to her father. Henry III and Henry IV of France were said never to have spent a day away from the *Prince*. Christian of Sweden composed a long commentary on it. When Frederick of Prussia was Crown Prince, he wrote an "Anti-Machiavelli" and Voltaire remarked that he had spat on his favorite tarts so that no one else would be able to eat of them.

Not only the founders of absolutism, but their opponents also saw the individual fibers of Power in general and the inner mechanisms of their particular enemies on the thrones of Europe nowhere so clearly as in Machiavelli's book. "I have written for those," Machiavelli had said, "who wish to retain the liberty of a Republic as well as for those who intend to suppress it." Jean-Jacques Rousseau said the *Prince* was *the* book for republicans. The Italian risorgimento made Niccolo a secular saint. He was the teacher of Cavour. And the men who rose to Power from the masses, those men of whom Machiavelli had written: "I do not believe that a man will ever be found who has raised himself from low estate and become a ruler without practicing deceit, solely by open and honorable violence"—those men also felt the spark of virtù which linked them to the Florentine. "Tacitus," said Napoleon, "wrote nothing but novels. Gibbon is a teller of fairy tales. The only readable political book is Machiavelli's." And Lenin recommended Machiavelli in his "Left-wing Communism, an Infantile Disorder" to his followers as an antidote to stupidity.

Famous as a master of political theory, Machiavelli is also remembered as the preacher of infamy. The popes of the counterreformation condemned Niccolo's writings, which the Vatican presses had first printed. They claimed that Satan himself had written the *Prince*. A few years after the curse of Rome had been pronounced upon Niccolo's work, a grandson of his desired to publish the works anew, purified of sinfulness. The censor would grant permission only under the condition that the ill-omened name of Machiavelli be omitted. The grandson would not agree to this arrangement. Instead, countless copies of falsified editions of Machiavelli, bowdlerized or aimed at scandalizing the reader, appeared. Probably no other book has had so many stupid comments written about it as the *Prince*.

The unshatterable mirror which Niccolo held before the soul of man may be scratched and blemished in the course of future years. But today it gleams as brightly as when it was first fashioned.

EPILOGUE

INTO THE seething cauldron of man's destiny, Fate throws the base ingredients of envy, desire, lust, greed, ambition, cruelty, and avarice, and brews therefrom the everlasting element of Power. Power is no more than the many times magnified will to live, which lurks and moves in the heart of every human being—the force that drives men on and lures them almost inevitably to their destruction.

Whether Power in itself is good or evil, Machiavelli does not venture to decide. But with his eyes wide open to things as they are, unblinded by romantic ideas of what they ought to be, he sets forth clearly for the man who hopes to attain Power, the steps to be followed in the pursuit, the attainment, and the retention of his prize. He looks about him with cool, unemotional vision and builds his philosophy of Power upon the foundation of man's nature as it is. The policies which he advocates and with which his name has come to be associated—deceit, intrigue, treachery, cunning, and cold-blooded cruelty—are, in his eyes, but the means to an end. They are never to be confused with the end itself, the law-abiding exercise of Power.

Schopenhauer failed wholly to understand Machiavelli's philosophy when he wrote, "The gist of his doctrine may be summed up as follows: that wherever between one individual and another, and so far as concerns the law and morality of their relations, the principle, *Don't do to others what you wouldn't like done to yourself*, certainly applies, yet the very converse of this principle is appropriate in the case of nations and politics: *What you wouldn't like done to yourself, do to others.*"

Compare this with Machiavelli's own statement in the *Prince,* "Now the main foundations of all States, whether new, old, or mixed, are good laws and good arms." Good laws are in themselves powerless; in nature it is Might that rules. To enlist Might on the side of Right, so that by means of this union Right may rule, is the problem of statesmanship. And this is the council that Machiavelli urges most emphatically in his writings. Since men are swayed less by reason than by emotion, it is physical power alone that has any direct effect on their actions; constituted as they are for the most part, it is for physical power alone that they have any feeling or respect. Moral force *per se* is powerless because of the fundamental nature of mankind which is prey to primitive passions. Physical force *per se* is equally incapable of ruling a people because oppression, sooner or later, fills its victims with despair and brings them to revolt. Only when these two forces work hand in hand for their mutual support, is a man truly vested with that Power in praise of which Machiavelli sings his paean.

The gospel of realism which reads, "In the beginning was appetite, passion, will to Power . . ." preaches also a despotism of the wise and noble, of the true aristocracy and the genuine nobility. Take away nobility and justice, and then, as Shakespeare cries:

> "The specialty of rule hath been neglected . . .
> And, hark what discord follows! . . .
> Then everything includes itself in power,
> Power into will, will into appetite;
> And appetite, an universal wolf,
> So doubly seconded with will and power,
> Must make perforce an universal prey,
> And last eat up himself. . . ."

Might, the domination by force, has had the advantage of having impelled man to action long before a sense of justice entered into him to restrain his baser instincts. Man's efforts to abolish Might have ever proved futile. It must be accepted as naturally as his appetite for food, and all that a man can hope for is that Power shall be found on the side of Justice, Might on the side of Right. And the nobler—that is, the more lawful—the Power that is wielded, the greater will be the pleasure that it gives, the more blessed the condition of that people over which it is exercised.

INDEX

DG
730
.14
.M2
M25
2010

LaVergne, TN USA
19 August 2009
155101LV00006B/72/A

9 781430 473299